WHITE MEN, WOMEN & MINORITIES

in the Changing Work Force

Anthony J. Ipsaro, Ph.D., Psy.D.

MERIDIAN ASSOCIATES

DENVER, COLORADO

As the author and publisher, I have exhaustingly researched all sources to ensure the accuracy and completeness of the information contained in this book. I assume no responsibility for errors, inaccuracies, omissions, or any other inconsistency herein. Any slights against people or organizations are unintentional.

Published by Meridian Associates, 3320 East Second Avenue, Denver CO 80206

Library of Congress Cataloging-in-publication Data

Ipsaro, Anthony, J.
    White Men, Women & Minorities in the Changing Work Force: Race, Sex, Power, Technology, Global Markets, Innovation.
    Includes bibliographical references and index.
            p.   cm.
        ISBN 0-9645723-3-8
        1. Male Psychology-United States. 2. Men, Women, Minorities-Employment. 3. Men-Work, Relationships, Family. 4. Diversity. 5. Business/Management.

First Printing: June, 1997

Printed in the United States of America
2000 99 98 97   7 6 5 4 3 2 1

Cover and text design: Shelton Design / Comm Arts

DEDICATION

To all the men
who have influenced my life;
To all the men
whose lives I have influenced.

CONTENTS

ACKNOWLEDGMENTS   *vii*

INTRODUCTION   *1*

1   UNKNOWN TO HIMSELF AND OTHERS   *11*

2   THE WHITE MALE WARRIOR   *29*

3   THE BIOLOGY BEHIND THE BEHAVIOR   *57*

4   CONFUSION IN THE WORKPLACE   *71*

5   THE DEMOGRAPHICS OF DIVERSITY   *89*

6   WHITE MEN IN QUIET DESPERATION   *107*

7   BENEFITING FROM THE DIVERSITY DILEMMA   *123*

8   SOME LEGS FOR DIVERSITY TO STAND ON   *141*

9   BECOMING AN AGENT FOR CHANGE   *163*

10   TRUST—A NEW WAY OF DOING BUSINESS   *189*

11   THE NEW FRONTIER FOR WHITE MALES   *209*

12   ORGANIZATIONAL CHANGE AND
THE MOTOROLA MODEL   *231*

CONCLUSION   *251*

SELECTED BIBLIOGRAPHY   *259*

INDEX   *279*

ACKNOWLEDGMENTS

I have been offering seminars focusing on white men, women, and minorities in the national and international corporate workplace for over twelve years. During that time I have shared, interacted, and learned from over 100,000 men and women of diverse backgrounds. Any success I have had generating ideas and communicating these concepts has been the result of many people who have richly impacted my life.

As a young adult in high school and college, I was deeply influenced by the Marianists, a Catholic religious order of men. My association with these educators has been life-long. This religious community was founded during the French Revolution by a priest, Fr. William Joseph Chaminade, who attempted to imbue the life and work of his group with the spirit and motto of that revolutionary time: liberty, equality, fraternity. The founders of this country adopted the motto for our pluralistic society at the writing of the American Constitution and Bill of Rights. It is this spirit I believe our workplace is striving to realize some 200 years later. I am grateful to the Marianists who in that spirit taught me so much about myself, who encouraged and supported my personal, professional, and spiritual development, who challenged me to use my talents in my community and in my work with others, and to dearly uphold the covenant that all men (and women) are created equal.

My thanks goes to the School of Professional Psychology at University of Denver in Colorado. The faculty there had the courage and insight to risk accepting me as a graduate student. I was fifty years old, had one doctorate already, and wanted to study men. In a time when there were no departments or courses focusing on men's issues, my request must have caused some curiosity, if not concern. Many of the faculty challenged and encouraged me to create my own program to explore the field of male psychology in a scholarly manner.

I also am grateful to US West, the Denver-based telecommunications giant, who long before diversity issues became fashionable, was courageous enough to attempt many new and creative concepts. My own initiative was to define and place the white male as a solid partner in the movement to bring equity to women and minorities in the corporate power system. Over 24,000 employees from US West have attended seminars and presentations at which I responded to the comments, experiences, and challenges the employees presented in their pioneering efforts to offer equal access of job opportunity to all in the workplace.

I also am thankful for the opportunities presented by other fine companies, notably Motorola, Hewlett-Packard, AT&T, Lockheed-Martin and dozens of others who have invited me into their white male power structures. Although my seminars are aimed at assisting white males to become more aware of their impact in the workplace and their capacity for growth and change, my presentations have focused on helping everyone—white males, women, and all minorities—to understand what workforce diversity means and the impact it has on our society. Constant questioning and probing by these participants have kept my presentations as vital and changing as the workforce they represent.

My clinical practice has had much to do with the stimulation for this book, since I have specialized in working with men whose male identity is so often determined by their work roles. I have been reaffirmed and strengthened in my work by assisting many men to integrate those unknown relational parts of their lives into a new definition of their manhood.

About three years ago, I began to see that my presentation schedule would not permit the creation of the book frequently requested by seminar participants. I knew I needed an infusion of assistance from editors, writers, and researchers. I received the help I was looking for from Victoria Cooper, a long-time publications editor and writer. Besides serving as an editor and project manager, Ms. Cooper conducted numerous interviews with individuals who had taken a seminar and whose comments I have incorporated. She also did a unique job of probing me for more clarity of some of the ideas found in this book. Within Ms. Cooper's group I am especially thankful to Thomas DeMers for his dedicated help with writing and research. I also am grateful to Roy Wood, Janet Whittle, Barbara Darling, Kathleen Campbell, Patrick Pritchett, Judith Aplon, and Paula Carroll who contributed their unique talent and skill to the writing of this book. I am most grateful to my general copy editor, Robin Coblentz, who smoothly balanced an insightful and firm professional intelligence with an understanding and patient personal sensitivity.

No acknowledgements would be anywhere complete without my expression of gratitude to those people who have significantly nurtured, challenged, encouraged, and supported me in the years of my life and work. My debts of gratitude first go to my father and mother. My dad, grew up an orphan in Italy, came to America as a poor immigrant. With little formal education, he became a shrewd and successful street-smart entrepreneur. His example and his wisdom showed me how a man can be passionate in living life. I forever will have warm memories of the "seminars" he frequently held at the family dinner table covering a variety of business topics, current world affairs, the economy, and whatever else might impact life. My mother was my original model of what full womanhood might be. She was my first experience of a true feminist. She balanced her life with that of a husband and six very active children while working in my father's businesses. She still found time for herself and a broad network of relatives and friends.

I offer a debt of thanks to my sister, Paula, who showed me that a man can enhance his respect, responsiveness, and effectiveness with others through his presence and grace, style and poise, appearance and manner; in a word, by being a "gentle man."

To my brothers, I also extend a debt of gratitude for offering me four different models of manhood given one common family upbringing. Through the give-and-take as male siblings in childhood and adulthood as well as the ways they have chosen to live their lives, they have been a constant reminder of how important reflection and education is in maintaining the freedom, responsibility, and power to shape and develop one's manhood.

To my wife Barbara, an extraordinary woman, the most important and influential friend I have ever had, I have an eternal debt. She has been, and continues to be, essential to my life and work. Her love and concern, her friendship and companionship, have been an irreplaceable source of strength and support as I grow and evolve in my personal and professional life. Her intellectual stimulation and her direct challenges have of necessity, grounded me when I have expressed "on the edge" ideas in my seminars and in this book. Through her keen wisdom, expansive reading, intense discussions, and reflected behavior she has taught me so much about womanhood and manhood.

I am indebted to her six children, their spouses and their children, for all the wonderful years of love and friendship. The many long discussions—sometimes intense and emotional—have challenged me to grow, to remain current, and to be fully alive. Our lives together have reaffirmed my convictions that the ageless journey of becoming a mature man or a mature woman, although occasionally confusing and painful, has everlasting joys.

Perpetual devotion to what a man calls his business
is only to be sustained
by perpetual neglect of many other things.
–Robert Louis Stevenson
An Apology for Idlers

INTRODUCTION

Women comprise the majority of the United States population and nearly half of the U.S. labor force. Immigrants and other minorities are expected to constitute a fifth of the labor force in another ten years. Today's interpretation of our founding documents promise equal access to the resources and wealth of this country. Yet white males continue to dominate leadership positions in America, in the corporate workplace, military, government, schools, churches, and the media. Women and minorities are asking,"Is this fair?" And white males are squirming. Their anxiety comes not because white men *think* they are the bad guys, but because others are treating them as though they *are* the bad guys: their partners, their children, women and minority co-workers, and younger men.

Over the past several years white males have seen government and corporations pressured to pass laws and promote the cause of women and racial minority groups. Businesses send out special recruiters who offer jobs to women and racial minorities. The white male perceives these minorities moving up the management ladder faster than he, because of minority quotas and affirmative action. And, perhaps, he has been told by his supervisor that if he is white and male, he has no future in the department.

Observing this cultural shift, the majority of white men in America feel confused, isolated, lonely, and alienated in ways they cannot voice. When white males do voice their concerns by bringing up "reverse discrimination" issues, they are seen as racist, oppressive, or clueless. They are labeled "honkies," or "male chauvinists!" In most discrimination cases white males believe they have no avenue for due process. They are considered guilty until they are proven guilty.

The white male sees women and minorities wave the equal opportunity banner and use gender, color, and difference to gain monetary ad-

1

vantages and power positions. He watches these same women and minorities support cultural institutions (e.g. churches) and societal norms (the man is protector) that practice discrimination and oppression. This is confusing.

The white male sees religious groups attempting to influence national views on issues like abortion and sex education in the schools. These same religious groups, when confronted about the subjection of women in their institutions, claim immunity from these democratic principles because of this country's guaranteed separation of church and state.

Faced with this confusion and overt onslaught by women and minorities, most white males have gone underground. White men use their present positions of power to defend themselves and covertly subvert women and minorities. White males withhold information, leave women and minorities out of key meetings and informal discussions, and avoid mentoring them. Without this powerful informal network, many women and minorities fail to move into upper management. If they do move into managerial positions, women and minorities feeling isolated, begin to make poor decisions, and move toward failure.

What is needed now is a new beginning.

Many others in this field of diversity in the American culture and workplace have focused on the oppression of the disenfranchised—women and minority groups. I would like to focus on those who are seen now as the *enfranchised*—white men. They are viewed as the *takers*, the *entitled*, and the *privileged*. Yet, these same white males, I believe, are now the essential element in this movement of creating a more prosperous United States of America that fully benefits everyone regardless of sex, race, or background.

This book focuses on males, especially those who are white.

It is important for men, particularly white men, to better understand themselves if they are to profit from a changing culture. It is important for women and minorities to have a good understanding of American white men if they are to be equal partners with them, join with them in effective alliances for change, and benefit fully from white males' contributions and failures. Dismissing or attacking the white male is naive. White males hold the dominant power in our society. As essential contributors to the success we have experienced in the workplace and in this country, white males now cannot be excluded. To profit more from a democratic and diverse culture, any societal change must include and enrich everyone, not just a select group. Furthermore, given the most recent happenings in American society, being male and white seems to be something one does not discuss, much less something of which to be proud. A more balanced view of white males, their contributions, their failures, their future in America in the 21st century is necessary. Learning more about the men categorized as "white males," may lead to an understanding and acceptance of who, why, and what they are.

Some of the questions this book addresses are: What is the definition of manhood? What motivates a man? What has been his heritage in the culture, in the workplace? How has he associated with other males, with males not of his own race or ethnic group? What has been his history with women—women of his own race, or women of other tribes? What has been his relationship to the family, to the community? What does it mean to be white and male in America? If today's American culture promises equal access to the resources, power, and wealth of this land regardless of gender or color, what does it mean to be a white man? How do such characteristics as color, race, ethnicity, sexual orientation, impact on the definition of manhood? What does a man have to do to feel strong and stable, content and confident, satisfied and safe within himself, within his relationships, within society? What have been the white male's contributions and failures in this culture? What is the white male's future in America, in the American workplace?

I meet many culturally isolated white males in my clinical practice and in my consulting work in the public and private sectors of the workplace. Individually, they like to come to my office because they can slip in (no public sign signals "therapy") to talk about the confusion and emptiness that have taken them over. Here is what they say:

"Why are they picking on me. I've never owned a slave. I've never killed an Indian. And, I think I'm pretty nice with women."

"How do I speak out when I see injustices heaped on me all in the name of their justice?"

"As a white male what is my future? What is my son's future?"

"I've reached the top; I'm successful. Is this all there is? Was it really worth it?"

"I don't understand why my job doesn't mean anything to me anymore."

"What happens to me when I retire? What do I have to face?"

"My relationships are ho-hum. I feel trapped by them."

"I'm not happy. Frankly, I don't know what 'happy' is!"

In trying to replace these feelings of restlessness, boredom and confusion, men have tried more work, drugs, sexual affairs, hobbies, sports, even religion or politics. All these activities simply distract most men from directly confronting the hollowness they feel.

Typically, when I see these men, they have reached a crisis, which is what it takes to move most of us to action. The crisis can be the loss of job, health, or relationship; their vulnerability or mortality overwhelm them. Frequently, these men are in their mid-thirties to mid-fifties when this crisis (sometimes called the mid-life crisis) occurs. Often these men are quite successful in their professional lives, and their personal lives appear to be stable and responsible. Yet, underneath they are confused, sad, suffering, and in pain. Even when many men recognize this condition, most are afraid to ask for help. Asking for help signals that something is drastically wrong with how they are fulfilling their roles as men. To avoid labeling oneself as being inadequate as a man is a major reason why most men deny they need help.

Most men are in denial. In the all-or-nothing world many men think that if everything is not right, then everything must be wrong! Rationally they know this conclusion is not true but use such mental gymnastics as a defense. Such thinking leaves men completely confused and anguished. Some men deny by recreating reality in an effort to blame someone or something for their inadequacies or problems. If others are made to be seen as ignorant, incompetent, or lacking, the male can continue to view himself not as bad as, or at least somewhat better than, others. Unfortunately, this mind-set leaves most males in the exhausting position of having to remember and reenforce all the details of their scenarios of reality. One of my purposes for this book is to address the predicament of these men.

In any discussion about men and women, terms such as sex roles, gender, masculinity, and femininity are frequently used as distinct and sometimes similar concepts. This can be confusing. For our purposes, a working vocabulary may be helpful.

In this book the *sex* of a person refers to the physical and biological—the body and reproductive aspect of a human being. This distinguishes a *male* from a *female*. It is this physical element of the body that is common to all people regardless of time or culture.

Gender and *gender roles* are terms used to describe how these male and female bodies function in the social order. Gender refers to how human bodies, male and female, behave in society. Gender roles are those behaviors and feelings of males and females that a society deems acceptable at that historical moment. As R.W. Connell states in his significant work, *Masculinities*, "In gender processes, the everyday conduct of life is organized in relation to a reproductive arena, defined by body structure and processes of human reproduction. This arena includes sexual arousal and intercourse, childbirth and infant care, bodily difference." Connell continues: "Social practice is creative and inventive, but not inchoate. It responds to particular situations and is generated within definite social relations." *Gender relations* are seen as the interactions among people and groups formed along reproductive lines. Impacting upon these relationships are the on-going events, both historical and immediate.

Masculinity and *femininity* are characteristics gathered by society from public and private gender behaviors. Masculinity and femininity are relational, interdependent, and independent. One concept cannot exist without the other. Given this understanding of masculinity and femininity, at any time in history and depending on the specific society, a unique definition of what is masculine or feminine is culturally affirmed. Therefore, we can have a multitude of masculinities present at one time. This diversity can enhance and enrich each definition of masculinity but also can cause confusion to men and to women.

In this book we will use the Western Civilization/European/ United States of America's understanding of masculinity and femininity. Not only are these definitions most familiar to me, but they remain the dominant influence in shaping men and women throughout the world.

This book will focus more on gender differences than on differences of race, age, ethnic background, religion, sexual preference, or physical abilities. Biological sex is the most basic element of a human being and is fundamental to all other differences. In most societies these biological elements—distinguishing who is a man or who is a woman—frequently determine, and limit, the gender roles that a man and woman fulfill in a culture or society.

Color, race, even sexual orientation, although extremely important, are secondary elements to the fundamental aspect of biological sex and the resulting gender role. People of different colors, races, and backgrounds can find many gender commonalities, from which to relate. However, even with these commonalities, gender can be considered a unique manner or way human beings fulfill their humanity.

Men and women seek common human goals such as love, acceptance, respect, dignity, and security. Gender sometimes has produced confusing and conflicting styles for achieving those common human goals. For example, although men and women use the same language and perform the same rituals (job, parenting, relationships), they frequently can mean something different. Many writers have successfully noted this phenomena, but few have given us reasons for this paradox, let alone a methodology to handle such confusion. To add more clarity to this communication problem between the sexes, I will propose that understanding cultural gender roles is key to interpreting what is meant by most men and women when they use similar language or rituals. Better communication habits in relationships between men and women are essential if we are to have greater success both at home and in the workplace.

Much of the information, reflections, and comments in this book focus specifically on white heterosexual males. Gender, race, class, and background all impact masculinity. Therefore, there are many types of masculinity. How one man relates to another man further impacts the multiplicity of how men can interpret their masculinity. Yet, all men share a great deal of sameness—they are human, they are biologically men, they live in a culture that has male role expectations and privileges. That sameness cuts across race, ethnicity, and sexual orientation. I hope that all men will find in this book some meaning and assistance in their unique journey of redefining their manhood in today's rapidly changing world.

In focusing on white males and their place in a democratic and diverse society, I bring all the positive elements of being a white male. I also bring the subjective and limited view of a white male. All of us are influenced by who we are. Our world is seen through those multiple moderators of gender, race, ethnicity, background, experiences. It is who we are—our identity—that affects how we view our world. Our worldview is *our* truth. It is from this limited world view as a white male that I share my truth.

I must say some words about the use of research in this book. At all times, and to the best of my knowledge, I have tried to report the prime research and statistics that amplify and support my material. I recognize that some people have difficulty with statistics and group standards since they cannot be accurate for each individual in the group. To the male, who gains great control by knowing the exact properties and dimensions of objects, this uncertainty of generalizations can be very disconcerting. Nevertheless, although each person is unique, we all share a lot in common as human beings. Statistics state what those commonalities are so that we can understand better the individual who is part of that group or collective. At the same time, understanding an individual member of a group can give us insight into knowing better the entire group.

Frequently, in their discussions about groups, statisticians report group profiles in an attempt to balance the uniqueness of the individuals in the group with what these individuals share in common. This information is commonly shown graphically by a bell curve.

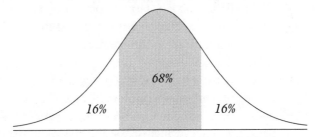

The bell part of the graph indicates that the large majority of unique individuals in a group—approximately 68 percent—share the *norm*. The norm does not mean *normal*, nor does it mean *right*. I can give you the norm for murderers, but in most cultures that behavior is not normal or acceptable. The norm leaves out some males—the far left of that population, some 16 percent, who *do not* exhibit that specific characteristic as well as the far right, some 16 percent, who *always* exhibit that specific characteristic. What the norm reports, then, is a generalization.

To make statistics meaningful, we need to *particularize* the generalization. This is done by taking an individual who is included in the group and adjusting the group norm to fit that specific individual. The adjustment is made by studying the individual and then adding or subtracting the amount of the specific characteristic or trait considered the group norm to fit that individual. If this important step of particularization is not done and each individual is identified fully with the group norm, we have what is called *stereotyping*. Stereotyping also results when you view a specific characteristic in one individual and then conclude that all individuals who share that specific characteristic are exactly the same.

Hence, when I cite group norms or generalizations, the reader should use the norm or generalization properly by remembering to add to or subtract from that norm depending upon the specific individual in question. Such words as *most, some, many,* and *frequently* will alert the reader to norms and generalizations.

Much information about the white male is found in a variety of fields and sources: anthropology, sociology, clinical and organizational psychology, theology, history, and political science. I have attempted to present some of this vast wealth of information, although at times somewhat simplified, in an understandable form and under one cover. For a more in-depth view of many of these topics, an extensive bibliography is included. Each chapter begins with a quotation that should trigger a moment of reflection. Reflection is a starting point to gain greater clarity and understanding which is essential for any growth or change. The first paragraph of each chapter is an abstract or summary of the material that follows.

Following each chapter is a recorded and transcribed interview—one of the oldest methods of research—with an individual who has attended one of my seminars. These individuals, whose true identities have been protected, offer real-life views of themselves and the white male in the workplace. Observations by others are essential if we are to have a more honest view and a better understanding of ourselves.

Finally, at the end of each chapter is a short section called *Workshop* listing three or four questions that can lead to further reflection, practical skills, or concrete behaviors which may help the reader integrate the ideas contained in the chapter.

Once we better understand who men are, we will discover new and different ways to define masculinity and femininity. Our relationship will become more gratifying and fulfilling. We will be less lonely and dissatisfied. We even will become more productive at work, more contented at home! In this technological world, in this American culture, men have taken on too much. It is time for men to share their burdens and their blessings. Men have been significant and major contributors, and, at times major obstacles, to the greater effectiveness of the Great American Experiment. Our American heritage offers us rich opportunities to explore and redefine manhood. The enormous possibilities presented men are beyond comprehension.

Now is the time for all of us—white men, women, and minorities—to join together in a new way to reflect on our past experiences of living and working in a democratic and diverse society. Let us all admit our successes and our failures. Let us all admit that each one of us is part of the problem and part of the solution. Let us all renew our efforts to accept responsibility for ourselves and for each other. Above all, let us all reach down deeply for that understanding, forgiveness, and compassion that is essential to free us so that we may move on.

Let us begin.

He knows the universe,
and himself he does not know.
–La Fontaine
Fables

1

UNKNOWN TO HIMSELF
AND OTHERS

Excluding white males from the process of achieving greater benefits from the inherent cultural diversity of this nation is a strategic mistake. A whole organism (the organization) cannot change if one of its constituents is not included in the change. It is similar to family dynamics: one individual member can have a significant impact on the whole unit. Everyone's actions count! White males need to examine their actions, their lives. The more men are developing and changing as human beings, the more society will benefit. Men are part of the organization and have major power positions. To be unaware of them, or to leave them out of the process of change, as power is being redefined and transformed in the world, stultifies and polarizes the process. It is a lose-lose dynamic for everyone.

History has played a joke on all men. Most cultures have promised men they will find their manhood by successfully performing their societal roles as resource producers—hunter, fisher, farmer; resource protector—warrior, soldier, defender; and resource director—be in charge, take responsibility, make the rules. Many men expend a lifetime of effort and energy on these exterior activities so necessary for the survival of the community. They believe that in fulfilling these duties and obligations they will attain their manhood, and, ultimately, happiness and contentment. But do they?

Lee Atwater, former national chairman of the Republican Party, provides a good example of men searching for the meaning of their manhood. Atwater was the youthful bad boy of Republican politics, who smashed Michael Dukakis's bid for the presidency as George Bush's campaign manager in 1988. At age thirty-nine, Atwater had helped elect a president and been named to lead his party. He was at the top of his career when he learned he had inoperable brain cancer.

Atwater was bright, combative, brash, and arrogant. Heading a South Carolina congressional campaign in 1980, he exposed the opposing candidate's history of electroshock therapy. When accused of running a dirty campaign, Atwater replied, "I'm not going to respond to allegations made by someone who was hooked up to jumper cables."

In a 1991 *Life* magazine article, Atwater wrote just before his death. He repeatedly describes himself in military terms, the resource protector: "I (and others like me) approach politics as only a slightly politer form of ground battle. We are hired guns. That's why I rely on three books of military and political wisdom: Plato's *Republic,* Machiavelli's *The Prince* and Sun Tzu's *The Art of War.* . . . Perhaps because I am so wedded to war strategies, a reputation as a fierce and ugly campaigner has dogged me."

Atwater's survival depended on winning, being the best. Anything less was not to be a man. Atwater confesses that he employed whatever tactic was called for to ensure victory. I believe he spoke for most white males when he said, "Like a good general, I had treated everyone who wasn't with me as against me."

The way Atwater approached politics is the way most men approach work and life: defend, attack, conquer. In this struggle to achieve manhood you trust no one. When cancer took the field against Atwater, the nature of the combat shifted. "My campaign-honed strategies of political warfare were simply no match for this dogged opponent," he wrote. "Cancer is no Democrat."

Cancer took Atwater out of the "attack dog" mode although he first approached his illness as though it were another political opponent. He looked for a weak point and struck hard as Sun Tzu had taught him. His first assault was a radical procedure that used steel tubes to insert radioactive pellets into the tumor. It failed. The tumor continued to grow. Atwater turned to alternative therapies, alternative philosophies, and religion, which, he says, he had never relied on "for much of anything." He spent time with friends, with his wife Sally, and with his children. He began to trust again. He read the Bible and committed himself to practicing the Golden Rule, which aide Blake Williams told him was a common thread in all the world's religions.

Reflecting on the campaigns he managed, he realized he had been "nakedly cruel" to Dukakis and made amends to many of his political enemies. He discovered the love he felt for his father, who was also fighting cancer.

To say that Atwater mellowed would be putting it mildly. He once told George Bush that his "kinder and gentler" theme was a nice sentiment but wouldn't win any votes. Later he wrote, "There is nothing more important in life than human beings, nothing sweeter than human touch."

Long before he was diagnosed with cancer, Atwater said he realized that "something crucial" was missing from the lives of Americans—Democrats, Republicans, and Independents alike. The gift of his illness was to see what that was: "a little heart, a lot of brotherhood."

His analysis is worth printing in full: "The '80s were about acquiring—acquiring wealth, power, prestige. I know. I acquired more wealth, power, and prestige than most. But you can acquire all you want and still feel empty. What power wouldn't I trade for a little more time with my family? What price wouldn't I pay for an evening with friends? It took a deadly illness to put me eye to eye with that truth, but it is a truth that the country, caught up in its ruthless ambitions and moral decay, can learn on my dime. I don't know who will lead us through the '90s, but they must be made to speak to this spiritual vacuum at the heart of American society, this tumor of the soul."

Cancer had two gifts for Lee Atwater: the awareness that he did not know himself; and, the limited time to discover what was really important to be a real man, to be fully human. Although he now had less time, he made the most of it. He used what time he had left to reflect and recover values that had been inoperative in the daily pursuit of being a successful resource producer, protector, and director.

With all the economic gains of the twentieth century, with all the labor-saving inventions, the paradox is that we have less rather than more time for reflection and depth, friendship and intimacy, beauty and sensitivity, even common decency. These values seem incidental in the quest for more productivity, more material things, more wealth, more notoriety, more titles and prestige. Some men have believed that the more they can accumulate for themselves and those special in their lives, the better men they are.

What contributes to this lack of awareness of those internal elements that are essential for a man's true happiness and contentment? Part of the answer is the individual male himself. Part of the answer is the culture that keeps men unaware.

White males are the unknown majority in American society. Yet, they are key to this country's economic life. White men are the leaders in the workplace. This is a workplace that is the subject of intense scrutiny as America's demographic profile shifts, the corporate world globalizes, and technology makes brain more important than brawn for the first time in human history.

White male power is real, permeating, and ever-present. Yet, women and minorities frequently shun, work around, or ignore such a force. Leaving white men out is a deferential bow to white male power. It automatically positions those who take that approach, as the victims of the white male, afraid of looking "the king" in the eye. Women and minorities hope the fairness of their argument and the reality of their statistics will persuade white males to play along without actually inviting them into the process.

Furthermore, creating parallel systems such as the "mommy track," or creating one's own business in the image of the successful white males' organizations, simply enhances white male power. The message sent to him is that his system is the only way to be successful. Unknowingly, power and support are given to the white male when he is perceived as the standard.

But let me tell you a secret: Most men in most cultures have no sense of their power! They have remarkable power. Since that power is inherited through cultural gender expectations rather than earned, it is an invisible mantle. Although each male has his own brand of masculinity, all men share a relationship that fosters an alliance of domination and subordination. This is achieved through practices that exclude and include, exploit and reward, intimidate and reaffirm. The entire cultural system supports, reaffirms, and colludes with white males to keep them in power. Yet, most white males do not think of themselves as belonging to a powerful, elite group until others label them that way.

It is a phenomenon of those in power that they never see the ramifications of the power they have. To understand how that occurs, let me put it to you this way: If you were to ask a goldfish in a bowl of water, "How's the water?" The goldfish would say, "What water?" The water has always surrounded the goldfish who is unable to compare its environment with anything else. The same is true of most white males: the entire system—institutions, society, culture—has always totally surrounded him. He is unable to stand back and see the system. Women and minorities readily see the system since they are on the outside looking in. They know that to be excluded from equal access to this country's resources is to be out of the privileged fishbowl.

The fishbowl in which the white male swims, however, rests in a large aquarium. The water from that aquarium flushes up into the fishbowl and keeps the fish alive, keeps the white male in power. That aquarium is the sum of our cultural institutions of family, school, community, churches, government, and workplace. In those institutions women and minorities swim and live. Unknowingly they support the cultural dominant role of males. They collude to keep white men in power and themselves oppressed.

Too often many of us want to give away our personal power and play the role of victim. We prefer to blame some other person or group for who we are, who we are not, and what we do not have. Such an attitude absolves us from any responsibility. It eliminates the need for us to change. Others may be partially responsible for our problems. But each of us needs to ask: Where is my responsibility for behaving in a manner that allows the situation to continue?

There is a strong tendency for many human beings to behave as children. We want to be taken care of and be provided with what we need. This attitude is at the core of the "you-owe-me" view of life. Individuals or groups expressing that approach want all the privileges of adulthood with the limited responsibilities of childhood. To behave as a child or to claim the role of victim, is to make oneself powerless.

Most men define power in a simplistic way. If you have power, you are in charge. You set the rules for order and control. You modify the actions and behaviors of others. Society looks to you as a male to take charge, to exercise power. Most men do not see themselves as setting rules that are really important. On the contrary, they see themselves following the rules made by others. As in many institutions in society, their bosses in the workplace set the rules. At home, men follow rules made by those whom the culture says are in charge—women. Many times those in power feign meekness and appear unintimidating. Yet, it is understood that unless you cooperate with their set of rules you can be replaced. With this confusing experience of power, most males believe they are powerless.

Yet, most men believe their societal role includes being responsible for those around them. The last one they are to consider is themselves. They see themselves as never doing what they would like to do; only doing what they should do. Or, if they do what they want, they are labeled self-centered and insensitive. Many men feel guilty for, or think that they have to justify, their needs. No wonder some men behave in childish, manipulative, and passive-aggressive ways to satisfy their needs. Most men do not know how to say what they want or need. They simply take! After all, aggressive behavior is seen as manly. Men have little experience and few skills for asserting themselves.

As we shall see in more detail later, societal power is maintained by two basic principles. If you are the right gender—male; and of the right color, clan, or social group, then you have inherent power in society. All institutions in society unite to support these concepts. In the American culture, when you are white and a male, you get a seat in the stadium of resources—wealth, power, and position. You may sit in the bleachers but you are in the stadium and have a reserved seat. That's power! If you are female or not white, you don't get a seat. You can get into the stadium only by running the concession stand, providing the entertainment, or cleaning up after the event. You assist, you support, but you do not receive the full reward. You are excluded from the real seats of power.

Simply put, to be part of the rule-making group—no matter how those rules are made—is to have power. When your group makes the rules, chances are you benefit from those rules. If, over time, these rules prove to be successful for the majority, rule-makers gain even more stature. With everyone following these rules or laws there is order. Law and order can become interpreted as: be reasonable, follow my rules and we'll all get along.

All white males are seen to have inherent power whether they want it or not. In the dynamic shifting of power which is taking place in the American culture, to leave out powerful white males is incredible. Left out of the plans, they feel excluded and plotted against. The shrewd few will sense the scheme. Exclusion is a backhanded tribute to their numbers and authority. Some white males will use that authority to protect their power and position.

At the same time, the majority of white males discover that to be excluded is to be dismissed. The situation quickly polarizes into those who are included and those who are excluded—the powerful and the powerless. Feeling shut out, many white males withdraw and go underground to fight their battles of survival.

Marilyn Loden, one of the authors of *Workforce America!*, has characterized this white male attitude as "vigorous indifference." In reality, the white male is hardly indifferent. Vigorous, yes; indifferent, no. What may appear as passive resistance to women and minorities is really part of a well-honed program of defense. Feigning inactivity to fool his enemies, he is constantly on guard for the next attack. He lies in wait to defend his cause using whatever means he can. Such an approach is a retrograde dynamic in any organization trying to benefit from cultural diversity.

This view of males as indifferent is a bias exemplified in the literature on diversity. White males are reported as feeling a loss of power—threatened and angry. Little is offered to white males who want new empowerment in a regenerated work force. Little is made of a number of men who are attempting to redefine their role given their historic heritage and today's realities. White males are frequently stereotyped as interested solely in the success of their businesses and themselves. I can assure you that is not the case. My own experiences as well as many studies have documented the serious commitment of a growing number of men who are making efforts to change.

The sudden surge of interest in the "Promise Keepers" program and the African American Million Man March are startling examples of how hungry men are to clarify their role. "Promise Keepers"—a men's movement that is rooted in the Bible—is now filling up stadiums with large numbers of men. This movement will soon be discarded by these same men. As with previous men's movements—Coalition for Free Men, the National Congress for Men, the efforts of Robert Bly and Sam Keen— "Promise Keepers" offers very simple and clear definitions of men and women.

While emphasizing timeless human values, this movement supports the expression of manly values with behaviors that were better suited for another time and a very different culture. For example, the Biblical values that should exist between men and women—love, honor, and respect—remain constant even today. To live out these values through the same behaviors of the historical time when the Bible was written becomes illogical and confusing in a technological, educated, and democratic culture. The spirit and laws of American society strongly promote the equality of women. Religious groups have attempted to negotiate these difficult societal waters by stating that their group does honor and respect women—but, in their place. This means that women are not the rule-makers but the supporters of the rule-maker.

At the same time, the popular press and media are rife with white male "backlash" stories. White males are rarely mentioned as people who have needs similar to anyone else. Little is said of white men who want to be part of a successful partnership in the culture and in the workplace. On the contrary, white males are seen as oppressive, greedy, egotistical, and power hungry.

To exclude the white male is to practice "reverse discrimination." Democratic equality in a diversified society will succeed to the degree that it promotes inclusion for all and benefits for everyone. This concept is precisely what women and minorities hold to be true! To exclude anyone, even the white male, regardless of his past history or present situation, is discriminatory and undemocratic. When white men cry "reverse discrimination," women and minorities simply say, "Welcome to the club. We have been discriminated against for hundreds of years. Now it is your turn." But, as Jesse Jackson has said so well, "Discrimination is discrimination, is discrimination."

Sociologically, whenever anyone in a group feels discriminated against, the whole group, including the one feeling disrespected, loses twice. First of all, rather than the whole group focusing its total energies on the common goal to benefit all, it siphons off its energies to manage internal conflicts. The total group loses. Secondly, when anyone feels disrespected by the other members of a group, he/she never contributes fully to the group's goal. Again, the entire group loses, even the individual who withholds his/her efforts.

Affirmative action and quotas are properly motivated. They attempt to terminate an historical, societal movement that excluded specific groups. The methods used to offer a more favorable access to the country's wealth and resources are through special privileges and designation of elite groups. The laws which attempt to promote this goal of equal access to the resources, while helpful in the short-term, are causing greater social hostility in the long-run. Colin Powell, in his autobiography warns: "Discrimination 'for' one group means, inevitably, discrimination 'against' another."

Very few cultures and societal forms in the world offer Americans a model of how best to offer access to the resources of a country regardless of gender, race, creed, and color. Most cultures still follow old world principles of right gender, right clan. America continues to write the book on the creation of a new world, a new democratic society, in which everyone, although different, is offered equal access to that society's resources. We need to be more bold and courageous in establishing new world formulas which benefit all Americans. In later chapters, I will offer some recommendations and solutions.

In a new world, like America, we are setting up new and creative models. We open ourselves to misunderstandings, hurts, and frustrations that occur in a trial-and-error approach. As we travel this unknown road, we need to be more compassionate and not just tolerate each other. Tolerance frequently means holding one's position while "putting up" with others. Compassion implies respect, understanding, interaction, compromise, acceptance, and forgiveness. We will better benefit from a diverse culture only when we discover compassionate formulas that will provide seats for *all* in the stadium of access and power.

As a nation we give great play to white male failures and exploitations. There is a strong tendency to hold white males responsible for the evil in the world. Inclusion of white males in this process of change begins with acknowledgement of their positive contributions. For better or worse, much of the progress in this country, in the present corporate workplace, is the result of the efforts of white males. This is not, in any way, to diminish the contributions of women and those of other cultures. White men's need for acknowledgment and respect is genuine. This acknowledgement is essential in assisting white men to better understand themselves. This understanding will better focus and balance the role of white men in the culture. This awareness will help to demystify white male power.

The diversity equation must factor in recognition of white males, both the good and the bad, of the decades of toil of all kinds that have created a society and a workplace to which everyone aspires. I say recognize rather than respect because respect may be construed as an attitude toward an authority to which others must conform at the expense of who they are.

I half-kiddingly state that we need to have a year dedicated to the study, understanding, appreciation, and celebration of white males. I am well aware that the cultural climate in America today fosters negative feelings towards white males. Some may believe that designating such a year would be a year nobody celebrates. We need to give white men appropriate credit for the talent, creativity, and old-fashioned ingenuity they have contributed to making the United States the world's economic pacesetter for most of this century. White males' corporate traditions need the respect accorded to an elder, especially as we move to radically reorganize the work force for the next century.

What is more, focusing on white males makes their aura more visible. This visibility allows us to better label and understand the different components of white male power. Once white male power is visible it becomes less threatening. It is no longer as assumed and as accepted as the air we breathe. We now can better reaffirm the positive elements of white male power and change those negative aspects.

After having a year of honoring the contributions of white males we need another year or two of reconciliation with the white-male system. Knowingly or unknowingly, that system also caused a great deal of pain and suffering to those who were neither white nor male. This reconciliation calls for acknowledgement, forgiveness, understanding, and change on everyone's part. The first step in reconciliation is for all of us to be educated in a greater understanding of the history of this country and its political system. We need to know and develop the skills of how individuals and groups interact in a democratic society. All of us must become responsible participants in this major movement toward creating a culture that fully benefits from the diversity of its people.

A diverse culture will fail to achieve its goals if we pretend we are the same. Denying our differences is a feeble attempt to remain unknown to ourselves. It can be disrespectful of others: there is nothing worth noting about you. I have a difficult time with those who say, "Let's treat everyone alike;" or "When will we have the day that gender, race, and ethnicity will not be such an issue and we see the person." I hope those days never arrive!

We do not want to treat everyone the same way. All of us equally deserve respect, dignity, understanding, and appreciation. Having another view—of being different—makes for a creative and dynamic mix, makes for a country that is alive and vibrant. I, for one, hope we will not all be alike. How boring! How uncreative! How unproductive! Most often when people call for everyone being alike, they are seeking a simple solution that can cover everyone, that requires little or no reflection but promises simplicity, safety, security, and reward.

In the workplace we all have a common goal, a winning product or an outstanding service. At the same time, we need some common parameters and rules. We need some norms to hold the group together in harmony as it seeks its common goal. Up until now that common parameter has been called performance evaluation. Most performance evaluations are the styles and ways that men, given their societal role, use to become successful resource producers. This male performance evaluation has become the American work ethic for everyone.

The male has set up workplace standards or rules based on his life, history, and role. If women want his reward, his conclusion is that women must be like him. Women should be educated the way he is, put in as many hours as he does, think as he does, produce as he does. If women follow these expected behaviors, the rules of the game, then they can be rewarded as he is. To most males everyone following the established rules makes the game fair, just, and orderly. This is how males treat everyone alike—treat everyone by their standard! No wonder women complain that they are losing their femininity in the workplace. No wonder women say that to be as good as the man they have to perform even better! Women need to be more critical of this male model. Learn from that male model and create a different model or style that would achieve equal success.

Individuals cannot be treated as though they were robots, operating on one program. Depending on sex, race, and background, people can use different styles to accomplish a common goal or to contribute to the groups' achievement of common goals. That difference becomes the essential ingredient of creativity. Creativity nurtures the dynamism of a system and keeps an organization alive and moving. It constantly discovers new ideas so that the group may improve its achievement of common goals.

The acknowledgement and inclusion of different styles for the attainment of common goals is a double-edged sword. The price of inclusion is scrutiny, not only by others but also by white males themselves. What stuff are we made of? What has been our history? What has been the impact on others of one group's power? These are questions we are reluctant to reflect upon for reasons clearly outlined in the remainder of this book.

Self-reflection and performance have been uncomfortable bedfellows in most cultures. To benefit from a diverse culture requires us to better understand ourselves as well as to learn from others, to grow, to expand, to change. Diversity is the face of change in people and in institutions. Worthwhile change, especially in our diverse culture, requires reflection. Men and women need to learn how to reflect. Many of us would rather drift through life. We want to simply follow the rules that some institution has established and we obeyed as children.

Reflection is the result of reading, traveling, discussing, thinking. Reflection asks us to study our history, to examine what our institutions tell us. Reflection requires us to be clear about what is good for us, what is good for the community—the common good. This is not a one-time process. Reflection is a way of life and is hard work. Reflection is essential for developing a conscience and for making good choices. Reflection makes changing to new behaviors less threatening, less frightening, more satisfying. Change without reflection can be change for the sake of change.

Such reflection will help men, as we saw with Lee Atwater, to discover another part of themselves. That newly discovered part can be a source of strength and true power. That unknown part is the world of feelings and emotions. That world finds life and form in the everyday relationships of human beings. The world of relationships, of emotions and feelings, is a world all people share. It is the major path of connection for all people. This is why effective communication skills are so essential. If white males wish to connect on a safe and common level with people who are different, it is essential that they become knowledgeable of and comfortable with their relationships. This not only will benefit men in the workplace but also in their personal lives. In ongoing relationships with partner, spouse, children, and friends men fulfill another part of themselves. They discover that they are energized and rejuvenated. Men will uncover and then discover the soul of their manhood.

Without those values of relationships, of feelings, of what can be called the spiritual (other than the material) world, life is meaningless. It is an empty exercise of getting, defending, increasing, maintaining, doing, and spending that has special implications for the male's identity today. This issue will be explored further in the next two chapters.

Without the limits of the common good, respect, kindness, and mutuality; without an attachment to values more noble than being "top dog," a man's military nature will take over. As conqueror he will continue to promote life as plundering for limitless material acquisitions—the result of intense competition and warfare. This conflict has no borders or safe havens. It is conducted, as we saw earlier, much as Lee Atwater ran his campaigns.

Lee Atwater has my gratitude forever. We have learned a great deal on his dime. He has shown us what men discover when they turn inward and access the truth of their reflection and their feelings. Unfortunately, it often takes something as threatening as cancer, an overwhelming crisis, to turn men in that direction.

The business world—a key area for men—is essential in promoting reflection. Companies must work to eliminate workaholism as a standard for men and women. Corporations must ensure that people have enough time to respond to all parts of their lives. This balancing of work life and home life, this interacting of the philosophical being and doing, rejuvenates the spirit and strengthens the individual. The investment return for focusing on the whole life of an employee will be value added to the quality of work and productivity. This is one of the hidden riches that comes from a deeper understanding of diversity.

INTERVIEW

Jack
37
White
technical researcher
11 years with company
B.S. in finance

I came into this company from a background in construction, working with my father. We were running a small business, and I was burned out when I came into this company. When I signed on, we were a small, entrepreneurial startup, but now we're about a fourth of a large multinational based in another country.

Even though I thought I'd only have my job for a couple of years before going back into small business, I got sucked into the security of a larger company. They paid me a little more each year. I've survived a lot of layoffs. And I have a tremendous amount of freedom in my job. To a large extent I get to decide what I'm working on when. Also, we're on the forefront of science and technology.

The work force is very diversified at our site—mainly immigrants from southeast Asia. The majority of workers on the production floor are Laotian, Cambodian, Vietnamese. We're constantly under the threat of suit for anything that smacks of racism, sexism, personal victimization, sexual harassment. It's the climate of the 1990s.

I've watched the company go from small to large, from an R&D orientation to a manufacturing orientation. The manufacturing emphasis has been a struggle from time to time. In the old company, people wore lots of hats; we were mutually interdependent; the principals went out of their way to build and support an innovative, friendly work culture. When we were bought out by a large company, they hired a corporate culture consultant to help us identify the norms of our workplace, to help preserve our culture.

All that got lost when we moved into our big new building; in the first month, in fact, I found a framed copy of the norms of our workplace in a trash can in the H.R. department. I retrieved it, and it's hanging in my office.

Since the acquisition, it has become clear that the company doesn't really care anymore about its employees, or even, for that matter, doing what's right for itself in the long term. The present management doesn't feel as vital about the company as the previous management. A lot of us have felt we care too much; we've been treating the company as a personal mission rather than as a job. It was sad to back down from that, to treat it as a job rather than, "we're going to change the world with this company." But that's what's happened now.

I feel that the people at the lowest levels of power in a large company have more real company loyalty than those at the highest levels of management. I think American managers are likely to sell a company's long-term future down the river in exchange for a short-term gain and another chance to promote their own careers. Their priorities are clear. Having sold out once or twice, these managers have less compunction to do it again and again. It destroys loyalty and creates a feeling of cynicism.

The worker bees, as managers call us, see the company as a boat, sometimes a life raft, and we're utterly dependent on our fellow sailors and the officers to keep it afloat. We don't flit from ship to ship as these managers do.

I read a lot about economics and business, and I've seen a tremendous importance placed on short-term gain. We've envied the Japanese because they have a five-year horizon, whereas Americans are always looking for a quick fix. Boards of directors hire managers and CEOs based on guesses, reputations. Trust is a matter of appearance and reassurance. I don't think managers of large companies want to exclude women from CEO positions. They just want to exclude everybody except themselves. The boards speculate, they want the hired gun, the short-term miracle worker. I think that's why top management salaries have been bid up in the last few years.

The startup people at my company were entrepreneurs, not professional managers. Not one person since the early days has shown the altruism to give up his job so that everyone else in the company could keep theirs. There are only a handful of the original people here now. As the dilution of the old work force has taken place, if you really act like you care, it's out of place.

A family reunion I went to last summer got me thinking about my loyalty to the people who started this company. I had never met my grandfather, but an uncle characterized him as "a boss's man." That's a pejorative thing to say now, but in the early twentieth century it was a statement of admiration for someone. Something clicked for me in that phrase, because I saw how my father busted his butt for his bosses, and so have I. My dad's loyalty was to the men, not the company, and so is mine. Maybe it's genetic.

I've been lucky to have two or three bosses who have been good friends in and out of the workplace. Sometimes it's scary to other people how close we are, because of the long working relationship. Yeah, I'd do anything for them. Our disagreements are straightforward because we have this history. Whether you win or lose the argument, there's agreement in the end. With newer people, people you're less familiar with, misunderstandings due to emotion come in.

American men have a background of teamwork: genuine team friendship and loyalty. My current fun sport is ultimate frisbee. We mix up the teams every day we play. You're intensely competitive on an individual basis, and on a team basis, but since the teams are mixed up all the time, you can't take it too seriously off the frisbee field. All the competition takes place within the context of the game only.

What I think men bring to the workplace, besides teamwork, is a tradition of getting things done in a practical way, as in "this is your job and you know it." Everyone's pretty mature about "no matter what my personal feelings are, this is the job, and I've got to get it done." I think women think, "My personal feelings will probably help me get this job done better."

Men also have the outlook of military hierarchy. They may not like their place in the hierarchy, but they understand it. They tend to see hierarchy as positions of power, and they recognize the position, more than the person filling it. Women tend to look at the person more.

In the workplace, if a team doesn't produce, it's not worth a damn. I think you put together a team for a project, with some new people, some experienced people, and they work together for better or for worse. No matter how well they do, I think you should keep them together for the next project so you don't throw away all that process. We live in a disposable society, with disposable people. Management thinks we should be lean and mean and start shedding people like paper towels. It's very important not to throw away experience gained on teams. People learn from their mistakes.

At my company, we draw our teams from a larger pool of people who have worked together. Everybody in this department has had some relationship with everybody else, at some level, whether it's playing frisbee at lunch or being in the same room for the department potluck.

I see empowerment as real, at least in the high-tech world. But, just like everything else in management theory, it will go in a cycle and it will be overdone. There will be a whole spate of books attacking it and latching onto the next new thing in a couple of years. From reading the literature it looks as though everyone's running from one thing to another in two or three year cycles.

WORKSHOP

1. What are five words that quickly come to mind that describe the white male for you? How do these words influence your behavior as a white male, or towards white males?

2. What is your definition of power? When do you feel powerful? powerless? Is there a way of always being powerful?

3. Is there one new behavior you can start practicing towards better balancing your home life and your work life? Your relationships?

4. Will you set aside fifteen minutes each day for private reflection on your life?

Tell me to what you pay attention
and I will tell you who you are.
−Ortega y Gasset
Source unknown

2

THE WHITE MALE WARRIOR

In our earliest agrarian and nomadic days men and women shared the same work; both were resource providers of food and goods to preserve themselves, their families, their communities. Anthropologists have shown that gender roles became more sharply defined as work roles became differentiated. What caused this differentiation? When one people invaded the territory of another for conquest, the stronger had to protect its tribe and its resources. Thus, men, because of their physical attributes, came to view their role not only as resource providers but as resource protectors, defending the lives and property of the community. Often, as we have seen from history, to the warrior-protectors went the spoils. Establishing law and order and being in power became entitlements for men. Men became resource directors—they made the rules governing the distribution of those resources. Only now men are learning that owning, distributing, and enjoying the spoils is no substitute for connectedness and community.

White men are the missing link in the corporate plan to successfully diversify the workplace. They must be drawn in as partners for change. It is that simple. But who are men and how did they get the way they are? What is this thing called masculinity? Why do men make so much of it? Or do they? We are most conscious of the abuse and violence committed by some men—behaviors society could do without. But what are the elements of masculinity worth saving?

Unfortunately, the people who seem to have the fewest answers to these questions are white males themselves. Why should that be? Men know who they are from their experience of doing. Their inherent lack of self-reflection means they often do not know things about themselves that others, especially women, easily see. The experience of doing has an interior component that men ignore or avoid, perhaps due to male conditioning. Most men are rewarded for performing, not for reflecting on what they are doing. Male mythology remains effective precisely because it remains unknown. Its power resides in its transparency—just as the goldfish cannot see the water in which it swims.

In my private practice I often meet with men who do not know this internal world of relationships and feelings. Most societal patterns for raising male children enforce—indeed, reward—males who ignore almost all of their emotions. The emotions that cultures encourage males to exhibit are anger, hostility, and bravado. These strong emotions are used to exact dominance and control. Dominance and control are associated with the cultural role of the male—resource producer, protector, and director.

Alexithymia is the technical name for this condition of being unaware of emotions. Alexthymia is the inability to localize emotions in the body and to distinguish among different kinds of common affect. In 1972, psychiatrist Peter Sifneos first used the term *alexithymia* to describe an individual's inability to consciously experience and communicate feelings. Dr. Sifneos noted two types of alexithymia: primary, which is genetic or biological in origin; and, secondary, resulting from psychological traumatic events. In their research, psychologists Fukunishi and Rahe suggest that alexithymia may be a personality trait. This trait may help to explain why subjects with the inability to express emotions, exhibit low social support systems, and show poor responses to stress. Might it be that many men suffer from alexithymia? Might it be that the definition of masculinity which society promotes is psychologically unhealthy and dangerous for men?

The inability to recognize and express emotions ultimately represents a loss of a part of self and consequently a loss of power. Reflection—looking within—connects actions and feelings and makes the personality whole. It raises questions that, if explored, lead to personal depth, self-knowledge, and personal strength. This is terrain men have avoided because it is unfamiliar and viewed as "unmanly."

Many men are terrified of this internal world. They deny such territory even exists because it threatens their most basic sense of who they are. This domain shakes men's fundamental allegiance to masculinity as external action and performance. But if men are to swim in currents over which they have some control, they must understand the waters flowing about and within them. To navigate the waters of diversity, the social waters in which we all meet, men need a firm sense of who they are. This is not only important for men themselves but essential to understanding others.

For thousands of years men have been attending to the questions of the material world, the physical universe. Physics, chemistry, mathematics, and engineering increasingly have focused men's consciousness outward and have helped make them, in many cases, strangers to themselves. My purpose in this chapter and the next is to make the unseen visible—to assist men to see the water in the fishbowls in which they swim. This invisible world will become more obvious as we talk about the cultural, historical, and biological roots of masculinity. This brief history of men should inform and help demystify what it means to be male.

Neither masculinity nor femininity is magical. As noted earlier, both are a mixture of hormones and history. What the proportions of these elements are, however, continue to be a subject of intense debate. Women in the American culture continually have redefined womanhood and femininity. Because of education, technology, and easy access to information during the past thirty years women have stepped up this redefining. This redefining of the female identity has brought the male identity under scrutiny as never before.

Let us begin with a woman's view of men, especially in the workplace today. In her book *Games Mother Never Taught You* Betty Lehan Harragan compares the business environment to the military. "It may come as a shattering revelation to find out that collecting a regular salary from a business enterprise means that you are part and parcel of a classic military organization. Not some slapdash medieval legion where knights-errant occasionally jousted off to defend the honor of their lady fair, but a modern, mercenary, well-equipped, scientifically staffed military operation."

The author continues to parallel military and business culture. "First and foremost among these values is the need for tight control. The resultant behavior that supports this value is authoritarian management. Drawing heavily on the military model, the traditional organization is structured along rigid, hierarchical lines. The corporate pyramid is the metaphor used to describe the basic structure of most large organizations.

"Successful movement up this pyramid or, for that matter, the ability to simply stay on it at all, requires absolute respect and deference to the individual on the level immediately above. Rank becomes the ultimate source of respect, although it is not always linked to ability or professional competence."

The accuracy of these observations arises from the fact that we, men and women together, inhabit a warrior culture. In sports, business, education, or even in personal relationships, men interact from the perspective of competition, winning, and domination. That is what warriors do. The warrior culture embraces not just white males but blacks raised in this country and in Africa, the Aztec tradition of Mexico, the samurai past of Japan, and the warrior past of Jews, Arabs, and Chinese. Certainly it includes Native Americans and the values fostered between warring tribes across this continent long before Columbus. This was not always the way.

Anthropologists teach us that the first humans lived in small bands. They survived by hunting and gathering, walking from place to place, and living off the land. They were not much different from our foraging proto-human ancestors at first except in social organization. The bands numbered fifteen to twenty-five men, women, and children. Without population pressure and with an abundance of food there was little reason for conflict. Men and women lived quite similar lives. Focus was on the well-being of the individual and the community.

This was a relatively long period, although its length is constantly being revised. The shin bone of a six-foot man found in West Sussex dates to half a million years ago, when England was still a peninsula of Europe. Human remains found in China may be 200,000 years old. Parts of a skull unearthed in Java, believed to belong to homo erectus, are thought to be two million years old, according to a *Time* magazine report.

The point is that for the overwhelming majority of human history a man lived very differently from the way he does today. Agriculture, believed to have originated only about 6000 to 8000 B.C. in the part of the world we now know as Europe, caused a major alteration in the hunting and gathering pattern. Early man spent a very long period living close to nature and in intimate relationship with only a few others. This had important consequences for the relations between men and women.

Anthropologists have learned from the comparative study of cultures that gender roles become more sharply defined as people differentiate in terms of their work. If we extrapolate backward, we can imagine a world in which men and women did much the same work and in which gender equality was the cultural norm. For the individual and the community to survive, be secure, and have a future, everyone needed to contribute.

Agriculture ended the nomadic lifestyle and centered life on harvesting and processing crops. The first cities developed in this agrarian period. With the use of bronze in 3500 B.C. and iron in 1000 B.C., technology acquired a harder edge. Technology of all sorts amplified human success. Surplus goods created the opportunity for trade and organized commerce. Trade-based economies were well underway in Eastern Europe and the Near East when the first of several waves of invaders, called Kurgans, appeared in about 4300 B.C. The towns the Kurgans invaded were relatively undefended and unfortified, but their incursions made defense a necessity.

Men, because of their inherent physical attributes, were pressed into the role of protector. Men defended those in the tribe who were less physically strong—women, children, the elderly, and infirmed. Not only did men defend the people but guarded the territory and their accumulated resources. The norms of human interaction were changed forever. Men now focused on the world outside the tribe. Their efforts served as the means to everyone's well-being. Acting as resource producer, resource protector, and resource director—now took up so much time and effort, it became the all-consuming end for men.

One controversial but insightful book describes the pre-warrior period as "gylantic." It was a time when women's influence was as great or greater than men's. The author of *The Chalice and the Blade*, Riane Eisler, calls this the partnership model of society. She argues that a deeply feminine social model prevailed before warfare became an instrument of policy. People worshipped the goddesses of fertility and equated power with nurturance and motherhood rather than conquest. Eisler finds in the culture of Crete, the most highly evolved of these societies, a place where the sexes lived in parity. "In Crete, for the last time in recorded history, a spirit of harmony between men and women as joyful and equal participants in life appears to pervade," she writes.

That may seem far-fetched to many people raised in our age of global competition, market shares, wars, and technology. The society Eisler describes certainly is not verifiable to many people's satisfaction, since the period is so remote and the evidence so scanty. Nonetheless, Eisler is certainly on target in describing the goals many contemporary women and some men are striving to reach. What do women want in the workplace if not equality and partnership—an equal shot at running things? What do they want but an end to strict hierarchy and the instigation of more flattened, circular, more community-like organizational structures?

Many women today are calling for a modification of the warrior model as our dominant social paradigm and the return to a civilization that values people equally. Yet, around the world, many women are too often viewed or treated as property. We continue this practice in our enlightened culture with women bearing the last name of their fathers and upon marriage frequently replace that last name with the name of another man, their husbands. Surnames indicate belonging and ownership. Men are designated by society to nurture, protect, control, and own the women.

Society views the male and his behavior as superior, the model, the ideal. In most cultures boy babies are the preferred choice of parents. The female is viewed to be weak and less preferable since her body has limited her societal contribution as the primary resource producer. Moreover, she does not have the physical abilities to defend the tribe, its territory, and its resources. Still, Eisler and others who write about early matriarchy draw a fascinating conclusion that our future is in our past. Even better, our future can be a blend of the best of our past (matriarchy), and the best of our present (patriarchy) into something new with greater benefits for all.

With the warrior came an entire social structure—patriarchy. Patriarchy is based on conflict, defense, and domination. The father, the male, with his physical attributes, produces and defends the resources so vital for life itself in the community. As author and originator of these resources, he automatically has the right and the privilege, the inherent authority, to make up the rules that govern the organization and the distribution of those resources. This is a major aspect of male power in most cultures. Patriarchy is based on force and the threat of force. It is a hierarchy with the most powerful individuals, originally the most physically powerful, at the top and the less powerful beneath them. Among the least powerful as a class are women regardless of race. Eisler points out that patriarchy thrives on inequalities of sex, race, and economic class, all ultimately based on the notion of power *over* as opposed to power *with* others.

As I view the long history of clans and tribes, I see two axioms guiding the use of this power in the distribution of resources and goods. The first: if you are a member of the right clan—the largest, the strongest, the richest, or the brightest—and the right sex—male, then you have primary access to the resources of a region or a country. The second axiom: if you are neither one of these, then you struggle and fight to survive.

In living and working with many cultures throughout the world, I found these axioms, although simplified, to be quite universal. When I worked with the Kikuyus, a prosperous tribe in Kenya, I soon discovered that if you were born male and Kikuyu, you had primary access to the job market. The Kikuyu culture and system prepared and maintained the entire society to support and affirm male's access. What is the system? It is all the institutions in the culture that organize, support, reaffirm, and condition its members into the norms and behaviors of that culture. The system includes the institutions of family, school, church, community, workplace, and government.

Thus, if you were born male and Kikuyu, you probably lived in the suburbs of Nairobi in a very fine home. Your parents, because they were Kikuyu, had good jobs and provided you with all the necessities. They also provided you with important societal contacts. They sent you to the best schools in Kenya, which happened to be run by Kikuyus. After receiving this superb education, on graduation day you were met at the school doors by recruiters who were Kikuyu. These recruiters represented businesses that were owned and successfully operated by Kikuyus. It was, therefore, easy for you as a Kikuyu male to enter the workplace and move up the managerial ladder. Once you married, you too moved out to the suburbs and continued the system.

If you were female and Kikuyu, you had less access to the job market, the wealth, and the power positions in the system. If you were the same color but belonged to another African tribe, you had even less opportunity. In Kenya, if you were as I was, definitely right sex, but definitely stand-out wrong tribe, you were lucky to get the crumbs of the system. You were a racial minority!

This similar pecking order appears in other cultures. It can be more subtle, but just as powerful. When I worked with an organization that had sites in Spain, Puerto Rico, and South America, I discovered that if you were a male, upper class, and spoke Castilian Spanish you had the best access to the resources. If you were female, upper class, and spoke Castilian dialect, you had less. And if you came from another Spanish-speaking tribe like the Basque group, or from a deluded Spanish culture, you had even less.

What is a *deluded* Spanish culture? The conquistadors who came to this new world spoke Castilian, a dialect of a region that became the nucleus of modern Spain. The mixture of the Castilian language and the native language of those whom they conquered gives us today different words, accents, and pronunciations such as Cuban Spanish, Puerto Rican Spanish, Mexican Spanish. These variations of Castilian Spanish were used by conquered people who had been proven less powerful and of less importance. Their language is seen as low-class Spanish.

Furthermore, the conquistadors mainly were white. The people whom they conquered in this new world were of brown or black skin. As one proud male of Castilian background said to me one evening after several hours of drinking: "You Americans can say what you want about equality, but we proud Castilians know that 'white is bright!' You fill in the rest." Thus, to be white and of Castilian heritage, or to speak Castilian Spanish—the standard literary and official form of Spanish—marked you with the necessary credentials of the powerful, the cultured, and the upper class.

Asian cultures are no different. When I was in Japan, I discovered the *keiretsu*. At the end of the Second World War, America aided the Japanese in rebuilding their country. Two very different worlds met. The ancient Japanese culture interfaced with a modern, industrial nation. The bridge between these two different worlds frequently was Japanese businessmen, many of whom, as a part of the Japanese upper-class, were educated in America or Europe before the war. They were the start of the *keiretsu*, business families, who now control the Japanese economy. The *keiretsu* are corporate groups that interlock through boards of directors and subcontractors. Estimates indicate that there are some three to five thousand of these business families in Japan that keep that country's markets closed or greatly limited to outsiders. The family names are: Toyota, Hyundai, Mitsubishi.

If you are a male and a member of one of these business families, you have the greatest access to the resources in Japan. If you are female, you have less. If you belong to the Leather People, the lower class Japanese, you have even less access to the wealth and power. And, if you are Korean, forget to come!

To this day, most nations continue to promote the "right gender, right clan" principle. If you are neither the right gender nor the right clan, you struggle and fight to survive. As I write, there are approximately thirty-two locations throughout the world in which a civil war is waging. In America the media only informs us of a few civil wars—Bosnia, Northern Ireland, Burundi, Chechnya. The media reports what is important to this country in the amount of space available.

Kenya is a good example of a quiet, unreported civil war. Until eighteen years ago the president of newly independent Kenya was Jomo Kenyatta, a Kikuyu. During his fourteen years in office many Kikuyus found their way into prominent positions in government and lucrative positions in business. To make some attempt at balancing the increasing power of the Kikuyus, Kenyatta promoted Daniel arap Moi, of the small, rural Tugen tribe, as his vice president. In 1978 Kenyatta died and arap Moi became president. During the past nineteen years arap Moi has been removing the Kikuyus and installing his own tribesfolk and friends. The Kikuyus and others are upset. History is filled with the overthrow of one group by another, only to be overthrown by another group, only to be. . . . You begin to see the pattern.

However, the unusual occurred in the history of how societies operated. Many colonists who came to this new land, we now call America, were part of oppressed groups in England and other parts of Europe. They believed that in this new land they could set up a new order regarding the distribution of goods. They would be different. They wrote documents containing the seeds of a political system that would directly counter the existing standards for old world societies. This new culture would formulate a society with democratic concepts.

Several major factors propelled the colonists to create this new social order. Two hundred years prior to the English colonists coming to the new world, King John had signed a charter, the Magna Carta, granting political and civil liberties to citizens. This document was the first major piece of legislation in Western civilization that guaranteed basic human rights. The years following the signing saw much struggle and strife as England tried to implement the promises of the Magna Carta. The British colonists coming to a totally new land believed that the

Magna Carta could work better in a country starting with greater civil liberties.

Thomas Jefferson strongly influenced the founding principles and formation of this government. As a political theorist and a scholar, Jefferson helped shape this new society with democratic concepts he admired in the republics of ancient Greece and Rome.

Jefferson produced the Declaration of Independence. He penned the most quoted statement of human rights in recorded history. These are the best-known fifty-eight words in American history: "We hold these truths to be self-evident; that all men are created equal; that they are endowed by their Creator with certain [and inherent] inalienable Rights; that among these are life, liberty & the pursuit of happiness; to secure these rights, governments are instituted among men, deriving their just powers from the consent of the governed.

Joseph J. Ellis, in his remarkable biography of Jefferson, notes: "The entire history of liberal reform in America can be written as a process of discovery within Jefferson's words, of a spiritually sanctioned mandate for ending slavery, providing the rights of citizenship to blacks and women, justifying welfare programs for the poor and expanding individual freedom." This was a seminal statement of the American creed. "No serious student of either Jefferson or the Declaration of Independence has ever claimed that he foresaw all or even most of the ideological consequences of what he wrote."

Yet, Jefferson has been a paradox that few can understand. Although he was brilliant and upheld such truths of freedom, he remained an owner of several hundred slaves even after his Virginia neighbors had freed theirs. Many historians have offered their views of such a glaring contradiction in the founder of American democracy.

As a history teacher, Thomas Jefferson has always been one of my heroes. As a psychologist, Jefferson personified for me human nature at its best and its worst. As a student of philosophy and theology I learned that Jefferson struggled with the human dilemma of which we are all afflicted: *What we say is not what we do.* His historical prominence spotlights Jefferson's foibles in a bold and blatant way. In the person of Jefferson we find that common human germ which he passed on to a nation.

What we now have is an American national disease of epidemic proportions. We are all infected with this political disease either by birth of by association. This disease is similar to schizophrenia. Simply put, schizophrenia is characterized by withdrawal from reality, illogical patterns of thinking, delusions, and hallucinations, usually accompanied in varying degrees by other emotional behaviors or intellectual disturbance. The burden of this illness is that people inflicted with it operate out of two different worlds at the same time: the world within their heads with all its characters, events, and history; and the world of reality outside their heads. The painful anxiety suffered by these people results from their confusion in knowing out of which world they are operating.

Jefferson was pulled by two worlds: the world of the intellect (head) with all its exciting ideas and stimulating schemata; the world of passions (heart) which he kept under lock-and-key only to reveal momentarily during his time in Paris and in the private luxury of Monticello. Even as a mature human, Jefferson failed to integrate the two worlds. We, too, are heirs to that human dilemma and to Jefferson's political thought: what we say is not how we behave! In common parlance, or in the jargon of the field of diversity: we don't walk the talk! All humans, all of us are guilty of this condition—white males, women, and minorities.

Another possible influence on the thinking of the founders of this new world could have been the cultures of several Native American tribes. Many of the colonists were familiar with the Iroquois Confederacy in New York. The Mohawk, Oneida, Onondaga, Seneca, and Cayuga tribes originally composed the Confederacy by signing the League of Five Nations. After 1722, the Iroquois confederacy added the Tuscaroras. The purpose of this Confederacy was to peacefully unite all these tribes. They had waged deadly combat over the rights to the resources in the land that they jointly occupied.

Separation of powers, checks and balances, rights of recall, and representative democracy at all levels are just a few of the principles of the Iroquois Great Law used to hold its Six Nations together. The founding fathers learned from the Indian law a structure that endured gender balance. Although all the chiefs nominated to the governing council were men, all the nominators were women, the clan mothers in each tribe. J. Mander writes: "The women also had the power to remove the chefs from office if they proved not 'to have in mind the welfare of the people,' as the law says." Furthermore, all the nominees were approved by votes at several levels, and women participated fully in the elections. American men took another 150 years before they approved suffrage for women.

Still, another possible influence on the colonists in their formulation of a new world order could have been the Native American concept of *berdaches*. *Berdaches* is the Spanish word for a special category of tribe members. Berdaches were women who assumed male roles with such activities as warriors and chiefs, or engaged in male work or occupations. If they were men, berdaches assumed female roles with such activities as caretakers and nurturers. Will Roscoe in his work *The Zuni Man-Woman* notes that over 130 North American tribes in every region of the continent had some type of *berdaches*. As a prime example of this concept, he especially focuses on the Zuni tribe in the American Southwest.

Roscoe notes that the European culture transplanted to America, with its Western view of sexuality and two genders, had difficulty with such a concept as the *berdaches*, a third gender, in the Native American cultures. In the European culture gender roles were based on physiology not on inclination or "a calling." Furthermore, the Spanish and Anglo-Americans who overran these Native American cultures came to know of the *berdaches* and reacted with confusion, dismay, disgust, and even anger. Some of the behaviors of the *berdaches* were interpreted by the Europeans as being deviant, perverted, and sinful. Few aspects of European and American Indian cultures conflicted as much as the definition of gender roles. Nevertheless, equality of men and women, regardless of their biology, challenged and attracted some of the colonists in the founding of a new world order.

This new Republic was very unusual. In most societies then, and in much of the world today, major decisions concerning an individual's life are made by that individual's tribe, sex, or government. For example, many European countries give each child an academic examination at age twelve, sixteen, or eighteen. If you score below a certain level, you are sent to a technical school. If you score above, you may enter the university. Your education indicates what career you will have, how much money you will make, what societal class you will inhabit, who you will meet and marry, how many children you will have, where you will send them to school, and where you will spend your vacation. All the major decisions in an individual's life are already made by age twelve! Some cultures even label distinct social groupings as caste systems. For all practical purposes your life is set, never to change.

Although the concepts of the New Republic were unusual and attractive, the colonists did not understand fully nor know how to implement these new political ideas. They could not look to their brothers and sisters in Europe for models of this new system. Even if they knew about the cultures in Africa or Asia, would they find any differences? These cultures followed the old order. The colonists were forced to set about discovering new language and new processes for implementing the freedoms promised by the Declaration of Independence and the Constitution. As their descendants, we continue their journey of discovery.

Although the colonists knew intellectually what sort of society they wanted, they were the victims of their history and culture. As the oppressed people of England, they came to this new land to establish a different society. Soon, however, they killed Native Americans, imported slaves, and persecuted those who were not of their religion. They quickly moved from being the oppressed to becoming the oppressors. This great nation offers people the conceptual ideals of freedom and democracy as contained in our founding documents. We do not know how to fully live out these ideals. We become the victims of the old world patterns.

This is the major cause, I believe, of the great tension in this country and in the workplace. What we proclaim as a nation is not always how we live. There is a difference between what we say and what we do. Many women and minorities rightfully focus on the stated promises of equality in the American workplace. Yet, these same women and minorities support other institutions in our society—homes, schools, churches, and government—which oppress and deny them their rights. Yet, women and minorities become frustrated when white males speak of the fine ideals of equal access, but behave differently. In turn, white males become bewildered with women and minorities who seem to use their sex and race to gain power and economic advantages, but behave differently at other times in their lives.

To many white males there seems to be a double standard. White males are expected to practice the American principles of equality in every institution of their lives. Women and minorities seem to choose where and when they want to practice the tenants of democracy. In reality, all of us—including white males—use either old world concepts or new world concepts when either one works to our personal advantage. If "equal rights" gets you what you want, call upon that American principle. If the way you have been raised or the concepts of your religion gives you the advantage, call upon that old world concept. One of the greatest struggles every individual experiences, every institution and organization undergoes, and every society sustains, is truly living out its stated ideals.

As long as women and minorities support old world behaviors, they unknowingly collude to keep the white males in power. As we have stated, a fundamental premise for the operation of the old world order is that the males of the dominant clan have supreme power.

Talk to men about changing this paradigm of proclaiming equality and living it, and they are likely to say, "You first." To the male it looks as if he is giving up his power and dominance—giving up his rightful place—in the culture, or is he? Of course, men were not just the warriors and the soldiers. Our American history shows that men were also the farmers, the fishermen, and the breadwinners. Such occupations facilitated men's roles with their families. In an agrarian society, achieving a balance between work and home was easier to accomplish since life and work were so intertwined. Setting priorities according to one's values was not as difficult.

All this changed with the industrial age. Starting in England in the late eighteenth century, the Industrial Revolution soon reached our shores. The Industrial Revolution solidified a growing movement in societies: the division of home and work. The roles of men and women became much more defined and separated. Many of the factory jobs required the physical strength of men. Men were now brought out of their homes, away from their families, to work long hours. Now they were away from their homes and families for most of the day. Women took charge of all the duties involved in the operation of the home and raising the children. From this historical context we obtained the phrase *a woman's place is in the home.*

While the country prospered in this new era in the workplace, we unknowingly planted the seeds for much of the emptiness, lack of meaning, and loneliness men feel today. By minimizing the time spent in relationships with those people closest to them, men began to lose sense of themselves. Why were they putting so much time, energy, effort, and even their very lives into the roles of resource producer and resource defender? Having lost their focus, men gradually made the means of their role their end. Men had re-defined their manhood. Masculinity now meant accumulating an abundance of material goods (resource producer), winning at all competitive efforts (resource protector), and seeking domination and power for its own sake (resource director). Herein lie the roots of today's definition of societal success. This definition of success is really the definition of manhood. It is a definition, a goal, to which most men (and women) subscribe unknowingly.

Throughout the changing workplace, then, muscle, brawn, and strength continued to be the distinguishing element that gave men their superiority, their power in society. The machinists and other factory workers were lifting and building things. Physical brawn was the unifying currency of competence in both the agricultural and the industrial eras.

The role of women also was determined by their physiology. They gave birth which bonded them to their children and focused them on their children's well-being. They did not have the physical strength of men to perform many of the important jobs in the workplace. Physiology defined role. Physiology gave power. Physiology could make for powerlessness. Which came first, the physiology or the construction of a gender role, is anyone's guess. A looping cycle of nature and nurture seems to be operative.

A half dozen major events and movements have occurred on the American scene in the interval since the beginning of the industrial age. Each one was part of a necessary progression in the process of becoming the American people we said we were. In 1920 women won the right to vote, a major step in the slow march to equality in American society. In the democratic process women now had an equal footing in determining who ran the country.

In World War II many American men experienced one of the first lessons of diversity in modern times. Soldiers were forced to fight and interact with those who were not of the same tribe or race. At the beginning of the war men in the military were segregated by race. Blacks were sequestered in units with other blacks, Hispanics with Hispanics. All those in power, the officers, were white. This division was very much accepted since it reflected American society at large. Americans were segregated with few means of contact. Television did not exist; cars were few; travel was limited. One could actually grow up in a racially specific environment without seeing "one of them." This segregation of races seemed to work in peacetime America. It did not withstand the pressures of life and death, stress and fear during wartime. Lacking an understanding between white officers and men of a different color, the armed forces soon experienced unrest and tension. This unrest even led to "fragging"—the killing or wounding of a disliked superior usually by means of a fragmentation grenade. This practice has been present in most societies since the beginning of time. Sometimes troops lacked any commonalities in background, education, or experience with their officers. There were no bonds of understanding to bridge the gap between the life-and-death intensity of wartime and the interdependence of camaraderie. Troops lacked confidence and trust in their officers' ability to keep them alive.

Without too much fanfare, the armed forces between 1942 and 1945 began to desegregate the officers' corp. In 1948 President Harry S. Truman, as Commander-in-Chief of the Armed Forces, officially desegregated the entire armed forces. This mandate allowed men of color as well as whites into leadership positions. The military, sixteen years before the civil rights movement in America, led the way toward desegregation of the American society. We have a Colin Powell today as a result of this factor.

Prior to the beginning of the war in 1941, about a quarter of the work-age women in America went to work part-time or full-time. Since men were at war, all women were encouraged to leave their homes and families to support the war effort. This happened in the same American society that believed for many decades a woman's place was in the home. In most cultures men who set the rules for the culture, many times change those rules when their lives or positions are in jeopardy. Isn't this what men do even in today's world—change or adjust the rules to maintain their power, position, and status?

After the war society expected women to return to their traditional domain of home and family. Having been the successful protector, men were expected to resume their role as the historical family breadwinners. However, with the right to vote, and a taste of the power and freedom earning money gave them, many women were reluctant to resume their former passive roles in society.

America experienced a tremendous period of prosperity after the war. We were one of the few industrial nations still intact. The world looked to us for raw materials, products, and information. America became a manufacturing workplace. Booming industries searched for workers, even women workers. Unemployment rates were at their lowest. In 1953, for example, unemployment in America reached an all-time low of 2.9 percent.

Women workers were in high demand by male employers. Working in factories during the war years, women had learned the latest technology that now was needed for business production. Besides, by paying women less, more money could be made. Offering women lower wages was culturally approved. Women were not seen as society's heads of family—the primary breadwinners. Furthermore, the growing number of home appliances freed many women to enter the work force. Women employees became essential to a company's competitive edge. Women were an essential element in achieving post-war business success.

Again, unknowingly the military promoted the principles of equality in American society. In an effort to help returning servicemen readjust to civilian life, the government offered them special privileges and opportunities. One of the monetary benefits of the Government Issue (GI) Bill was to encourage and support men in their effort to further their education, to acquire more skills. The pressures of a Cold War, Sputnik, and the race to space, underlined the importance of math and science and the necessity of education. Everyone was encouraged to become educated. With more free time on their hands and excess energy, women, too, pursued an education. In the past fifty years, in fact, the number of women with advanced degrees has more than doubled. In the mid-1990s the number of women graduating from undergraduate colleges has surpassed the number of men.

The women's movement and the civil rights movement understandably emerged strikingly in the 1960s. To me, it was no accident that these two movements gained prominence at the same time. Women and minority groups had been brought up in new world ways. They possessed the right to vote. They won their independence by making money. They were exposed to new ideas in education. It was only a matter of time before women and minorities directly confronted the institutions based on old world order. What supports the old world culture is the principle that the male of the right clan or tribe had the power, the wealth, and the position. America promised a new democratic world. Racial groups protested white power. Women protested male dominance.

Notwithstanding some progress, women and minorities still lacked equal footing with the white male. Something was missing. That missing component was to be found in the American workplace, the economic heart of this new world republic. In 1948 two white males, John Bardeen and Walter Brattain, at Bell Laboratories in New Jersey, stumbled upon the physical principle of PNP—positive, negative, positive interaction. This PNP principle led to the development of the transistor which became the heart of the computer. With William Shockley, these three scientists received the Nobel Prize for physics in 1956. By 1976 it is estimated that the computer had transformed the workplace. The world of technology and information exploded.

Not only has the computer changed the workplace, it has changed the gender roles and the culture forever not only in America but the world over. In the past, physical strength was needed to have had access to many of the jobs in the workplace. Men had that strength, and therefore, had exclusive rights to the job market. Computers do not require physical strength. To operate a computer you need intelligence and training. Intelligence is blind to one's sex, gender role, race, ethnicity, age, physical ability, and sexual orientation. The computer has given women and minorities a major tool in their quest for equal footing with the dominant male. Ironically, the work of three white males facilitated this equality of women and minorities. A greater twist of fate was the fact that one of these three white males, William Shockley, became a controversial figure in the '70s with his white supremacy views.

The long period when muscle equaled power has now drawn to a close. Access to information is admission to wealth and power. Access is more democratized. The infrastructure for the new digital world should be in place for mass interactivity by the turn of the century.

There is one fundamental reason for the lack of greater progress and change in today's technological workplace. Many employees and employers, attempting to maintain old world ways of gender roles and class power, try to harness and direct a technological world for the year 2000. Performance evaluations, management procedures, and leadership styles basically were developed by and are geared for the white male—old world right sex, right clan.

Many of the white males in the leadership positions at American corporations are now in their late 40s, 50s, and early 60s. Their worldview is often different from the younger generation who has been raised on music television, video rentals, and personal computers in the home and office.

For this older generation of men, sitting in the top seats of power in major corporations around the country, the '60s revolution seems never to have happened. Their mothers were their role models, and they married replicas of them. They went to work, as did their fathers, to be with other men in an environment that they designed to replicate the warlike atmosphere of the male-dominated worlds. Listen to the lexicon of many of these men in the workplace: "business is war"; "it's a jungle out there"; "fight to the death"; "officers of the corporation"; "top brass"; "rank and file"; "bite the bullet"; "take no prisoners"; "what's happening in the trenches"; "are you a good soldier?" Or, from competitive, team-functioning sports: "Let's do an end run"; "full court press"; "one on one"; "what's the score"; "it's a slam dunk"; "what's the game plan?"; "who's up to bat?"; "be a team player"; "you're only as good as your last win"; "you win some, you lose some".

As providers—the hunters and the fishers; as the protectors—the soldiers and the athletes, men have always believed it was their inherent right to write the rules of life's games. The answer to the original question of this chapter, "Who are men?": they protect women, children, the helpless, and the powerless; they provide goods for their families and communities; they procreate the next generation of the tribe. These are the three functions of the male that anthropologist David Gilmore cites in *Manhood in the Making* as nearly universal among cultures worldwide. All three roles are to be carried out at the expense of self if that is what it takes to get the job done.

The warrior virtues prepare a man for war, the combative corporate world, competitive sports, and physically dangerous situations, but little else. Men are not prepared for human interaction. The world of family and friends, of feelings and emotions, of intimacy in relationships, of raising children for most men is, at best, confusing, at worst, chaotic.

The warrior resides at the core of male identity dealing with the most fundamental human issues: survival, life, and death. Asking a man to surrender his competitive drive and aggressiveness is like asking a woman to transcend her mothering instinct or her menstrual cycle. Even in times of peace and prosperity the warrior instinct governs the male desire not only to survive, but to be the best. In school he wants top grades; in sports, first place; in bed, all night long. The course is rigorous. The race belongs to the swift.

Conditioning men with warrior values restricts their human potential. It dehumanizes them by cutting them off from the full range of emotions, chiefly those in the softer mid-ranges of human expression. In war, soldiers are not supposed to talk about their fears. They believe that to acknowledge those fears is to be overcome by them. You keep your feelings bottled up. Your attention is focused on survival. All combat soldiers collude to avoid any emotion other than those associated with preserving your life and taking that of your enemies.

The man who comes home from the office responds similarly. He does not want to reveal to his family what is bothering him at work. He bottles up his emotions. He sees this behavior as protecting those less strong from the rigors of everyday warfare. Besides, talking about one's fears might shatter the hope, confidence, and security of those depending on him. Battlefield conditioning is not confined to the battlefield. The true warrior switches from one kind of survival to another.

In a warrior mentality, every other male is a potential adversary. Even though you have the same rules, you are not sure the other always will follow them. You trust no one. Any sign of lack of control or diminished domination of self and others is considered weakness. You are prey to the strong. Emotions, compassion, or understanding might be used by your enemy to his advantage. No wonder the warrior role as we practice it limits men from bonding with other men. This distancing is partially accomplished through competition, but more fully by homophobia.

As a result of the socialization process, many men learn that those who fail to live up to accepted masculine norms, to show warrior characteristics, are not fully men. Real men are in control. They maintain an emotionless expression, particularly in the presence of other men. Those who are not fully men, those who are not in control, are woman-like. They are called softies, sissies, prissys, homosexuals. The warrior is to be strong, competitive, and tough with other men. He is not caring, warm, and expressive. The sensitive and affectionate traits of a macho male are reserved for his mating game with women—a prelude to sex. It follows, then, that using those same mating behaviors with another male would be a prelude to sex. That is homosexuality! That is the antithesis of the heterosexual warrior! It is no wonder that the Armed Forces have so much difficulty accepting the policy of homosexuals in the military. Homosexuality is a direct attack at the core of manhood, the warrior-soldier.

Given their limited understanding and experience with their emotional side, most men see the world in very simplified, black-and-white, all-or-nothing terms. The life of any person is more than biology. There are other levels of humanness. You can connect, even to other males, through the expression of feelings and emotions.

Homophobia is a classic double bind. It teaches a man that closeness with other men is disgusting. It assures him that shutting off his sensitivity towards men is a good thing. Shutting down natural male softness can leave men unsuited for the company of women too. Intimacy in any direction is blocked. Effective homophobia can imprison a man in emotional solitary confinement bearing a life-long sentence of self-imposed loneliness.

One cost of this emotional constriction is the enormous anger many men carry but dare not express. This often unfocused rage usually has no source in a man's immediate reality. Its true source is the confinement and isolation he feels because he is deprived of part of himself, his own feelings. Rage is not always generated by the events of adult life but can be traced many times to infancy and early childhood. Those deprivations and abuses over which the child had no control are now experienced as uncontrollable emotion. Often this rage erupts with relatively powerless men, women, and children as its targets. Here is a chance for a man who may feel powerless to express raw, male power through domination. Besides, the anger one may feel for being weak can be expressed in the anger toward those who are similarly powerless. His lack of skills necessary to live in the world of emotions leaves a man with no control over his own emotions.

Associated with that anger and rage can be enormous fear, confusion, and pain. Rage can protect the man from the pain, cover his fear and confusion, and serve as a culturally acceptable manly emotion. Remember: "Big boys don't cry." But big boys can get angry! Unbridled anger and violence frequently are mistaken for strength and power. Sometimes this anger and rage is found in the workplace in ruthless behavior with employees or competitors. In reality, anger is for men what tears have been for women—an acceptable emotional release.

Many times when some men go beyond their anger, they find the pain and unshed tears of that little boy being hammered into a durable warrior forcing him "to act like a man." On top of this he learns to endure pain to gain strength, to gain manhood. Endurance of pain can make one strong in character or body. Endurance of pain can foster courage and self-sacrifice. Yet common sense and good judgment need to temper the ability to endure. There are many other ways to develop strength of character besides endless endurance of pain.

Stephen Shapiro writes about this in *Manhood*: "The inability to re-spect pain results in the inability to feel compassion or empathy, for it means that a person will be out of touch, both with his own felt values and with others' needs. So, respect for pain, as simple as this may sound, is fundamental to the whole structure of human reality. Life lived on the basis of denying pain is life spent in the illusion of invulnerability; it is ac-tually life unlived, unfelt, like a story that is merely skimmed. Allowing pain to penetrate our deepest being and taking responsibility for that pain: That is suffering.

"The pain I speak of here is the pain of the hurt child inside us . . . of loss of childhood . . . of realizing that no one—neither idealized parents nor ever new mates—can protect us from time, from the pain of our vi-olent, envious, twisted hearts, the pain of acknowledging the pain we have carelessly inflicted on others, the pain of knowing we can do other-wise, the pain of admitting that we have no control over our own vul-nerability to loss and death."

The cost to men of keeping all that feeling suppressed is enormous. There is a cost to one's physical well-being, one's relationships, and to the individual's own humanity. Many men are well protected from the pain and sadness that lies beneath the surface.

Helping men change is like peeling away the layers of an onion. As we saw with Lee Atwater, when men reach those depths, the tears will come, and wash away the pain. The wealth and richness of human emo-tion will surface to balance, temper, and complete the warrior who has not allowed himself to feel. These emotions provide the deepest links white men have to women and minorities who suffer the indignities of their lives in sadness and pain. The truth is that a disproportionate share of tears has been shed by people who are allegedly different from the warrior norm.

When I work with men, I ask them to start reflecting on what they are doing and what they are feeling. Many times I have to help men learn how to recognize their feelings since usually they say they have no feelings. This is partially true, since for years they have been trained to ignore, repress, and suppress those feelings. One way that is helpful for men to come in contact with those hidden feelings is for me to say how I feel.

Since psyche and body are very much connected, another way to dis-cover feelings is to explore what parts of the body seems most sensitive in the situation. For example, backaches can speak of fatigue; headaches, confusion; inability to breath, fear.

Most men seem to operate with four basic feelings: mad, glad, sad, and scared. That is it. There are no nuances to their feelings. This comes from a lack of experience with the world of feelings. Most men need to feel something more: frustration, exhilaration, anxiety, comfort, disappointment, calm—the hundreds of shades of feeling that make us human. Delineating shades of feeling helps us achieve a better understanding of ourselves and the world around us. For example, Eskimos have twenty-seven different words for *snow*. Snow is a vital factor in an Eskimos's life. They select the word indicating some special quality of snow— humidity, color, texture. We simply call it by one name *snow*. Demarking emotions gives them depth, shades, and variations. Women sometimes call this variation the gray areas of life. This world of gray lies beyond the world of black or white, of win or lose, which governs the lives of most men.

Male feelings are critical to living in a diverse society. Once men relate to the diversity in their own emotional lives, they can make the generalization of appreciating the variety of feelings and experiences of others. At the same time, they can see that people who are not like them by sex or race are very much like them in human feelings and emotions.

We know men can be different because we see the variety of masculinities in men around the world, even in other warrior cultures: the softness and depth of Africans, the emotionalism of Italians, the expressiveness of Arabs. When men experience the variety of their emotions and the reality of their emotional choices, then the reward for change is evident: an inner power and strength. This blending and balancing of the inner power of feelings with the outer power of performance will provide men a fullness of being, a new sense of personal power.

Transforming the notion of power is the ultimate shift. It is moving from control to cooperation, from power *over* to power *with* others. This is how truly effective teams work. The workplace of the future will be dominated by successful teams that are more than a grouping of related talents and functions, sharing information and tasks. Teams are also made up of human beings with emotions, feelings, visions, values, hopes, and dreams. Organizations, with their diverse work force and customer bases, will limit their success unless there is a basic understanding and appreciation of the full humanity of people.

Companies change when the people in them change. It would be simpler to start by changing the way we raise our children and condition our young men and women. To do that, society would have to change the reward system for behavior. We would need to create incentives in school for gender role expansion so that men like me do not have to do remedial work when they are adults.

The good news is that men are changing. Studies have found fathers choosing flextime in large numbers so they can spend more time with their families. The Catalyst Institute for Research found that the number of American companies offering paternity leave has climbed rapidly to almost half. Still, greater support from men and women to change the cultural definition of man beyond that of the warrior is needed. The greatest need, however, is for a new breed of men. We need men who reflect, struggle, and mutually support each other in their day-to-day lives.

This struggle to re-define manhood and power can be enhanced by the present movements of women and minorities. They, too, are seeking their new identities and power in America's diverse society. Who would have ever thought that the enticement for white men to enter into this national journey would come by focusing on their loneliness, their need to relate, their need to prize their feelings, their need to reclaim their souls?

INTERVIEW

Ron
48
White
project manager
27 years with company
high school education

I always wondered about upper management, which in my view is pretty insulated. And I'm probably insulated from what goes on in their little world too. I think it's interesting that even in trying to create a diverse work environment, there's a sequence to the way upper management promotes people. First they promoted women. Then they promoted blacks. Now they're promoting Asians. There's even a hierarchy to the promotions. The pecking order still exists. I wasn't prepared for it.

When I started working for my company right after I got out of the service, I had a personal experience with discrimination. There were people who wanted to promote me, but I was not promotable because there was such a large emphasis on correcting the imbalance of minorities and women in management that they were only promoting them. It was quite a setback in my own aspirations. It affected my career for a number of years. My wife, who works for the same company, was promoted long before I was.

It was a shock, a big letdown. In retrospect I see there was no other way it could have happened. Every change is going to affect somebody. There's no getting around it. At the time I was a technician; I'd work my eight hours and go home. Your view of the big picture is somewhat limited in that kind of job. When I became a manager, I looked at things in a different light.

I've worked for women during the past fifteen years. A woman promoted me. Most of what I have today I can attribute to women. If there's any resistance to women in the workplace, I think it's mainly in the nine to five occupations, where someone comes in, puts in his eight hours, and goes home, interacting with a limited number of people. If people live in a small bubble and don't get out of it, they don't have the opportunity to change.

When I was losing out to women in promotions, I was single, raising my seven year old son by myself. I was so busy, the time was a blur to me. I remember all the things I had to do to get him ready for school and things, that you would normally share with another parent. Three years later I remarried, and we became a blended family. My son had difficulty in school and had some unresolved issues with his mother, and they manifested themselves against my wife. So we went into counseling. My wife helped me accept this. Now I know we couldn't have done what we did without counseling.

I was more communicative with my son than my father was with me. I've tried a lot of different things that my father never had available to him. My father's position was "you owe everything to the company." He was raised during the Depression, when having a full-time job was a rarity. He worked for the same company I do. When I was a kid, any derogatory word about the company was taboo. There was phenomenal loyalty. In my case, when I came of age, I was more interested in self development and not taking things at face value. You know, the "never believe anyone older than you" mentality. My son is having more difficulty than I did at finding what he wants to do. I've never been without a job. He's not worried about working. It bothers me, but I've reached the point where it's none of my business anymore.

I've altered my thinking about the place of work in a man's life. I'm appreciative I have a job in these times and that I like what I'm doing. I'm not trying to look for alternatives. At times I feel I am right where my dad was standing.

Now that my son is grown, my wife and I spend a lot of time at work. She has a more demanding job and has commitments to clients or customers. I have more flexibility in my work schedules. We've had discussions recently about spending more time together, doing things for ourselves and not just for the company, so we can continue our relationship.

I thought that was interesting when Dr. Ipsaro brought up that issue of loneliness, that hole in the chest for men. Man, that really hit home.

I think it has to do with connecting, having that connection with your spouse or not. That sense of connection isn't something you get off the shelf.

I think the sense of loneliness men feel comes from the whole emphasis on being male. You perform, you go out and you do your job, and you do it well. It's easier to do that than build a relationship.

But we've gotten to the point now where it's more important to build our relationship. A lot of people my age are getting divorced. It concerns me for my own personal survival. I see it's a distinct possibility. But we have the power to take care of that.

WORKSHOP

1. List five items (people, concepts, etc.) for which you would give up your life. How much time each week do you devote to developing, supporting, or sustaining those five elements you say are important in your life?

2. Make a time chart of your week. List how many hours you devote to work, family, friends, personal time and leisure, and the community. What does this indicate about who you really are? Are you satisfied with this? If not, what is one thing you can change in each of these categories?

3. This evening sit down for a few moments and list the two or three special events of the day. Try to list all your feelings surrounding each of those events. Was your body giving you clues of how you were feeling? What do those feelings say about you as a person? What can you learn from those feelings about the way you live your life? Do you need to reaffirm those ways; adjust them; or, change them?

4. One way to examine your experience of pain is to focus on your losses. What are those major losses you have suffered in your life? How

have you handled the pain of loss? Do you still carry that pain with you? What other emotions surround those losses? Did you allow yourself to grieve? Do you know how to grieve? What have your losses told you about yourself?

Inferiority feelings, the power drive, anxiety, possessiveness,
envy, jealousy, and the compulsion to subdue and conquer
are the mainsprings of the patriarchal ego.
–Edward C. Whitmont
Source unknown

3

THE BIOLOGY BEHIND
THE BEHAVIOR

Men have become dissociated from the reasons they were fighting for re-
sources—to provide for their families and their communities. Fixated on
competitiveness and protectiveness as values in themselves, they have lost
their way. They have misread the warrior code, forgetting that the war-
rior fights for a larger purpose: to serve others and for the common good.
Self-interest has become a substitute for service in our culture. Bereft of
bonding with other men, white American males can as easily become out-
laws as they become organization men.

Change does not mean that everything male gets thrown on the scrap
heap. The warrior tradition embodies much that is worth keeping. The
loyalty we mentioned in the last chapter and the capacity for self-sacrifice
are virtues in any age. Change does not mean cutting off parts of ourselves. Rather, it means loosening our grip on those parts, becoming less
automatic in our judgments and more thoughtful in our responses.

Real men have choices. For example: Can you evaluate the new woman manager on her own terms, her achievement, and performance,
rather than on the basis of your own behavior and how you would act in
her position? Another way of asking that question would be: Can you
see her performance outside of your biases? Do you even recognize
your biases? That requires some insight and self-awareness. Not evaluating her on her terms is like designing an IQ test for black children based
on examples known primarily to white children, something that has
been done for some time in our society.

Change means becoming less robotic. Knowing that you have choices means having more choices. Change means taking your life off automatic pilot. It means working less and reflecting more so you discover more choices. Making time to appreciate a sunset can enrich you even if your bank account sags a bit.

The change I am talking about will take the tarnish off your surface. Some teachers call it "polishing the soul." The beauty of the warrior is well-expressed in a book by Robert Moore and Douglas Gillette called *The Warrior Within*. "The fully expressed Warrior has the capacity to anesthetize us against pain and suffering," they write. "He gives help setting goals and then gives us the energy we need to achieve them. . . . Self-discipline is the hallmark of the Warrior . . . [who] imparts to a man the capacity to be faithful."

In speaking of Japanese warriorship, these authors find tenacity. "The Samurai held that a warrior's method is to attack and attack, always moving forward. He never gives up the vision of his mission. This defiant human quality is the essence of the human drive to conquer new frontiers. It is the Warrior's willingness to charge into the unknown that moves the mind and soul of our species forward, claiming new territories both mental and physical, and eventually perhaps even new planets for homo sapiens to inhabit."

One could write a book about the value of men, but if we are so great, what has gone wrong? Moore and Gillette argue that in America today we have a "pseudo warrior." This is a version of the warrior that has been degraded by the loss of the inner warrior, the spiritual component of the warrior which balances his action with inwardness and reflection. Unless the inner warrior puts himself at the service of the highest ideals of the culture, they tell us, the warrior serves only his own self-interest and becomes a liability. "The Warrior's aggressive potentials must be dedicated to some power beyond his own, or he becomes purely destructive, creating unnecessary conflict instead of serving and protecting the human community."

Ideals are critical to the healthy functioning of the warrior. "The masculine self is never stronger or more cohesive than when it is clear about its mission and when its vision of the world and related ideals that it serves are worthy of the supreme commitment," say Moore and Gillette.

When I read this, I thought of the Vietnam veterans I counsel. Vietnam was an economic war made to appear like a "defending the country" war worthy of the supreme commitment. Fifty-eight thousand men made the supreme sacrifice. But clearly this was a war fought to gain economic and political ground, not the more traditional ground of war. The vets ask, "Is it my job to defend someone's business with my life?"

Without a commitment to the highest values, Moore argues, the boardroom is little different from the streets of East Los Angeles or the killing fields. "Men in the business world often seem to be treading water, padding their resumes, and looking for an out rather than working to improve products, services, or the quality of their leadership for their corporation and community. They are happy to enjoy the salaries and benefits their firms provide. They like their suspendered uniforms. But when they make decisions, increasingly the end results are short-term windfall profits and not the long-term health and integrity of either company or community. If the Warrior is on-line at all in these circumstances, he is only supporting personal gain. And the men who are using his energy are merely mercenaries."

Moore and Gillette believe the warrior is "hardwired" into the male psyche as a biological component of masculinity and that aggression is also innately male. My reading and training bring me to a different conclusion. I think the warrior model is made from the basic male "stuff": cultural conditioning in the face of environmental pressure (predatory animals, cold, scarcity, competition for available resources). I think warrior masculinity is a conditioned response to life on earth.

What is the basic male stuff? And the basic female stuff? Knowing what a man is involves knowing the hardware nature has installed. Learning about some of the female stuff will help to respect the differences. Those differences begin *in utero*. For the first six weeks the newly conceived fetus is neither male nor female. At that point the mother's body enters a series of hormonal changes that create a male child if the changes are fully implemented. The Y chromosome from the father carries the genetic signal that the embryo is supposed to start masculinizing. If none of the changes occur, the fetus will grow to be a fully female child. If only some of the changes occur, you may have an anatomical male who is psychically female. John Money and Patricia Tucker, who did groundbreaking work on sexual identity at the Johns Hopkins University, conclude that the greater sexual variety among males (gays, transvestites, transsexuals) is the result of the way male children are formed during gestation. It also may explain the higher mortality rates of male fetuses and infants, the greater vulnerability of males, including weaker immune systems and the well-known difference in longevity.

The father contributes an X chromosome to a female child. His X duplicates the X contributed by the mother and also helps cancel any deadly genetic anomalies on one of the female's X chromosomes (Alzheimer's disease, Parkinson's disease).

An article in *U.S. News and World Report* stated: "Genesis was wrong: Women came first—embryologically speaking at least. Genetically, the female is the basic pattern of the species; maleness is superimposed on that. And this peculiarity of nature has the side effect of making males more vulnerable to a number of inherited disorders."

The *in utero* distinctions include differences in the way the brain is organized. The hemispheres of the male brain are more specialized, with language functions located in the left hemisphere and visual/spatial functions located in the right. Women tend toward left/right distinctions also but have these functions distributed more equally in both hemispheres. After strokes or damage to the left hemisphere, for example, women are three times less likely than men to suffer language deficits.

Some researchers found the corpus callosum, a bundle of nerves that joins the two halves of the brain, is wider in women, allowing for better integration of the two sides of the brain. Furthermore, they found the hypothalamus, a kind of master control unit at the base of the brain, is markedly different in the two genders. One recent study has shown that gay men also have a more female-constructed hypothalamus.

Estrogen keeps the female body prepared for childbirth. It keeps blood vessels pliable so they can accommodate the extra blood needed during pregnancy. Estrogen stimulates the liver to produce high-density lipoproteins which allow the body to make better use of fat. Testosterone, on the other hand, causes men to have the low-density lipoproteins which can clog blood vessels.

These innate biological differences show up as gender tendencies in infants and children. We have all heard that white females (white children have been the main subjects in these studies) tend to be more sensitive to touch and sounds; white males tend to be more sensitive to light. Males tend to be better at visual-spatial activities; females have better fine-motor control. Studies have shown that females, starting as early as five months, are more attracted to people, and males are more attracted to objects. This may explain the tendency for girls to have superior verbal skills and boys to have better mathematic skills.

These differences are not a problem unless they become interpreted as superior and inferior. That is exactly what happens when purely biological traits cross into the realm of culture. They get evaluated according to the needs and biases of particular cultures. For example, an increased ability to do math will be rewarded in a culture that values math and science. The person in that culture who is better at math might be regarded as superior. Likewise, physical strength is valued in a culture that emphasizes force and "dominion over." It is no accident that a culture that aligned itself with exploration and conquest came to value the male musculature that produced superior strength and speed. The success of Arnold Schwartzenegger is the direct result of biological factors interacting with cultural evaluation.

Puberty is another biological fact and one that has wide ramifications for male and female identity. Emily Prager puts the difference succinctly: "We women believe that when a girl sprouts breasts and gets her period, she becomes a woman. But in the rugged terrain of manhood, there is no such surefootedness." Prager examined seventy-four "About Men" columns published in *The New York Times* and concluded that manhood is an uncertain and ongoing test for American men that lacks the humor and delight women find in their condition. Women are blessed— and some would say cursed—by having their identity embodied in the condition of motherhood. Their value, their importance in society, their identity as individuals are, in a sense, guaranteed by the fact that they bear and nurture children. Today, whatever women achieve in any of the several worlds they choose to enter is built atop the fundamental certainty that they are females with an assigned place in the natural scheme of things.

Men have no such assurance. Their procreative value is fleeting at best. Only very recently have men been valued as parental nurturers. In sports, in school, at work, and at play men are constantly having to prove themselves. We are continually subjected to our own performance judgments and the judgments of others. Prager calls this "the dogged Alp climb of male uncertainty."

One of the key ways modern man establishes himself is, once again, by analysis. Since he wants to be the perfect man, he figures out what he is lacking. Perhaps he is not short, or tall. Perhaps he is white, perhaps not. Perhaps he is educated, maybe not. A set of standards is essential to labeling one's perfection. In learning to label himself, he learns to label others as a form of identification. They are not like him. They can be a little more perfect or less perfect and that's a little discomforting. It is scary to the psyche to live with people who are not like us, perfect or not. To create order, we categorize, and our categorizations become our prejudices, our labeling of differences as "better than" or "less than." Every human being does this categorization. To be human is to be prejudiced!

Earlier societies helped their young men and women attain their identities in a group process. Initiation rites for men, for instance, separated the young men from their mothers and attached them to a brotherhood with a distinct and revered male identity. This rite served as a counterpart to the natural female ritual of menstruation, which began at about the same time and was marked by tribal women with coming-of-age ceremonies. In fact, several commentators have noted that male initiations, with their reliance on pain and the shedding of blood, closely parallel the biological initiation of women. Commentators also have noted that the hardships endured in male initiation rites (which include the possible death of the initiate) prepare young men for the rigors of combat and the hunt.

Anthropologists have shown us the ways initiation traditionally provided young men with the skills needed to carry out their cultural responsibilities as providers, protectors, and procreators. In addition, initiation attached them to the tribal gods and secured their allegiance to self-sacrifice for the tribe. This initiation rite established a societal role, in Gilmore's words, that "men are expected to produce and give more than they take," including the sacrifice of their lives in war.

Initiation was neither pretty nor easy, but it achieved its purpose. The initiation ceremonies served to create a valued masculine identity that, in tandem with the female powers, might serve the needs of the tribe. The loss of specific initiation rituals in technological societies around the world means that men are constantly having to construct and reconstruct their identities when adequate models are not available. Men have no commonly agreed upon definition of manhood and no point in time at which they know manhood has been attained. Therefore, they are in a continual state of becoming and must take their initiations where they find them: at college, in war, in the boardroom, in the back seat of a car.

With this much freedom, without some sort of guidelines, we usually find confusion.

Bereft of the kind of initiation women come by naturally, men are un-bonded to their maleness and in that isolated condition must face life, both its hardships and its joys, relatively alone. The natural result of this is that men become overly dependent on women to satisfy a host of in-terpersonal needs. There are emotional needs, such as belonging and re-spect, that have traditionally been the province of the male community. Men promoted their needs as they hunted or worked or sat together in a kiva (a special underground chamber designated for the men in Pueblo villages) or in other places of male association. Without this male forum, undue stress has been placed on marriages and other male-female associ-ations. With the absence of an initiation rite that establishes manhood, male anxiety is carried into relationships. The result is the current flood of books and articles on male-female relationships and the difficulties of cross-gender communication.

Even these difficulties have their roots in environmental adaptation. Let us look at the way men and women confront situations. I like to say men have a cultural built-in radar to focus on a goal or project. Women see a wider perspective. They have a cultural built-in periscope to learn about their environment. When a man was confronted by an animal, he had to kill or be killed. He didn't have time to gather data and reflect on the impact of his actions. He put all his thoughts and feelings aside to focus his energies on completing the task at hand. Women, lacking the strength of men (and the testosterone levels leading to aggression) have to use their wits. They "read" their environments. They are open to de-tails and clues that trigger telling information stored in their brains. They quickly reflect and intuit what might happen. Woman construct their reality from a wide variety of sources and resources, interacting with them in a fluid manner.

The cafes of Europe, the chai shops of Asia, and the male-only clubs of the United States and England (often criticized by women as bastions of old boyism) have attempted to fill the gap for safe male relationships. These are the substitutes since initiation passed away with the break-down of tribal life around the world. In some cases these attempts at male bonding have worked.

The male community must struggle against its own tendency to dis-integrate. In most cultures the male community always is threatened by homophobia. Competitive urges caution men to view each other as rivals for goods, status, and women. In fact, if you think about it, you will notice, as I have, for safety reasons men choose their friends to match their identity as providers and protectors. Their friends are typically work or sports buddies.

Without much support for brotherhood, the male community tends to splinter into isolated males in search of meaning, who they are, and their purpose. This condition was most directly addressed in the literature and philosophy of existentialism in postwar Europe, in the work of Camus, Sartre, and others. With its death camps and millions of battlefield casualties, World War II communicated the same message: Man was alone in a godless universe. The existential image of man as an isolated individual crying out for meaning in a cosmos that gives back only "the still, cold silence of the stars," in the words of Camus.

I do not think that image or that stance could have been created by a woman. It is the legacy of the warrior, who, like the Tin Man in "The Wizard of Oz," is looking for his heart. When he finds the Emerald City—the community he was born to live in, be enriched by, and to serve—he will find his heart.

With discussions of initiation and the effects of its absence, we have crossed once again into the realm of historical and cultural influences on masculinity. But no discussion of biology would be complete without mentioning the influence of testosterone and aggressive behaviors as critical factors in male development. The one difference which is constant across cultures is that males are more aggressive than females.

Testosterone is a sex hormone found abundantly in males. But it is also present in females where it figures prominently as the hormonal stimulus which forms a male fetus. It is responsible for the changes at puberty which deepen male voices, cause the growth of facial hair and muscles, and attract men to contact sports and sex. In fact, some studies cite testosterone as responsible for the female sex drive as well.

The testosterone factor cannot be ignored, but it can be managed. This hormone is responsible for many things, for example, as a factor in baldness. Its role in male aggression most concerns us. Here is Kenneth Purvis in a recent book on male sexuality: "Deep within all men is a Rambo imprisoned and shackled by society's rules and regulations. This anachronism, this prototype of maleness, is created by a strange union between the primitive areas of our brains and the male hormone testosterone produced in the testicles. This hormone is the reason for maleness, affecting not only how men look, but is to a great extent the fuel for those primitive male pursuits. It may be at a soccer match, with angry hordes of youths tearing each other apart. It may be at a discotheque, with men indulging displays of courtship to entice the defenseless female into their webs. It may be on the road, driving mechanical steeds in life-and-death ego races. It may be at work, involved in power struggles for status and salary . . . and when man does his male dance, it's his testicles and their released hormone, testosterone, that usually call the tune."

In a study of American ice hockey players, Purvis describes coaches that ranked players on the basis of how much aggression they showed. Players were tested for blood testosterone levels. The correlations between high test levels and the coaches' ratings were very close. Anabolic steroids used by bodybuilders mimic the effects of testosterone in both aggressiveness and sex drive (although they ultimately lead to sexual deterioration).

At puberty the bodies of young males are suffused with testosterone at levels thirty times higher than in females. In primitive societies that energy was handled by initiation rites, which provided both boundaries and direction. Gilmore's work describes initiates pushing razor-sharp sawgrass up their nostrils and bleeding without crying out. These rites of passage represent a barrier those young men had to surmount. Indigenous cultures required their young men to face pain and death. They knew they could not afford to have unbridled male aggression loose in the countryside. Initiation harnessed testosterone for social purposes. Some of them were quite violent but always in the service of what Moore terms "a self-transcending public commitment."

Testosterone and the aggressive potential it carries are not debatable. The hormone is part of our body chemistry. It will always make us more aggressive as a group than females. It is an important form of human energy. But how we socialize this aggressive tendency will determine whether we use it or it abuses us, both in society and in the business setting. In today's atmosphere of social breakdown, violence and the raw power needed for survival are in many cases the only ideals young men are offered. In an environment of compromised values and corruption in high places, raw power and survival may seem the only ideals worth holding. With such a degraded tribal vision, the results are disastrous. In the inner cities, the breakdown of family and economy is most severe. Young males form gangs, like outlaws, to provide themselves with initiation rites. These ceremonies provide connection, boundaries, and rituals of achievement and respect.

These outlaws, however, are by definition lost to the uses of the larger community. They represent an untamed human resource in rebellion from broader cultural purposes. They do not recognize the kinship uniting them with anyone beyond their narrow pod of self-interest, be it a gang, a union, or a country club.

What has gone wrong with men? Many of us have retreated into the safety of our clans, sometimes convinced that no wider associations are workable. Diversity calls on us to widen our circle beyond "right clan, right gender." Diversity challenges us to expand our vision if only because the social experiment that is America cannot keep working unless we do. That call goes particularly to white males, who have held a disproportionate share of economic and political power for hundreds of years.

Our world is out of balance because decisions have been made over a long period only from the white male perspective. For political office we usually choose between two white men whose points of view differ only slightly. Our cultural vision has been constricted by this one culture/one gender approach. In government and business we need the different perspectives of women, blacks, gays, Hispanics, Asians, and all the others who comprise our society. Different hands need access to the tiller if the ship is to sail successfully.

Native Americans have many gifts to offer from their cultural perspective. The Sioux have a phrase that is often translated as "all my relations" which offers their view of diversity. "Relations" in the Indian sense are all those beings of earth, air, and water that accompany them in the world. The term acknowledges everything within which the web of life is possible. "All my relations" calls upon us all to remember that we are not alone. It spells an end to isolation that many white men experience.

Chief Seattle of the Suquamish tribe, evokes the spirit of "all my relations" in these words: "We know the sap which courses through the trees as we know the blood that courses through our veins. We are part of the earth and it is part of us. The perfumed flowers are our sisters. The bear, the deer, the eagle, they are our brothers." "All things are connected like the blood that unites us all." Today we might want to add the information superhighway to this list of connections. Chief Seattle's vision of diversity typifies the kind of insight we need to capitalize on the positive elements that diversity brings to the workplace.

INTERVIEW

Richard
49
White
computer installer
23 years with company
high school education

I was in the Air Force before I joined my company, and, though the comparison is often made between the military and the workplace, I don't think it's true. The military is more stable than the workplace. I stayed out of management because I don't like the politics. I'm not a politician. I don't have the time for that. I'm more "go to work and get the work done and to hell with the paperwork."

I enjoy my job; it's probably fifty percent or more of my life. My job is my number one priority mainly because there is so much to be done. I put in twelve to fourteen hours a day, because me and my partner (who's a woman) have over 500 people to service. We have to keep a lot of systems running. There's a lot of movement, a lot of activity every day. I have to wear about ten or fifteen different hats every day. We joke and say "we do everything but light, heat, and water."

My boss gives me a free hand to do what we need to do. He doesn't Mickey Mouse with us at all. My partner has just joined me. She doesn't have the confidence that some guys do, but I don't blame that on her. A lot of the guys she worked with before have contributed to that. The old timers she worked with are real protective of their jobs. They got between her and what they were doing, didn't let her see what they were doing and how they were doing it. But, then, they do that with everybody, male or female. Not me. I say, "Here, you can take half of this. It's right here."

There's a lot of women in this company that are not in the upper ranks. In the upper echelons, they're very cliquish; they're careful about who they let in. As far as I'm concerned, they should let women run the whole show. There's too much of the old-style thinking around here, and women seem to be more willing to try other things.

It's time for a big, major change. We see things going to hell in a handbasket since our reorganization. We're all working seven days a week and going thirty, forty, sixty days without a day off; yet upper management is sitting up there making $2–$3 million and complaining about our working overtime. And yet they want you to work overtime. But it's like they don't want to divide the spoils, so to speak. They've run this company into the ground. Right now, the morale is bad. I've never seen it like this.

I don't think my company reacts to EEOC [Equal Employment Opportunity Commission] issues in a decisive enough way. People who have had complaints filed against them get moved or promoted, not fired.

Everyone's edgy. We joke and say that everybody in this building is having PMS everyday. They should hire more people; they laid off a bunch before the reorganization, so everyone's having to do his own work and the work of those they laid off. It doesn't make any sense.

Management says we're all a team, but they don't let us in on the team plan. They just try to jam it down our throats. It's hard to be a team player when you're not in on the team action plan, you know. What's the team's goal here?

I think everyone in the company feels powerless. I stay because I don't want to throw away my retirement. And I still like working my job. I can absorb myself in my work. When I retire, though, I might go back to Vietnam. I want to do something humanitarian to give back to them.

I have five daughters, and I tell my kids to get a college degree in telecom or some technical field. We're a service-type community. "Pick a job with a future," I say.

WORKSHOP

1. How do you react to change: little changes, like changing scheduled meetings; big changes, changing jobs? Do you "go with the flow," feel mildly uncomfortable, or feel out of control? What do you think is at the root of these feelings? Does this emotional response need to be changed? Where can you get some assistance in changing?

2. Did you have an initiation rite for your manhood or womanhood? If so, what impact did it have on you? If you didn't have an initiation rite, when did you know that you entered manhood or womanhood? What impact has the lack of such a passage have on you and your view of yourself as a man or as a woman?

3. If you have male and/or female children, what kind of model do you present to them as a man or as a woman? Have you thought about the symbolism of an "initiation rite" and the role it plays as a rite of passage in your children's development?

4. What role has the community, friends, media, religion, played in your concept of your manhood or your womanhood? What role have these played in your children's view of manhood and womanhood? What behaviors can you exert to support, neutralize, or negate some of those influences?

Confusion is a word we have invented
for an order which is not understood.
–Henry Miller
Tropic of Capricorn

4

CONFUSION IN THE WORKPLACE

The model of more money, more power, more prestige that has driven white male behavior in corporations during this century is no longer enough. The model that some women and minorities are introducing in the workplace may be the key to a more prosperous and holistic future. It is one that balances the notion of competition with collaboration and quantification with quality. This balance is not just another mechanical process to produce a better corporate product. It is the intertwining of a new understanding that relationships can enhance profit when the different talents of employees are focused on a common goal benefiting all.

The agrarian work model has heart and soul, intricately intertwined with the human and nature. The entire agrarian family lived and worked together. In an atmosphere of constant contact, each member of the family contributed to the physical and emotional well-being of the family. The roles of man and woman, husband and wife, mother and father, were intertwined, inter-related and mutually beneficial. So, too, with the historic male's role of intertwining the means (producer, warrior, rulemaker) with the end (the benefit of the family, the community).

The problem is that the jobs promoted during the Industrial Revolution required the natural strength of men. Those jobs took men away from home and hearth, from the community. What was a means to his life now became his end. To be a male now was identified by your level of success at work. The absence of a holistic view of life in the generations that followed the industrial revolution have left many men feeling restless, bored, disengaged, empty, and without purpose. In a word, he is lonely.

Many corporations have tried to give a substitute meaning to men's efforts by focusing on increased productivity through different mantles of management. The longest lasting of these styles is that of a patriarchal, military organization which fitted so well men's societal role. The trouble with that model is that to work, it needs individuals who are blindly obedient, like children. This model may have worked in previous decades where the majority of people were uneducated and uninformed. Today's world is nothing if not a more adult one filled with constant exposure to new options and choices, a plethora of diverse opportunities.

There is no heart in the corporation today. That is why so many employees feel restless and fatigued. They lack enthusiasm and easily burn out. There is little purpose or true meaning. Although they rarely speak of it, men know this as well as women and others flooding the workplace. Many workers are asking themselves, "Do you work to live or live to work?" Managers are asking themselves, "Is all of this really worth it?"

Many of the management ideas that have swept the workplace in the past fifteen years have been organizational attempts to breathe new life into workers so they would produce more. These efforts have been a feeble attempt to deal with the loss of purpose originating in the industrial age. Reengineering the work process was expected to reestablish the ties between corporate product and corporate purpose. Restructuring was meant to regain the efficiencies lost with the gargantuanism of the naturale. "Small is beautiful" was an elegant phrase for the more human-scaled endeavors of groups that are smaller than typical corporations.

Some gurus have promised increased corporate success by simply focusing on individual growth and development. This approach promised a more personal way to recover the worker's heart and soul. This would give the worker a reason to work—himself. This is not the answer either. A fusion of both the individual and the organization is needed. Unfortunately, few suggestions have been forthcoming to blend these worlds.

Thus the "more is more" mentality of the unbridled warrior-producer has run amok in corporate America today. Every good corporate manager knows that corporations still define personal and corporate success as: do what you can to increase employee productivity; more productivity brings you more money, more power, more prestige—more success. Unfortunately, many women and minorities unknowingly have bought this definition of male success. They have become silent partners colluding to maintain and intensify the male status quo.

There is a growing number of men, women, and minorities who are finding the old definition of success too costly, too demanding, too empty. They are bringing into the workplace a new and modified model. What they are asking for is the strength of community and the benefits resulting from the unique talents of all workers. They yearn for a balance of work and home. They seek a world that respects each individual and offers equal opportunity for a quality life. In sum, they are seeking to bring back purpose for one's expenditure of efforts at work. With the soul of the worker alive and well again and acting as a great motivator, greater productivity will tend to promote itself in an ongoing fashion.

This new wave of workers is compelling companies to look at other ways of doing things in this global, technological, informational, and diverse world. To thrive economically, corporations need to drastically update the old patriarchal, hierarchal model of the Industrial Revolution. That historic model is one of master and slave. Management and labor are adversaries. Life and roles are discretely divided into work and family.

An understanding of the humanity of workers is needed. This must be an appreciation of men, women, and minority groups who have different talents, who yearn for a deeper meaning to work and to life. One way the corporation can promote this is through partnership. Stewardship and delegation are variations of that theme. True sharing in the responsibility for the success of the corporation means worker participation and ownership of the product and the process.

The product/process schism is as deep as the nature/nurture one, and as intertwined. We see men clamoring for accountability to the bottom line, for profitability, for efficiency. They want to solve problems with immediate solutions. There is no time for frills or sidetracks. This is typical of the way men handle the world of objects. This is the way men view their lives. For most men life—including relationships—is a set of discrete steps to follow, problems to be solved, and challenges to be met. For many men, life is one long series, like the World Series. Each episode has a distinct beginning, middle, and end, leading inexorably to a conclusion and with one winner.

Perhaps this approach explains men's reliance on words. Words are concrete and can be directly interpreted as objects. "Read my lips!" "I am listening," says the male; "I'll repeat everything you just said.";

"How can anything be wrong? You never said anything!"; "You have my word." Men understand the concrete world around them through the spoken word. They listen with their ears.

Most women view life differently. Their lives and societal role have been intertwined with people, family, and relationships. People are not objects. People are very complex, growing and changing ever so subtly. Women, therefore, see life as a series of issues—most often about people. People need to be addressed and discussed before and during action. People are not problems that need to be solved. Once action is taken, the results again are addressed, discussed, and acted upon. For women, life is an epic story—an ongoing process—continually changing and unfolding. Somewhere in the past was the notarial. Here and now is the middle. Somewhere in the future is the ending. The spoken word gains even deeper meaning through physical gestures, facial expressions, and tone of voice. These signs better express the emotions and feelings of individuals. Women gain greater understanding of the complex world around them by listening with their ears as well as observing with their eyes.

Physical contact says a great deal about the confusion many men have with issues of sexual harassment. Many women use numerous gradations of touch and physical closeness to make contact with another. Many men immediately interpret a woman's touch, her closeness, her just wanting to chat, as the beginning of the series of behaviors leading to a conclusion, sex! When men respond to their interpretation in a sexual way, women clearly view their response as unwelcome behavior. Sometimes, however, men *will* use sexual behavior as a power tool toward women whom they might find threatening in the workplace. Making the woman a sexual object can dissipate his feelings of anxiety, role confusion, and loss of power.

Men need to expand their view of the world and of how others see their actions. They need to be more conscious of the nuances in personal interaction that can enrich their lives with women at work and at home. Women bring to the workplace a wealth of relational gradations that have enhanced their quality of life. No wonder men are running scared. They thought they had the right rules, the right operational methods. It is time for men to change.

A request to change comfortable habits, comfortable behaviors, pushes everyone's "fight or flight" button. Our identity is partially grounded in a set of behaviors which we believe expresses our values and how we view ourselves. Many males value the behaviors of hierarchical structures which give them a sense of their manhood. When these structures do not produce any longer many companies downsize. They simply restructure the same hierarchical behaviors for cost effectiveness. Most corporations do not work smarter by changing the hierarchical male behaviors. They work harder and longer to maintain those same behaviors but with fewer people.

Women can compound the problem by requiring men to change some of their behaviors in rapid time. This is understandable. Women have been adapting and waiting for men to change for too long. They have no more patience. Their frustration has moved to anger. Their anger has progressed to rage. Most men, on the other hand, have not thought about what is happening around them. They have been too busy trying to follow the same male rules to survive. Few men have reflected on the need to change their behaviors. The system always seems to have worked for them.

Living in a democratic and dynamic world of men and women asks us to embrace reflection, choice, and change. The privilege and responsibility of living in a democratic society is the freedom to choose. Democracy means the freedom to participate in a process to make rules and to choose to follow those rules. If you do not participate, democracy can feel like a loss of control. To the woman who accepts the choice of supervising men for the first time, benefiting from that democratic option can feel equally unnerving and unstable. In a democratic society, new choices are constantly offered and change is always happening.

Most processes of change have four key stages. The first step in achieving comfort with change is simply knowing it is under way. This is the stage of basic information. Information that is gathered from reading, discussing, seeing what institutions have learned over the ages. The second step is understanding what the change is and why it is happening. Is it a fundamental value change or a behavioral change? The third step is the realization that change stimulates emotions. One emotion is the fear of losing an old, comfortable, and safe behavior. Another is the anxiety resulting from not knowing how the new behavior will feel or work. If change is to take place these emotions must be addressed. The fourth step is to deliberately share that change with others by becoming a change agent. A good change agent recognizes that you cannot change people or organizations directly. The most you can do is to behave in a manner that provides a comfortable environment in which others can reflect, chose new behaviors, and feel safe in trying those new behaviors. This fourth step requires an attitudinal change. You are active and passive in the change process. You implement advantages and minimize disadvantages. In Chapter Twelve we shall see how Motorola, a corporation, is living out all these steps of change.

In an authentically diverse workplace a change process is implemented for the benefit of individuals and the organization. You can only change in an atmosphere of trust. It is a trust that comes in knowing that others are acting for your benefit. This is the trust of inclusion. You are seen as valuable. You are respected because of your value. You are accepted as a partner in achieving mutual goals. This trust which precipitates inclusion is the antithesis of hierarchical one-upmanship.

In addition to the influx of growing numbers of women and minorities in the workplace, global forces threaten the historical white male power structure. We cannot overstress the role of the computer revolution in shaping corporate America. American companies enjoyed a thirty year hegemony in world markets after World War II. That advantage ended when the information technology white men had invented turned on them. Technology leveled the playing field almost overnight. The rules of the game changed because information became widely available. Many international players entered the arena of competition.

At first, such change was dismissed as a corporate pursuit of cheap labor. It was not long before the quality of foreign products, Asian automobiles and electronics, for example, became evident. This fact was fortified by a worsening trade balance. Like it or not, we exist in a global economy. This interfacing with other cultures and different people became the counterpart and, to some extent, one of the causes of workplace diversity. The products, skills, raw materials, and services of many cultures are widely available in today's business climate. The international pool of knowledge filled by many different workers is now a resource for companies smart enough to lead from that strength.

However, the availability of information is only useful to the extent that we are aware of it. It is only useful if people can act quickly on what they know. Speed and responsiveness become indispensable assets in this climate. Barriers to flow of information become distinct liabilities. Like the skin of a dinosaur, layers of management become excess insulation between demand and supply. As Michael Hammer and Jim Champy put it in their book *Reengineering the Corporation,* "America's business problem is that it is entering the 21st century with companies designed during the 19th century to work well in the 20th."

For the sleeping giants they were supposed to be, American corporations responded with surprising vigor to the challenges of the new business climate. At first they did what they could to stop the hemorrhage of profits. They downsized the work force and contracted many services. They grasped at restructuring. Often changing nothing fundamental enough to make a real difference. The measure of change was unfamiliar to the operational dimensions of the hierarchical organization white males built and maintained.

"Bigger is better," was one of the first assumptions to die when American companies faced global competition. Tom Peters hit bigness hard in *Thriving on Chaos.* He quoted liberally from *The Bigness Complex,* an earlier book by Walter Adams and James Brock. Brock and Adams dismantle the myth that massive companies could do things cheaper and better. They found smallness an advantage, when regarding innovation. "Reality and the available evidence show that small firms are more efficient innovators than industrial giants. . . . Small firms are more prolific inventors than giant companies; small firms exert significantly greater research and development effort than large ones; small firms devise and develop inventions at substantially lower costs than large firms; and the giant organizations seem to suffer a number of debilitating and apparently endemic disadvantages as regards invention and innovation."

What did the largest corporations do? They fought back by restructuring into smaller units. IBM, Motorola, and AT&T are companies that have made big shifts into smaller business units in recent years.

Men and women, not surprisingly, are leaving corporations to start their own smaller companies. If their leaving is not because of the reasons stated above, then it is for the personal rewards and challenges of more direct ownership found in smaller firms. My concern is that these entrepreneurs simply recreate the organizations they left, the white male system. But it is on a smaller scale. How can you become an adult when you are trying to be like, or trying to outdo, your parent? That keeps you a child.

In my consulting to several women's organizations in different fields, I soon discovered that they mimicked the white male system. Not only did they imitate many of the good ideas of the system, but they unknowingly incorporated the bad ideas. When a job opening occurred in one of the companies, I suggested that the management hire a male. I was quickly told: "They don't get it!" The content of the organization had changed from men to women but the exclusive context was the same.

One of the new ideas in the workplace today is flattened hierarchy—getting rid of the layers of management. Another is self-organization—freeing workers to create methods and processes to get the job done without hierarchical control. These concepts fit nicely with the style of work most women bring into the workplace. Flat companies and self-directed employees empower workers. They free people whose ability and loyalty are respected company assets. Such workers are tied into the success of the company through the sharing of information about company goals and objectives. The company keeps very little from them about its hopes for their future, its marketing and sales objectives, and its results.

Flat companies and self-organizations are predicated on the need to share information widely and quickly. They are fundamentally democratic but for very pragmatic reasons. Carol Hymowitz in the *The Wall Street Journal* describes the key characteristics of such organizations: "[They are ones] in which information flows quickly from top to bottom and back again, decisions come fast, and teamwork is the rule."

In *Business Week,* John Byrne describes the radical shift the flat or horizontal corporation presents from the old, hierarchical model: "In its purest state, the horizontal corporation might boast a skeleton group of senior executives at the top in such traditional support functions as finance and human resources. But virtually everyone else in the organization would work together in multi-disciplinary teams that perform core processes, such as product development or sales generation. The upshot: The organization might have only three or four layers of management between the chairman and the staffers in a given process."

"Process" is the hot word in company reorganizations these days. Process engineering, or reengineering, calls for an end to vertical structures of authority that channel upward through layers of management. Process engineering substitutes a team approach for handling an entire business process. Fundamental to these new teams is the confidence and trust of upper management. As Hammer and Champy write, "In some sense we're only putting back together a group of workers who have been artificially separated by organization. When they're rejoined, we call them a process team. A process team, in other words, is a unit that naturally falls together to complete a whole piece of work—a process." Process orientation is sensitive to customers and focuses outward rather than upward. It is centered on the team and depends for effectiveness on good communication, interpersonal relations, confidence, and trust.

One of the biggest obstacles to change is getting companies to narrow their processes to a manageable number. With that problem, writes John Byrne, is the challenge of getting people to change the way they think about their jobs and develop multiple skills. "In all cases, the objective of the horizontal corporation is to change the narrow mindsets of armies of corporate specialists who have spent their careers climbing a vertical hierarchy to the top of a given function," he says.

Process is a historic redefinition of work that inherently values the worker. Hammer and Champy explain it in terms of the Industrial Revolution. Tasks were broken down into their simplest components so that unskilled and uneducated workers could accomplish them. With our polyglot work force in America at the time, such simplification was essential. However, as the authors point out, if you fragment the lowest levels of work, you must have complex layers of management above them to coordinate all the parts and pieces. The downsizing and restructuring of the past decade have cut out much of middle management in America. Although a skilled work force has the capacity to take over many management functions, investment, education, valuation, and trust are necessary to produce such a work force.

As for the remaining managers, "Many," writes Carol Hymowitz, "must adapt to fuzzier lines of authority and greater emphasis on teamwork. Low-level managers accustomed to carrying out orders suddenly are asked to set strategy. For most, a leaner structure means not only increased workloads but also diminished chances for promotion and the frustration that fosters." The rules by which the male has learned to be successful as a resource producer are now changing all around him.

Interestingly enough, process—whether a concept, a function, an orientation, or a managerial style—focuses on evolving, constantly changing, moving towards a definite goal. Women, by their historical role in many cultures, may have a great deal to contribute to the success of the process lines of twenty-first century corporations. Women are much more comfortable with relationships, with their ambiguity and their uncertainty. They read the other, understand and appreciate the other, and connect with the other. Blended with the success of the male's focus on goal orientation these female traits may provide the competitive edge of the future.

What is happening in the workplace today? Women and minorities have been frustrated for years by exclusion and so-called glass ceilings. They are now being joined by a growing number of white men who are outside the upper echelons of power. Their frustration comes from the personal emptiness of the corporate struggle for more production and profits. The corporate solution to this restlessness is to talk about values in leadership. "If you're not thinking all the time about making every person more valuable, you don't have a chance," Jack Welch, CEO of GE, told biographer Noel Tichy. "That's what boundarylessness is: an open, trusting, sharing of ideas. A willingness to listen, debate, and then take the best ideas and get on with it."

Free-floating sharing of ideas—sometimes called boundarylessness— works hand in hand with the diverse work force because it actively seeks input from everyone. It glories in its diverse and creative environment. Its assumption is that most of the traditional hierarchical walls—formal and informal—must be eliminated to promote the free flow of ideas. Many companies have laid off workers, but few have taken this critical next step. The getting on with it will not be as easy as many leaders think.

General Electric has begun. In a *Fortune* article Byrne reports, "GE's $3 billion lighting business scrambled a more traditional structure for its global technology organization in favor of one in which a senior team of 9-12 people oversees nearly 100 processes or programs worldwide, from new product design to improving the yield on production machinery. Major changes in GE's training, appraisal, and compensation systems were necessary. Employees were evaluated by peers and customers as well as others above and below them." Pay scales were reconstructed on the basis of skills developed as well as work performed.

This sounds like a good plan. I question values leadership as it is implemented in most companies. Does it really value workers with all their differences? Does value leadership simply prize workers for their ability to perform the job? Does it appreciate varied talents as an enrichment of the workplace and the work process? The way to value people is to treat them as adults. Give people the chance to express their ideas. Help them to take responsibility for their choices. Be eager to rejoice in their rewards. Assist them to learn from their failures.

Massachusetts Institute of Technology economist Paul Osterman estimates that nearly 80 percent of employers across industries have adopted quality circles, total quality management, team-based systems, or some combination of these relatively recent approaches to work. Knowledge workers, a designation first used by Peter Drucker in his book *Landmarks of Tomorrow,* work in teams. In an article appearing in *The Atlantic Monthly,* Drucker predicts a society of team-based organizations, with teams and organizations symbiotically related. "Only the organization can convert the specialized knowledge of the knowledge worker into performance," he says.

Teams are hardly new. The farmer and his wife were a team. "But until now the emphasis has been on the individual worker and not on the team," says Drucker. "With knowledge work growing increasingly effective as it is increasingly specialized, teams become the work unit rather than the individual himself."

"We will have to learn to use different kinds of teams for different purposes," Drucker continues. "We will have to learn to understand teams—and this is something to which, so far, very little attention has been paid. The understanding of teams, the performance capacities of different kinds of teams, their strengths and limitations, and the tradeoffs between various kinds of teams will thus become central concerns in the management of people."

One way to better understand teams is to redefine them to fit today's workplace. As noted earlier, most men and women define teams differently. The new team is a blend of those different definitions. This team is a collection of different and unique individuals. They perform their particular functions in a professionally competent and creative manner. They unite their talents to better attain a common goal.

Increasingly, then, the new teams will be diverse. They will offer companies a different dynamic from the military and sports concept that has presided for decades. These new teams will have women, minorities, and individuals who are different in a variety of ways. All will be required to bring new and different styles to a common plan that will enhance success.

Once you accept your workers with unique backgrounds and talents, the role of the manager becomes one of accessing and facilitating that richness. Many of today's managers, trained in the old model, must now deal with workers more as peers than as subordinates. They must act more like coaches than like bosses. They must see themselves as facilitators of a process rather than as overseers of production. They must work as well as manage, as Peter Block points out in his excellent book *Stewardship*.

Drucker sees an even more critical role for managers in the new workplace: "All managers do the same things, whatever the purpose of their organization. All of them have to bring people—each possessing different knowledge—together for joint performance. All of them have to make human strengths productive in performance and human weaknesses irrelevant. . . . Management is a social function. And in its practice management is truly a liberal art."

This is the new role of middle management. Indeed, technology is flattening the organization and reducing the role of the middle manager as we have historically understood it. In the past the middle manager set the organizational rules that would fulfill the corporate vision. Then middle managers supervised lower management in the implementation of those rules. These middle management procedures can now be done through e-mail, conference calls, fax machines, telephones, and jet travel. Now you can have twenty lower managers, located in twenty different locations, reporting to one central middle manager. You do not need one middle manager in each of these twenty locations.

Witness the present rash of layoffs among white-collar workers. With the emphasis on teams and the use of technology, many corporations rush to eliminate middle managers. This also is a quick way to save money by eliminating larger salaries. Many of the left-over responsibilities of middle managers have been passed down to lower managers. They now find themselves overworked, pressured, tired, stressed, and discouraged.

A new definition of a middle manager in the Drucker mold is needed—one who is the active liaison between organizational vision and implementation. This new middle manager has a keen sense of how the parts fit into the whole. This middle manager recognizes and appreciates the changing work force and how differences can be the necessary ingredients for creative solutions. This new middle manager is not only technically and professionally competent but a facilitator of diverse people who are working towards a common corporate goal. The new middle manager takes seriously the responsibility of teaching, fostering, and encouraging lower management to become facilitators of a diverse work force.

Finding managers who can succeed in this new environment is not easy. University of Michigan management specialist Andrew McGill says that only when managers think about employees as valued assets can they really begin to value their customers. "Getting close to customers is something that is unknown to many of them," he says, "and you can't have a long-term relationship with customers . . . if you don't have the same rapport with your employees, because they're the ones who are going to carry the mail for you."

Teams as they are now conceived are implicitly self-managing. UCLA management professor David Lewin estimates that about one in five U.S. employers operates such teams today, up from one in twenty a decade ago. By the end of the century he believes we could be looking at 40 to 50 percent of all workers managing themselves.

Of course, as the structure reconfigures, the rules change. All the news is not comforting, at least if you are looking for the security of the past. Job applicants will no longer focus solely on experience. They will be asked what is different and unique about them that can contribute to corporate creativity and success. Advancement used to depend on longevity, loyalty, and the development of relationships with upper management. Promotions now depend more on flexibility, innovation, and personal responsibility. Seniority in and of itself will not guarantee job security. Pay for knowledge will replace annual increases as the measure of your worth. Employees will be asked to continually update their training for a constantly changing workplace. The patriarchal environment took care of many employees as though they were children. Now employees will be challenged to act as adults taking responsiblity for their own careers and development.

It is no wonder white males are confused. Their old world has been turned upside down. The civil rights legislation of the 1960s and the women's empowerment movement of the last three decades have identified minorities and women's issues. These groups have been struggling to bring about the necessary changes. During this time most white males have been going along, filling the roles that have been "hardwired" into their old world identity. Many have hardly stopped to reflect on any of the changes listed in this chapter. Meanwhile there was an influx of workers who were not like them. Men thought if everyone followed their same rules nothing would change. Besides, white males were still in charge of rewarding those who did follow their rules.

Women and minorities are asking for new rules. They have asked for parental leave policies, flextime, day care, and elder care. Companies have instituted many of these programs. Still, most men keep their noses to the old grindstone. For them more is better. Putting in more hours means more success, more money, more glory for the company and themselves. White male management continues to reward this behavior.

Generally, flattened companies are more congenial to the flexibility of women. Most men have far less flexibility than women, for reasons specific to their socialization process. The early gender identification process for boys is profoundly (and sometimes painfully) different from the experience of girls. Girls remain closely identified with at least one person, generally their mother, throughout life.

In indigenous cultures boys also stayed close to their mothers for a long period. In industrial cultures boys are forced to choose early between mothers and fathers. When they turn from their mothers, as most of them do, they do not attach to their fathers. Their fathers are often physically and emotionally unavailable. Boys are left to attach to the cultural idea of masculinity frequently found in the media.

As Harvard Medical School psychiatrist Stephen Bergman points out, identifying with a set of values and behaviors is distinctly different from identification with an actual person. "Identity comes before intimacy, the self before the self-in-relation-to others. . . . Male psychology becomes fixated on achieving a separate and individuated self, a self based on separation from others, of self 'from' others which may then become self 'over' others. There is an emphasis on control and power—ego control, control of feelings—and on the basic Western paradigm of comparison, competition, and aggression."

Achievements—doing things and fixing things—become important as a way of proving a male's identity. "The fantasy is that by achieving a man will win love. But no achievement can win love," Bergman writes. Seen in this light, workaholism is an endless quest for love and acceptance that can never be attained.

What shaped the relationship between daughter and mother was interaction, reflection, and expression of feelings. When a woman is asked who she is, she looks within, to what she feels. Ask the same question of a man, and he will look outward and tell you what he does, his job, and his achievements. He *is* his achievements. No one ever taught him he *is* his feelings as well as his thoughts and behaviors.

Harvard psychologist Ronald Levant claims that many men recognize their emotions only as a physical buzz, a tightness in the throat, or an increased pounding of the heart. Emotions are foreign to most men as part of their self definition. Often emotions are sensed as a dangerous barrier to effective action.

All of this has significant implications for flexibility in today's workplace. Most girls grow up identified with a feeling person. Since feelings are fluid and non-rational, most girls are comfortable with ambiguity and process. Most boys grow up increasingly identified with a definite set of behavioral norms and rules. Patterns and rules are concrete. Following rules promises an orderly conclusion, a goal, or a product. Most men do not need to understand or agree with the rules. They follow them as loyal soldiers do in the military arena.

Because females are grounded in relationships, they have moved with relative ease into today's ambiguous, flexible, intuitive, customer-oriented workplace. What women have found is that most men are still playing by the old world producer-warrior rules. Setting aside the historical norms for which men and women have been conditioned requires a significantly deeper personal shift for men. I think this goes a long way toward explaining why men have such difficulty with ambiguous flattened structures, self-organizations, and process teams. Without structure men have moved much more cautiously in the fluid relational arena of home and family.

Men and women can learn from each other in this evolving new world. Women can learn from men how to be more successful resource producers. Men can learn from women how to better interact in the many relationships in which they find themselves. Men and women together possess the solutions for clarifying the existing confusion in their work lives and personal lives.

INTERVIEW

Randy
52
Hispanic
marketing manager
25 years with company
B.S. degree

I came from a very bad neighborhood in the inner city. Out of that neighborhood, I believe ours is the only family, with 10 kids, where several of us graduated from college. I'm real proud of that. I often wonder why. We were all in the same environment, but many kids from other families went to jail, etc.

I decided it has to do with my upbringing. I'm the oldest boy in the family. We had parents who had no more than a sixth grade education, yet I think my father was the smartest person I ever knew. He was a truck driver, but he always valued education. We didn't have the newest car, but we had Encyclopedia Britannica.

One of the values he taught us was "think for yourself." Other kids would try to pull you into their clan. My dad's advice was, "If you do it, then you belong to them; you have to think for yourself, and you have to stand by what you think." It hurts sometimes. You get beat up, but they can only beat you up for so long before they see you're not going to change.

I brought those values into this company, but they didn't always help me. One of my values is to be polite, not to argue with authority, whether it's age, position, or gender. I noticed when I went into the boardroom and I participated in a meeting, I was being looked at as passive, nonaggressive, not a team player.

It was a shock to me. I realized I had some options. I could change me. But I didn't want to change me. I like opening doors for my sisters and other women. I don't like to argue with authority—I like to discuss. Is that good or bad? Do I have to change to get ahead? Do I have to use real aggressive language, to fight, to get ahead?

Rather than change, I developed a theory. Here is what it is. You go to the boardroom and right before you open the door, there's a coat hanger on the wall and there are suits of armor on it. A lot of people don't even see the suits of armor because they wear them all the time. I don't have a suit of armor, so if I'm going into the boardroom, I better be wearing one because everyone else is. So I put it on, and now I'm equipped like everybody else. I go in there and I fight and maybe I'll lose or maybe I'll win, but I'm protected. So I use the same tactics because that's a war room and that's what they're doing in there—fighting.

Now when I come out, I can leave the suit of armor on and wear it all the time, which says I've changed, or I can hang it up and be myself.

There are a lot of minority kids out there from my old neighborhood and other places around the country who don't know that. They're thinking they're being polite and they're thinking I can't do what the others are doing, play the game the way it's played. But they have to. If you expect to move up, you have to do that. I like to help those kids by telling them they have options. They don't have to do it all one way.

WORKSHOP

1. What is your definition of a successful team at work? At home? How would men, women, people of different cultures and backgrounds fit into this definition?

2. List three positive behaviors you can learn from the other sex that will increase your effectiveness at work or at home; from a person of another race or different background?

3. To better appreciate the difficulty of changing, place the hand you most frequently use in your pocket and negotiate with the other hand for a half day. What did you learn? How can you use that learning for yourself? in relationships with others?

4. If you have children, how can you teach them about change, about teams, about balancing family and outside activities like school, work, friends?

The most universal quality is diversity.
–Michel de Montaigne
Essays

5

THE DEMOGRAPHICS OF DIVERSITY

The United States has a pluralistic work force. Women outnumbered men voting in the 1996 election, and they may overtake them in the workplace in this decade. In 1995 46.1 percent of the total U.S. labor force was female, although women accounted for less than 5 percent of upper management. In 1995 women held 48 percent of managerial/executive positions and comprised 52.9 percent of workers employed in professional specialty occupations, up from 33.6 percent and 48.5 percent in 1984, respectively. The demographics of corporate markets are changing as quickly. The new customers, both at home and abroad, are from diverse populations and diverse cultures with diverse ages and diverse desires. Meeting their needs will take every bit of creativity the American work force has to offer.

If you think the issue of diversity can be ducked or put on hold, take a look at the projected demographics in America. Over the next ten years, ethnic and racial minorities in the United States will grow seven times faster than the white population. By the year 2000, 75 percent of those entering the work force will be minorities and women. In the years from 1992 to 2005, the Bureau of Labor Statistics estimates that non-Hispanic whites will become the largest of several minority groups entering the labor force. They will add 10.9 million new workers or 46.5 percent of all workers. More than two-thirds of these white workers will be female. Notice that white non-Hispanic male workers will not be a majority but will become one of several large minorities in a pluralistic work force.

In some cities and states pluralism is already the norm. Open to migration from the Asian Pacific and the Hispanic south, California leads the way. In Los Angeles today eighty different languages are spoken. By the year 2000 there will not be a clear majority population in that city. White Americans will still be the largest minority, but five to ten years into the next century, Hispanics will occupy that slot. Given current demographic trends, Hispanics by estimate will become the largest ethnic population in the United States sometime before the middle of the next century.

According to the Population Reference Bureau, nationally, there were approximately 32 million African Americans, 27 million Hispanics, 9 million Asians, and approximately 2 million Native Americans living in the United States at the end of 1995. These three groups alone made up 26 percent of the U.S. population.

Although Hispanic growth will be significant in the long term, Asian Americans will be the fastest growing ethnic group over the next decade. Asians in the work force will almost double their numbers in the next ten years, up from 4.6 million workers in 1992 to 8.3 million in 2005 or about 15.8 percent of all new workers. About half will be female. Based on census data trends, "Work Force 2000," the landmark study published by the Hudson Institute, predicts that by the year 2000 immigration will account for 22 percent of all job growth, native non-white men and women for 20 percent, native white females for 42 percent, and native white males for the least in growth, 15 percent. Since the study's publication in 1987 we have discovered that the percentages continue to be on target. The predicted pace of these trends, however, has slowed.

Immigration patterns have changed. Twenty-seven million new immigrants from southern and eastern Europe arrived in the half century from Lee's surrender at Appomattox to America's entry into World War I in 1917, as Arthur Schlesinger Jr. tells us in *The Disuniting of America*. Predominantly white and Christian, they formed the backbone of industrial America through the early part of this century. Today's immigrants bring customs, behaviors, expectations, and skills into the workplace that differ substantially from those of the big European migrations.

As San Francisco-based diversity consultant Leonard Copeland explains: "This country is no longer a great melting pot where newcomers are eager to shed their own cultural heritages and become homogenized Americans." "Now most immigrants are from very different cultures, predominantly Asian and South American, and they are not blending so readily into the mainstream of American life. Rapidly changing demographics are forcing more and more Americans to interact with people different from themselves, people whom they do not understand, who have unique values and ways of doing things."

These assertions are confirmed by the numbers Schlesinger quotes. "Immigrants were responsible for a third of population growth in the United States during the 1980s. In 1910 nearly 90% of immigrants came from Europe. In the 1980s more than 80% came from Asia and Latin America. Still, foreign-born residents constitute only about 7% of the population today. Black share has grown from 9.9% in 1920 to 12.1% in 1990." Schlesinger points out, "We have shifted the basis of admission to the United States three times this century, from national origins in 1924 to family reunification in 1965, to needed skills in 1990."

The whole issue of immigration is receiving needed examination. Several states are calling for a revamping of immigration laws and the federal government is answering. Many of the present immigration laws were passed at a time when the modes of transportation restricted access to this country. Seventy-five years ago a major way of entering this country was by boat. Few boats were available in few port cities for this long transoceanic trip. To secure passage one needed money—another limiting factor. Given our modern means of traveling today, one easily can obtain an inexpensive plane ticket, fly from most major cities in the world, and be in this country in a matter of hours.

Control of individuals entering the United States urgently needs to be updated. The government reports just under half of illegal immigrants enter this country by obtaining a legal visa and green cards then "disappearing." The majority of illegal immigrants cross over the southern border of this country.

Few poor countries offer any help to America in the protection of this country's borders. And, why should they? Each time one of their citizens enters the United States, it is a double bonus for their government: they do not have to support the person and his/her family, because the American system will provide necessary aid, and since their former citizens remain bonded to their families, they send money home. It is as though these foreign governments have a cadre of workers in the United States.

I am in favor of legal immigration. My parents were immigrants; I am a first-generation American. The key to American cultural success is the influx of legal new immigrants and the continual enrichment of other cultures that they bring. The concern is the *illegal* immigrant. Time and time again, the histories of cultures and nations have shown that when the laws of the land are blatantly ignored or broken the destruction of the society is imminent.

Illegal immigration can be stopped simply by corporations and businesses not hiring undocumented workers. Businesses' unbridled ambition and greed to become financially successful can have a severe impact on American society. It is the worst of the warrior spirit: plunder the community for personal gain. Businesses must be held accountable to the American public and follow the law. With government aid businesses must bear responsibility to seriously address on-going employee verification of legal status. We use the best of technology to verify credit cards and checks; why not verify immigrant documentation?

Serious repercussions, swift and heavy fines, must be meted out to employers who hire illegal immigrants. The American public must unite to protest and boycott businesses that hire illegal immigrants.

The influx of unskilled workers from abroad drives down wages and deprives America's poor of the jobs they need. Do we have a responsibility to provide jobs for the world's poor or America's poor? American corporations and businesses must spearhead the training of our workers. The business community must take leadership in raising the level of workers' education and training so that illegal immigrants with low-skills cannot compete with a well-educated and highly skilled work force.

The ways in which this country incorporates immigrants also needs reevaluation. In the past the limited numbers of those entering the country were cared for by their own cultural group. Many of the ghettoes became the support systems for those new would-be citizens. Frequently members of their own culture would protect them from the American culture. They would speak for them, act on their behalf, and negotiate for them with government, schools, and businesses. Only the next generation, brought up in the American language and the American ways, became Americanized.

Today, with the rapid influx of immigrants, old socialization processes have broken down. The American government needs to create programs that deliberately and quickly integrate these new people into the American culture. Such programs should include mandatory American-English language classes, classes on the history and political system of this country, information about the operation of this government, job opportunities and training. Furthermore, we need to assist and support these people to maintain those parts of their native cultures that may add richness to the American culture. We need to assist these new citizens to understand that certain practices of their old world culture may not fit into the American new world culture. This process can be confusing and difficult for new immigrants as well as Americans born and raised here. Most people are attracted to America by the opportunity and prosperity this new world has to offer. However, they want the safety and comfort provided by their old world customs and behaviors. It has little to do with values, but a great deal to do with customs and behaviors.

All Americans need to become multicultural and multilingual. As noted, those who come here speaking only their languages need to learn the American-English language. How can we expect to run a unified country with immigrants coming from over 198 different countries speaking over 6,000 dialects unless we have a common language and a common culture?

The American language fits our American heterogeneous culture. It is a culture that is best served by the practices and policies of integration. The American language is the most integrating language in world. Many of our words come from other cultures and subcultures that keep the language ever-changing and dynamic. This is very different from homogeneous cultures that seek a unified and unchanging language. The Chinese characters in the Japanese language have remained the same for thousands of years. Some time ago the French Parliament decreed that American computer language would not be acceptable in France. You express yourself in pure French or you do not say it at all!

William Safire of "The New York Times Magazine" reminds us that in America "we borrow words from everywhere." Not only does this integration of words into one language bind cultures in America, but in turn, binds the countries of the world. By incorporating words and phrases from other languages into the American language, an international language is created joining people throughout the world. As Safire notes, the language we Americans speak ". . . is equipped to strengthen and extend its second-language lead in the coming century."

The workplace also can benefit greatly from this multi-cultural infusion. Today's legal immigrants often are not for the most part "your tired, your poor, your huddled masses yearning to breathe free." They are skilled and educated workers seeking the opportunities and prosperity that this country offers. Many of these skilled immigrants will have worked for American companies based in their homeland. In many cases these are the new knowledge workers of whom Peter Drucker speaks. They easily cross borders and set up shop with the skills and education they bring with them.

Yet, the biggest change in the work force is the entry of women on a massive scale. Projections are that 56 percent of all new workers will be female by the year 2005. This amounts to a peaceful revolution. At the same time we are undergoing a shift of the traditional roles of men and women that is causing a transformation in family life not unrelated to what occurs in the workplace. Most importantly, women bring a new culture, many similar values, and some new behaviors that have worked for them. This contribution can narrow the distance between work and home while challenging men to relate at work and home differently.

Statistics from the Family and Work Institute and the Work/Family Directions group in Boston, reported in the *Wall Street Journal,* show:

- In 1975, 40 percent of the U.S. work force was female. By 1985, that number had increased to 44 percent, and by 1992, to 46 percent. This means that the percentage of white females in the U.S. labor force increased 6 percent in just seventeen years, a dramatic change.
- By the year 2005, the percent of participation for men and women in the labor force will be similar, reaching 63.2 percent for all women eligible to work and 74.7 percent for all men. The numbers of women in the work force are closing in on the long lead held by men.
- From 1983 to 1993, the percentage of white male professionals and managers in the work force dropped from 55 percent to 47 percent, while the group of white female professionals jumped from 37 percent to 42 percent, according to statistics published in *Business Week* in January 1994.

Most of these women in the labor force work in traditional companies and in government, but the numbers also show that women have a strong entrepreneurial bent. The Small Business Administration counts about 5 million women-owned businesses. Women will own nearly 40 percent of the small businesses by the year 2000, predict Patricia Aburdene and

John Naisbitt in *Megatrends for Women.* "In 1990 women-owned businesses employed 11 million people and the *Fortune* 500, 12.3 million. From 1980 to 1988 the number of entrepreneurs increased 56 percent overall, but female entrepreneurs grew 82%," say these authors.

When I read these figures, however, I see women leaving large companies where they are dissatisfied. They are starting businesses with the skills they learned while seated at the corporate table. Many women have what my father called "the guts and ambition" that would shame many males. Often the businesses these women start invade the markets of their former employers, drawing revenues from companies that failed to take advantage of their innovative energies. You can be sure that the vast majority of the companies women start operate in a climate that they find more congenial than the one they left.

The report is not all rosy, however. As noted in the previous chapter, women can take with them into these new businesses the good of what men have taught them, but unknowingly take the bad. Too often they tend to mimic many men's exclusive tactics, workaholic behaviors, unethical practices, and cut-throat methods of competition. In a word, they unknowingly have bought the male's historical definition of success rather than adjusting it. They have colluded with the male in keeping his model of success as the only standard to be attained. Furthermore, even if women do fulfill all the requirements for this male model of success, they cannot obtain their full reward in the man's world since women continue to be seen culturally as inferior to men. Under this system women cannot win no matter how successful or talented they are. Men and women need to be aware of the impact of culture and gender roles. New definitions of success have to be developed that go beyond the historical male definition of workplace success.

The fact that women are going to work in large numbers spells a host of changes in family life and the raising of children. Day care, for example, is a social experiment for which we have no precedent in this country. Research on the effects of day care centers is spotty at best. Throughout most of human history, mothers spent long periods of time either in the home or in the working fields with their growing children. Many of these mothers also were supported by extended family members who lived close by. Now many children are sent to non-family members for care, often within a few weeks or months of birth. Many of these working women are single parents.

The emphasis on family issues is relatively new to the workplace. It is an issue that companies must address if they are to draw on the talents of women and a growing number of men. Family leave, elder care, flex-time, and other options that can accommodate the changing American family need inclusion in organizational planning.

The Census Bureau's definition of family may surprise you: "two or more people related by birth, marriage, or adoption and living together." Its analysis revealed that there were 96.4 million households in the United States in 1993, including 68.1 million family households, or 71 percent, down from 81 percent in 1970; 34.9 million family households were childless.

These changes in the structure of the American family have produced both positive and negative results. We all have benefited by the steady growth in the quality of life of most of our citizens. Yet the negatives of violence and crime, of teenage pregnancies, of drugs, and of the homeless are very much in our national awareness.

Interestingly enough, when I talk to men about these negative elements in our society, they frequently point the finger of blame at women. "If it weren't for women coming into the workplace and wanting it all, we wouldn't have all these social problems. Our families would be stronger. Our children would be raised with more morals! Women need to be in the home as they always were! Let's go back to way things were!"

What is happening in our society is a dramatic shifting of the historical roles of men and women. Women are coming into the workplace, becoming more independent, more equal to men as resource producers. Their presence must force men to reevaluate their historic roles, especially in their families. Indeed, children of all ages do need adult supervision. Men seem unwilling to change the role most of them have had in family life, in raising the children. Besides, few men have had a father who was a model of this new family man. We have not discovered satisfying options for raising the next generation and the roles that fathers and mothers should play. For women to succeed in redefining their role to include the workplace, men must redefine their role of parent and care-giver.

Women are coming into the workplace with their unique contributions. But this shift will not succeed if husbands and fathers remain at work for ten to twelve hours a day, working weekends, and spending a great deal of time away from the children. Men will have to consider shifting dramatically some of their time and effort from the workplace as a resource producer to their home as that of partner and parent. Both men and women need to examine, explore, and experiment with new and shifting roles, schedules, and responsibilities in today's world. Family life is not simply a woman's issue. It is an issue which affects all of us!

The fact that there are fewer children in most American families these days, especially white, two-partner families, is an interesting phenomenon. Contrary to what we may sometimes think, whenever tribes or clans have greater access to the resources of a region or country, their populations may tend to decrease. It makes good sense. If you have access to the resources, why not put both partners to work? In a primitive society you doubled your efforts to get more of the necessary goods to survive. In a modern society more income can bring a better quality of life.

But when both partners in a family are working for material goods, providing for themselves and their families a quality life, they expend a great deal of time and energy. A lack of time and energy can cause them to have fewer children. Working parents can focus on their own lives, frequently becoming involved in their education, their careers. They want bigger homes, newer cars, more clothes. They want to travel. They want to educate their children well. Although children are important, working parents find they are only one of the major ingredients in their lives. Finally, one way to give your children more time, guidance, and material goods is to have fewer of them!

For these three reasons we find those families that have better access to material resources usually limit the number of children they have. It is the best birth control method I know! Give members of a clan or tribe an education and a job, turn them loose to prosperity, and they will stop having so many children. We have not learned that lesson in America. We keep withholding education and job opportunities from different clans and tribes in America and end up taking care of their children.

Not surprisingly, in this diverse climate more diverse families are appearing as well. Interracial marriages are on the increase. Schlesinger reports "around half of Asian American marriages are with non-Orientals, and the Census Bureau estimates 1 million interracial—mostly black-white—marriages in 1990 as against 310,000 in 1970."

The permanency of marriage is under fire. In the 1950s the divorce rate was 9.2 per thousand married women each year. In 1988 it was

20.7 per thousand. Today, almost one-half of marriages end in divorce. The numbers of failures of second and third marriages also has increased. Fifty-seven percent of those who divorce have children under eighteen. Out-of-wedlock births have risen from under 4 percent of children born in 1950 to 27 percent in 1989, according to a report in *Fortune.*

The aging of the work force is another important demographic phenomenon. The newsletter *Managing Diversity* reports that in 1991 there were six million fewer teenagers in the work force than in 1980. The labor force is not expanding from below as it once did. Rather, it is ballooning in the upper age brackets.

In 1992, 71.4 million workers, 56.2 percent of the labor force, were thirty-five years or older. The Bureau of Labor Statistics projects that in 2005, 95 million workers—63 percent of the labor force—will be over thirty-four and that 21.3 million of those workers will be over fifty-five. Between the years 1992 and 2005 there will be 23.5 million new additions to the work force. The vast majority of these new entrants will be over thirty-four, and nearly 60 percent, or about 14 million of them, will be women. Since we can extrapolate that by 2005 14 percent of the work force will be over fifty-five, these figures suggest we ought to start planning now for a day when the older worker is a significant component of a diverse work force. What this means is still unclear. As with other diverse groups in the work force, however, businesses will occupy their most competitive position if they count older workers among their members.

Taken together these figures predict significant changes in consumer markets. Currently, older Americans spend more than 50 percent of all discretionary income, a figure that is rising. More older workers, retirees drawing on pension funds, foreign-born and their descendants, as well as more women with salaries, indicate a customer base that is not as white or male or young as it used to be.

An appreciation and understanding of these dynamics is important in today's market, as well as future global markets. Customers all over the world are interested in choices and want to be served. As management consultant Tom Peters says, excellent service in a customer-oriented market must be excellent from the customer's point of view, not based on an internal business standard. As the customers and customer preferences profile changes, a diverse, flexible, and well-integrated staff, including its component of white males, will be critical to the quality of product or service.

A follow-up analysis to the "Work Force 2000" report by the Department of Labor in 1990 found that many businesses have been slow to respond to changes in work force composition. Reporting on that study in the *Wall Street Journal,* Gilbert Fuchsberg says: "Although 39% of surveyed companies are boosting starting salaries, fewer than one-quarter are rehiring retirees or recruiting the elderly, disabled, and other nontraditional workers.

"Companies also have been slow to make a strong commitment to training the workers they do hire. Two-thirds of the surveyed firms spend less than $2,000 for classroom and other on-the-job education for first-year workers."

Other factors may alienate workers, too. "One-fourth of all surveyed companies said their corporate cultures weren't 'open to diversity,' while 29% said discrimination was a problem, and 155 reported 'overt harassment' of minorities as a concern. Such results suggest 'organizations' readiness to manage the changing work force is mixed at best,' the study says.

"The study indicates that diversity is already a reality at many companies. Minorities constitute at least one-fifth of the work force at some 39% of surveyed firms, while women make up more than half the employees at 47% of the companies. Still, just one-fourth of the companies are training supervisors in the complexities of managing `a disparate group' of employees, the study says. Even fewer are adopting innovative ways to ease conflicts between work and family and lower the `glass ceilings' that many minority and women workers face.

"While 42% of companies engage in 'explicit' minority recruiting, for instance, just 125 train minorities for supervisory positions. Only 11% have created minority support groups, and 10%, mentor programs. Meanwhile, 81% of surveyed companies have formal policies banning sexual harassment. But management training for women exists at only 32% of firms, while 85% of the companies have created support and mentor groups for men. Under one-third of companies offer extended maternity leave, and just 15% have on-site or near-site day care."

In an arena of continual upheaval or constant transition, no matter how enriching, many unreflecting individuals feel very frightened and insecure. What some individuals may be experiencing in society is a multitude of conflicting choices. Unable or unwilling to reflect, they chose basic and simple answers. They seek a fundamentalistic approach to life. Unthinkingly, they freely accept what they are told.

Frequently, simplistic concepts have just enough truth in them to be attractive. Who would disagree with certain fundamental concepts of the Bible? Who would deny that education should include reading, writing, and arithmetic? Who would deny that the Second Amendment of the Constitution allows citizens to bear arms? These societal behaviors were expressions of cherished human values for a specific historical time. To accept those past behaviors today in the exact same form because they are clear, straight-forward and seem to work, is to deny the present accumulation of knowledge and understanding of individuals and society. What is needed is to discover the human values behind those historical behaviors. Update the behaviors to fit those values as they are lived in today's world. Values do not change; behaviors do. When one behavior is promoted as the *only* way to express that value, then the behavior or the rule become more important than the value. The means becomes more important than the end.

One mark of a psychologically mature person is that he or she negotiates articulated values with the changing environment to obtain satisfactory results. Such negotiation is not available to the victim who doggedly accepts whatever comes his or her way, or who seeks to resist change. In a climate of constant change you must be clear about your values and priorities. One must stay aware of choices and their consequences. One needs to be flexible in adjusting choices to new information. Complete comfort and safety in such a fluid climate is not possible. That kind of safety only results in a never-changing, static environment, as in a homogeneous culture. Such an environment, although safe and secure, leads to atrophy. In a static society one sacrifices all change and movement for total security. A degree of necessary safety and growth can be maintained even in a constantly changing environment.

This security is the result of continual personal reflection, on-going social discourse, and an evolving world-view. This process is then experienced in practical, every-day behaviors. These are the characteristics of mature adults. These are the life-skills essential to survive and blossom in a heterogeneous society.One cause for the great tension and unsettlement in America is that many want all the advantages of a dynamic and ever-changing heterogeneous society, but with all the safety and security of a never-changing, always predictable homogeneous society. Long ago, Jefferson warned that the only way this new republic could survive would be with educated and enlightened citizens.

The costs of an ever-changing environment and the denial of societal diversity and all its implications in the workplace are devastating. Corporations will experience lower morale, employee absenteeism, high turnover, stress, and tension. The results will be lower creativity, lower productivity, along with equal opportunity or harassment suits. People are capital. When people are encouraged to reach their full potential, with all of their glaring differences and remarkable similarities, businesses will be a smart investor of this capital.

INTERVIEW

Nancy
54
White
human resources staff
7 years with company
B.A. degree

I've been working for about twenty years, and I have to say I've been really disappointed with my career in the corporate setting, although I enjoyed my previous experiences in teaching and sales.

I started with this company seven years ago in a lower level management position and have had only one promotion from one level to another. Also, my compensation has been disappointing. But I'm sure if I were a different sort of person, I could have done better. I have the type of personality that doesn't make waves. The white males I know are feeling resentment too, but theirs is because they had to work three jobs to make it during their career, and they didn't expect handouts from anyone, and now they see women and minorities getting breaks in the workplace.

White maleism lives at my company. I attribute it to the fact that we all come from that environment—it's kind of like, "you can't take the country out of the boy." Even though we have a new [diverse] culture, we have been steeped in years of conditioning. We're preconditioned: you can dictate someone's behavior, but you can't dictate their attitude.

I've felt the effects of white maleism in my career. There has been covert sexual harassment on a minor level, especially back in my sales days when I had all those white male bosses. If I would sum up the attitude, it was "you're an ornament, you're a pretty little thing, and you really don't understand what business is all about." That view of women was prevalent when I was in sales.

The other way was in the kind of sexual references and jokes. Things like that. The covert stuff, the pats on the head, for instance, were more rampant than the other kind of thing. Though I would call people on their sexist remarks or jokes, I didn't call them on the covert stuff, the insidious attitude of "there, there, dear." I was too steeped in the conditioning myself.

I still see white maleism today, despite the very tolerant workplace I'm in now. In the operation I support, there is a mentoring going on of our boss to his "successor," who is a young man and a clone of the boss. He has the attitude, everything. No one can challenge the [favored] position of this young man. One very strong woman in my department voices her opinion and clashes with the boss; several others feel the frustration.

I see a big difference in the communication styles of men and women in the workplace, especially in leadership. The women who are leaders have a softer style of delivery. The oldest male in my group speaks with the assumption that he is always right; he expects everyone to accept his authority. The young man being groomed to be boss's successor is mimicking his style, except that he has to exert more force sometimes.

I've noticed too that the top females hit against something. Yes, I believe there is a glass ceiling. One strong black woman in my organization dares not embarrass her boss in any way. She's having to move out laterally to extend her influence and competence.

Another problem I see in the workplace is addictions. I heard a consultant talk about the fact that organizations have addictions too. I think there's an addiction to turmoil and change at my company. I have been through so many different policies and campaigns that I've had to communicate to everyone in the workplace. You lose your credibility; saying "This is it. This is the way we're going," and then, the next year, saying, "Oops, that wasn't it. This is it."

But if you keep confusion going, it distracts people from any "me" issues they might be concerned about. There's always a war someplace— the idea of the common enemy. If you create a common enemy outside the company boundaries, like the competition, then all the people inside get in line to fight it.

The changes that have been lasting here have been driven from the top, which put the mechanics into place to make the changes. Unless that happens there is less support for change. It's rarely a grassroots effort. I've attended meetings of various resource groups (women, ethnic, racial, etc.) that have grown up in the workplace, but they haven't effected change. The resource groups tend to placate people. The compa-

ny gives them a place to be, then they're happy. They give them their little area to play in and then that makes them happy.

I think we've all created the white maleism in the workplace, though.
My awareness of women's issues and how I defer to men or not has
grown. When I was in sales I relied on feminine wiles, being cute and
charming, and that is certainly what got rewarded. I don't defer to men
anymore. But when I was married, I was the boss's wife. That marriage
was very damaging to me. I was married twelve years and had two daughters. I don't have a lot of trust around intimacy because of my marriage.

Marriage is not something I need anymore. I don't seem to let people
get that close to me anymore. I was very angry, I was raging for ten years
or so, and the men in my life had to pay. That was very selfish of me, but
that's the way it was.

There was a period when I left teaching that I became a workaholic. I
loved my work. I threw myself into it, and the men had to fit into that
or not.

My attitude toward men has changed in the last ten years. It's more
human and softer and allowing them in, allowing their humanness and
realness to be there for me as well. The reason I'm not interested in
marriage is I've had wonderful relationships without the give and take of
a marriage, without having to put up with the small idiosyncrasies.

When you ask me how I would want to be remembered, I could tell
you what it would not be. I get this acknowledgment all the time about
how good and warm and wonderful a person I am, but it's a hollow acknowledgment. That's not what I'm motivated by. I'm motivated by
getting the job done.

WORKSHOP

1. Name a significant male and female (parent, grandparent, uncle,
   aunt, brother, sister, friend, etc.) in your early life. How would you
   describe their roles? How did their roles affect how you see the roles
   of men and women today? your own role? If you have children, ask
   them the same questions?

2. State your views of immigration in four or five sentences?

3. Examine your home environment. If you live with a partner and/or children, what is the breakdown in time and types of domestic duties? If you live by yourself, how much time do you spend on domestic duties? Do you feel that the time spent on domestic duties affords you enough satisfaction, leisure, time to be with others important in your life? What can you do to make your home situation more satisfying?

4. Can you list four ways how a multicultural society has affected you? your family? your workplace? Are you and your family multilingual (foreign languages: French, Swahili, Thai; informal languages: Ebonics, computer, adolescent)? Have you or your children friends who are culturally different. If so, what have you/they learned from the experience? If not, how can you develop these friendships?

The mass of men lead lives
of quiet desperation.
–Henry David Thoreau
Walden

6

WHITE MEN IN QUIET DESPERATION

The stress men are feeling from their isolation and the ignorance of their own inner needs is evident in their health statistics, their rates of suicide and divorce, and their confusion and insecurity in the workplace. To cope with this stress they are doing what most unwitting individuals do when faced with change: become anxious, try to avoid uncomfortable situations, or retrench to historic behaviors that are known and safe. Yet the old marching orders are not working any longer. Women and members of other groups who are not white nor male now can compete as resource producers. They have earned the right to have a say in how things are accomplished in corporate America.

Everyone in the workplace seems to be pointing the finger at the white male as an oppressor. Yet he often views himself as a victim of history or a bystander to the rapid social changes around him. Mixed messages are everywhere. On the one hand, he is being urged to spend less time at work and more time at home with family and friends. However, a study reveals that those who do take a break in their careers lose an estimated $15,000 a year over the course of their working lives.

Despite the establishment of family-friendly programs at many companies, relatively few men take advantage of them. They are wary of the unspoken and unwritten rules of success that have governed corporate life for generations. For those who buy that definition of success, the competition is intense. To achieve that kind of success you need to be completely devoted, focusing almost all of your time, energy, and talent on your job. Anything else—family, children, friends, leisure, hobbies—is a distraction from your goal of workplace success.

Most males, when they intensely focus on their work, tend to be seen by their superiors, and by themselves, as committed, dedicated, loyal, and responsible. These are the qualities of a real team player. These are the qualities of someone who can be trusted to get the job done. These are the qualities that bring you raises, rewards, new corporate titles, and recognition. These are the qualities of a successful businessman. These are the qualities of a real man.

Although complaining that work takes them away from their personal lives, most men get seduced by the excitement and the challenge of job. Competition, strategizing, rewards, risk, adventure, and the feeling of accomplishment entice them. At some level, being so successful at work fits with all the expectations most men have of themselves, as well as what others have of them, for being the classical man.

But the work world is a place of rapid response and "lean and mean" attitudes. Companies are trimming staffs to protect their bottom lines and their carefully constructed ranks of women and minorities. The last hired now is not necessarily the first fired. Today's workplace is emphasizing intellectual and business talent, up-to-date training, increased technological skills, keenness in understanding corporate goals, and responsiveness to global marketing and sales shifts.

Does this sort of work environment make for craziness? You bet it does. What have men done to protect themselves in this fast-changing workplace? What have men done to redefine what it means to be a successful man in today's American workplace? Frequently, little. That is just the point.

I've met these men in my practice and in the seminars I give around the world for corporations and professional groups. I read about others in Jan Halper's book *Quiet Desperation: The Truth About Successful Men*. Many of the participants in my seminars are like the over four thousand corporate executives she interviewed. They are all human, concerned, sad, and often in pain. Most of them, she writes, "have been making changes quietly and often in isolation. Few have opened up to their wives or talked to one another about intimate feelings. Instead they have handled their inner turmoil in the proper male fashion, stoically and silently. So they have suffered inside. And the source of that suffering comes from the fact that men are cut off from who they are. They have been taught to deny their inner world, to avoid their feelings, to live according to prescribed ways of being."

In my years of working with men, I find that this inner pain frequently exhibits itself as boredom and restlessness in their work and in their personal lives. Most men are taught to show an unflappable external strength. If the truth be told, the majority of men believe they are the exceptions to this rule since they do not think they have it together nor have all that strength. What I discover is that a great many men talk about being the perfect, the successful, the strong male. With all this male bragging, some men conclude that they must be the only weak, inadequate males. So they maintain their silence and stoicism, never disclosing to anyone that they believe themselves to be less manly.

Stoic suffering in isolation is a rotten way to live your life. Most men feel the tension rising from the new demands being made by this diverse and democratic new world around them. They are finding the old world behaviors that automatically entitled them to wealth and power useless. These tensions play themselves out in most men's lives through the upsets in relationships, the divorce rate, increased health risks, and higher suicide figures. Although women attempt suicide more often than men, men achieve it more frequently—at four times the rate of women. This is due partly because men choose more deadly means. Even success in suicide is a sign of being a real man. Women attempt suicide more often; men get the job done! In fact, when many men hear about another male who attempted suicide and did not succeed, they label him a wimp, a loser.

Being male is a prescription for earlier death from all causes: health issues, risk-taking, adventure-seeking, living on the edge, and attempting to fulfill unrealistic expectations. Yet it is the way the mass of men experience their lives. Changing the image of manhood becomes more than a matter of expediency or political correctness. It is a matter of life and death!

Coming in contact through the global workplace with numerous cultures very different from the American culture also has forced many males to examine what it means to be a man. In my work in Africa, Asia, and Europe, I frequently am confronted with the confusion that many of these men have about the American male. In their cultures, the role of males is strongly defined. Most of these men see the American male as weak, unable to take charge of his society, allowing himself to be pushed around by women. In a word, most American males are seen by their foreign brothers as first class wimps!

This bewilderment is being fueled also by a new American tendency to focus on one's self. As Daniel Yankelovich found in his research for the book *New Rules,* by the late 1970s seven of ten Americans were spending a great deal of time thinking about themselves and their inner lives. This is not to be confused with the form of reflection to which I am referring in this book. In her book, Halper found that 62 percent of the men between twenty-seven and forty-five she interviewed placed a high value on personal growth, while only 6 percent of the men over forty-five did.

Historically most men have had a deep bond with their work. The turmoil in the world caused by the shift from an industrial to an information age, from a national to a global economy has had deep repercussions. Mergers and acquisitions, rightsizings and downsizings, restructurings and reengineerings, strategic planning and value-oriented leadership in the corporate world have caused intense reverberations through the very foundations of most males' identities.

Of comfort to most men's fathers was the adage, "Your job is your best friend." Men of the 1990s are wondering who and where their best friends are. In what or whom can they believe? Many men have lost their traditional source of a secure identity—their jobs. Those jobs are being recast constantly. They are told to be a team player. Yet many men view each team player as struggling with the other to protect his own job and stay alive in this "dog eat dog" world.

Men are wondering who their wives, girlfriends, and male friends are. In a word, whom can they trust. Formerly the women in most men's lives could be depended upon for unwavering support. They could count on women to need them, depend on them, praise, and adore them. During the past one hundred years things have drastically changed. At the turn of the century women did not have the vote. Now women are in the U.S. Senate, on corporate boards of directors, and coming into the workplace in great numbers. They compete just as hard as men to survive.

Ask a man today how he feels about women and he might respond: "Women? I don't understand them. They are hard to keep up with. They make movies, conduct orchestras, write books, lead companies, and still they have babies! They have all these choices. They can be and do whatever they want. How am I supposed to compete? How do I stay in the same room, not to mention the same bed, with this person? Do I need to win a Pulitzer Prize or a Super Bowl ring before she will look at me, before she can look up to me? What's going on?"

Joseph Pleck insightfully articulated the ever evolving relational maps from traditional to modern men in his classic, *The Myth of Masculinity*.

"In the traditional male role, masculinity is validated ultimately by individual physical strength and aggression. Men are generally expected not to be emotionally sensitive to others or emotionally expressive or self-revealing, particularly of feelings of vulnerability or weakness. Paradoxically, anger and certain other impulsive emotional expressions, particularly toward other males, are expected or tolerated.

"In the modern male role, by contrast, masculinity is validated by economic achievement and organizational or bureaucratic power. Interpersonal skills and intelligence are esteemed insofar as they lead to these goals. Emotionally, the modern male role strongly values the capacity for emotional sensitivity and self-expression in romantic relationships.

"The traditional male prefers the company of men to the company of women and experiences other men as the primary validators of his masculinity. Though bonds of friendship among men are not necessarily emotionally intimate, they are often strong. In the traditional male role in marital and other relationships, women are seen as necessary for sex and for bearing children, but these relationships are not expected to be emotionally intimate or romantic, and often seem only pragmatic arrangements of convenience. The traditional male expects women to acknowledge and defer to his authority. There is also strong adherence to a sexual double standard that views sexual freedom as appropriate for men but not for women.

"The modern male prefers the company of women. Women, rather than other men, are experienced as the primary validators of masculinity. Men's relationships with women are now expected to be intimate and romantic. Men now see heterosexual relationships as the only legitimate source of the emotional support they need. Women now soothe men's wounds and replenish their emotional reserves rather than defer to their authority in the family. Though it still persists, the sexual double standard is less marked. Masculinity is now proved less by many sexual conquests than by truly satisfying one woman's sexual needs. Men's emotional relationships with other men have become weaker and less emotionally important, though a high level of competence in conducting work relationships is expected. Men now disclose more to female than to male friends.

It is now men's relationships with other men—rather than with women—that seem to be only arrangements of convenience."

Indeed, studies by the Roper Organization and others have shown that men have come to respect women more over the past twenty-five years and women have come to respect men less. As reported in *American Demographics*: "Women were most likely to say that men only value their own opinions, that they find it necessary to keep women down, that they immediately think of getting a woman in bed, that they don't pay attention to things at home." Yet a scant generation ago, in 1970, women were describing men as "basically kind, gentle, and thoughtful." What has happened to men, to women?

My weekly seminars support the findings of the Roper Organization. A simple exercise that I ask the participants to carry out produces results replicated in every company worldwide, regardless of the organization, whether everyday worker or upper management. I ask seminar participants to divide into single-sex groups of four or five and list the five adjectives each group thinks best describe the other sex (I use "other sex" to avoid affirming the negativity inherent in the word "opposite"). Among the adjectives that men frequently use to describe women are: sensitive, nurturing, soft, intuitive, loving, talkative, emotional, unpredictable, attractive, confusing, and manipulative. What women frequently say about men is that they are: insecure, egotistical, possessive, controlling, demanding, domineering, logical, strong, insensitive, emotionally limited, macho, and competitive.

It appears that most men view women in a more favorable manner than women do men. Most men see themselves as being positive about women. When I probe further, I find that frequently women see men as having the ultimate power. Men set the rules. And, a world where you set the rules from which you benefit is satisfying. Most women are upset with men because their rules exclude them and tend to put them down.

At these seminars almost all the men are unprepared for the negative adjectives women use to describe them. How could this be since most men see themselves as nice guys? They are loyal, dependable, responsible at work and at home. They go to religious services on the weekends. They give to the local charities and devote their time to civic organizations.

These men conclude that if women feel so negative about men, it must be some other men who are at fault. This negativity by women must come from their poor experiences with other men in their personal or work lives. Those other men probably were not good examples of true manhood. Those other men were definitely quite different from us.

This line of reasoning may make sense to some males. Yet, it is one of the major roots of the difficulties men and women have in communicating with each other at work and at home. Men and women view the same situations and use the same words to describe them, but mean something quite different! Men and women use similar words and behaviors based on their historical gender roles. Males as resource producers and protectors tend to focus on objects. Women, as family and group collaborators, are more relational oriented. From their relational world women label men's behaviors as controlling, demanding, and oppressive. From their world of objects, most men will label this same behavior as assertive, ambitious, confident, and definitive. When women label men's behaviors as egotistical, self-centered, and narrow-minded, in their world, most men will label them as focused and goal-oriented. The opposite is also true. From their world of objects men label women's behavior as confusing, unpredictable, manipulative, and illogical. In their world of relationships, most women will call these same behaviors flexible, spontaneous, and explorative.

It is especially noteworthy that very few men or women indicate that the other sex is intelligent. If you recall, we had stated that intelligence is the key ingredient for today's technological oriented workplace. Furthermore, although most of the adjectives men used to describe women are wonderful qualities—soft, nurturing, loving—they are hardly the qualities one would expect to see in a help-wanted advertisement for an employee, let alone a manager. Most men and women still label themselves and the other sex by those characteristics that might have been valid in our society forty years ago. No wonder our workplaces have so much difficulty updating and upgrading. We have men and women conditioned to be emotionally comfortable in 1960 trying to operate in a high-tech workplace geared for the year 2000!

Most men have never viewed women as the major breadwinner (resource producer), combat defenders (resource protector), and societal leaders (resource director). They persist in viewing women in the historical cultural role of wife, mother, daughter, sister, or romantic liaison. In her book *Sex and the Workplace* Barbara Gutek addresses what she calls sex role spillover in the workplace. She defines sex role as "a set of shared expectations about the behavior of men and women."

"Sex role expectations are carried over into the workplace for three reasons," she suggests: 1) Society insists that gender role makes a difference in every domain of human experience. 2) Women may feel more comfortable with stereotypical female roles in some circumstances, particularly if they feel men at work will only accept them in a female role. 3) Men may feel more comfortable falling back on their familiar role relationships as "spouse, lover, parent, or child."

Two trends that contribute to sex role spillover are historical segregation of the sexes in different kinds of jobs and the differences in status, prestige, and power assigned to men and women at work. Gutek notes that there are very few sex-integrated occupations. Surprisingly, most men still have not had a female supervisor, and most women have not had a male subordinate.

The prominence of sexual harassment cases in the 1990s, the notorious Anita Hill-Clarence Thomas confrontation during Thomas's nomination hearing for the U.S. Supreme Court, and the recent disclosures of major sexual harassment problems in the corporate world and in the armed forces, prove that sexual roles and their spillover in the workplace remain a critical area of misunderstanding. Many of us want to see ourselves as modern or liberated, but old world words and behaviors are hard to shed. The Hill-Thomas matter was a vivid example of how men and women see the very same incident and interpret it from their own perspectives. Thomas, as a lawyer, should have been keenly aware of word interpretation. Yet he indicated that his words and his behaviors were flirtatious, somewhat naughty, and irreverent. It was not sexual harassment. For Hill, his words and behaviors were disrespectful and degrading. It was sexual harassment!

Here is how one executive in Halper's *Quiet Desperation* put it: "Men judge themselves by the women who want them. There are enough ways men compete in business without adding the 'get the beautiful woman' game. It only forces us to compete in yet another way, a way we would like relief from. In our company your power position increases based on whose secretary you are screwing. But we also have to maintain the facade of being happily married so the boss thinks we are stable."

Another Halper interviewee described his quandary in dealing with women differently in the workplace than at home. "I have three daughters and I want them to be able to do anything they want. I'd rather they aren't dependent on a man. I know my wife's not happy with counting on me for the bread and butter. But that's how it was for us. I tell my girls they'd better think about how they are going to support themselves. Yet at the office I don't encourage any of the women to go for it. If they do, they might get a position or project that should have been mine. It's crazy for me to think about it this way, but I do."

Amid this changing environment, men are also asking, "Why don't I get the respect for all I've done?" The answer is: computers have changed everything. To operate computers, brain, not brawn, is needed. Although brawn will always be needed in the workplace and on the battle-field, it no longer will be the norm. Computers will run the workplace, do the lifting, do the work for which the physical strength of men was so necessary. Computers will fight the wars, send off the rockets, fly the planes, secure the land. The physical strength and the killer instinct of the combat soldier will always be needed, but it will be the exception not the norm of warfare. The brawn factor that gave men their roles, their identities, their power, their privileges and entitlement, is rapidly disappearing.

Women are now major resource producers along with men. Now women also can be resource protectors along with men. Being resource producers and resource protectors, women want to be part of the power role of resource directors. Women want to make up the institutional rules with the men.

Men see women sharing their power in the workplace and on the battlefield. Making up the rules—being the resource director—is the last bastion of their historical definition of manhood. Without a new description of manhood these men frantically will protect their old ways of being in charge. They will fall back to fundamentalistic cliches: This is the way I have been raised. My father wasn't that way. This is not manly. The Bible says. . . !

The quandary men experience becomes clearer. Why are they being lambasted and released from their jobs when they were the ones who built the refrigerators and designed the computers? They were the ones dying in the wars in which women learned the power of work. They were the ones who invented what we know as the modern, democratic world in which people of different races want its benefits. They were doing what they were told, by their government, their employers, and, yes, by their mothers, wives, and women friends. Why should they now be punished?

One possible reason for this confusion is that men were not changing with the times and the technologies. Although Freud subjected our psyches to scrutiny in *The Interpretation of Dreams* (1900), men have continued to follow historically acceptable norms and behaviors. World shattering events such as walks on the moon, penetration of the ocean floors, cracking the DNA code, have mostly been developed by men. Despite these developments, men have continued, unabated, to follow the cultural marching orders of previous decades: provide, protect, rule. Women's rights and civil rights are someone else's agenda. Real men go to work, bring home the bacon, defend society, take charge.

But times in America have changed and the profile of the changing workplace cannot be reversed. Growth in the work force is coming from others: from women and from the nontraditional immigrants, mainly Asians and Latin Americans.

Management ideas and fads alone cannot deal with the issues and challenges of this new diverse and democratic environment. Why? Because they do not address workplace dynamics holistically. Just as physicians have learned that it takes a panel of drugs, not a single antibiotic, to attack bacteria successfully, we are learning that individuals and organizations are inextricably linked. Most of the organizational ideas have been just that—organizational! Since most men find their identities fulfilled in the organization, we must treat simultaneously organizational structures and the identity or description of what it means to be a man. If you change one, you must change the other. You can not just change some of the organization's members, but all men, women, and minorities.

The values many people learned from the sensitivity movements of the '60s focused on the individual and did not carry over into the corporation or everyday life, as some leaders had hoped. Even many of the diversity sensitivity sessions of the '80s and '90s failed to be incorporated in the workplace. The individual may seem to have changed but the everyday organizational environment had not. As John Naisbitt points out in his book, *Reinventing the Corporation,* social institutions, like corporations, do not readily respond to change instituted by individuals. Corporate change comes, instead, from the confluence of two forces: economic necessity and changing human behaviors. All the company's members—white males as well as women and minorities—must support the organizational and individual power shifts that are going on in society and companies today.

INTERVIEW

Bert
36
White
business development, process improvement
10 years with current company
B.S. Mechanical Engineering, MBA

I had a strict upbringing that focused on what I did wrong, versus what I did correctly. My social skills and self-esteem were initially very weak. I was painfully shy. Despite my religious background, I found myself divorced twice before the age of thirty. I found my dissatisfaction and/or personal pain was a powerful motivating factor to seek and implement change.

I have worked at four major U.S. corporations, typically starting in engineering, moving to business roles, and finally creative "change agent" roles. I am currently chartered to "improve our capability to improve our capability." I am recognized as being very effective in this role. Our company used to be very rigid and would not share "ownership" via empowerment. They are really progressing towards using empowerment. That motivates me and deepens my commitment to the company. I have been involved in several significant outside entrepreneurial efforts and find great passion and excitement in these efforts - and, also a chance to become more independent, both in terms of work and financially.

I feel very motivated to explore options in my life - music, relationships, expanding my intellect, and defining my spirituality. I have pursued such options with a near obsession. I have great dreams of productive, interactive relationships with people whether male-to-male/female, as friends. Ultimately, I seek one that is male-to-female as life-partners. I would like to fulfill these dreams. After my second divorce when I was twenty-nine, I quit being a workaholic and stopped being someone who "worked too hard" to please others. I literally had to learn to like myself. The shock of the second divorce was truly a watershed event. Why did it take that many years of frustration just to start the process of "waking up," or to achieve self-awareness? Had I really been unconscious that long and just not known better? What other items have I yet to wake up to in this world?

I seem to be a person who reflects heavily - in fact, I have to prioritize it at times. From my viewpoint, I started life with some deficits and capability gaps which left me feeling "underaverage." My father made me ashamed of gaps he saw through his combined sergeant/IBM corporate eyes. Overall, he was probably an average guy. He had some good vision and could structure things well, but he did not seem to act on them or implement them. He does not have a clue on how to have fun. I am still learning how myself.

My father is reclusive. I used to be strongly introverted, although if I had had more confidence, I would have acted on strong urges to approach people and "join in." I chuckle to think how far I've come. I used to actually get nauseated due to tension at high school social events. It is much better these days. Mr. Shy became president of his fraternity's international organization - largely just to prove to myself that I could overcome the perceived deficit in terms of my social skills.

My father had a mistrust for people and an unwarranted financial insecurity that rubbed off on me. I note annual progress in the area of spending money on myself more freely. I reacted to my father's disapproval and my own doubts and desires with a combined emotional force of shame and anger. I channeled these emotional energies into a structured, obsessive program of self-improvement in a self-competitive manner. I note people with world-class abilities and seek those abilities, often failing to achieve even above average status, but sometimes hitting success. I truly got good at "getting better."

I still long for things or capabilities I do not currently possess. I am becoming aware of the possibility of just accepting myself as I am. I feel like some life options are passing me by with no second chance. Having a loving wife and 2 or 3 loving children is one. I feel with all of the counseling and self-study I am truly prepared to be effective in that scenario, but it doesn't seem to be happening. I wonder, can men and women get together, on a large scale, and create varied examples of marriages that really work?

To me, success is maximizing the number and quantity of caring and loving relationships where people truly and productively support self-competitive personal growth. Traditional standards of male success are unfulfilling. Achieving macho, competitive goals like being a workplace success, benchpressing 300 lbs, becoming a millionaire, etc. have not made me happy. To top it off, the effort to achieve and maintain these goals/capabilities can drain your passion for the rest of life's possibilities, especially relationships.

Despite being near mid-life, supposedly intelligent, and having a very successful and balanced life, I find myself asking many questions such as: Where is the passion in people? How can we get people of "all creeds, color, nationalities, genders, religions, etc." to work together undefensively? How can we be more direct and open while avoiding being "politically correct" in an ungenuine and unproductive manner? Why is it so hard to truly and deeply connect with other people? Where are the mentors? How can I better self-mentor? Why do people stay with unsatisfying careers, raise children to whom they are unconnected, and participate with spouses in mutually unfulfilling marriages instead of initiating change? Where can I go, realistically, with my capabilities and accumulated "life-assets"? What is happiness? What are good criteria for measuring true happiness? If I were raising a child, how would I help create their thirst to seek and understand truth, for the benefit of humanity and themselves? How do you translate that into spirituality? What is spirituality? Is there a point where I will be satisfied with the "answers" I've found and my life as it exists, such that I will then seek change on a less-often and more selective basis?

WORKSHOP

1. What is your definition of manhood? What roles do work, relationships, color, control, and power play in that definition of manhood?

2. What is your definition of womanhood? What roles do work relationships, color, control, and power being perfect play in that definition of womanhood?

3. What is your definition of success, contentment, happiness? How does your present allotment of time at home and at work match your definitions?

4. How do your definitions of those concepts in #3 impact your relationships with adults, children, and the community? What behavior can you try that speaks of each one of your definitions?

A single arrow is easily broken,
but not ten in a bundle.
–Japanese proverb

7

BENEFITING FROM THE DIVERSITY DILEMMA

Differences tend to divide, and commonalities unite. In America since its beginning, we have been focusing on our differences. This focus has led to separatism and divisiveness. Isn't it time to see how our differences can be integrated into a working organization, a working society? America was founded on the principle of e pluribus unum: the many united. We tried an assimilation model to get this accomplished, but it no longer serves us. It is time to adapt the principle of e pluribus unum to the new realities of the twenty-first century.

Until most recently, many companies have approached our changing demographic profile in the workplace in the spirit of a blind date that must be tolerated. In fact, according to a *Wall Street Journal* article as late as September 5, 1996, some companies have gone so far as to limit severely any training programs for a diverse work force. They mistakenly believe there is no longer a need to focus on the diversity issue. White males' anger has cooled down. Women and minorities, although not cooled down, are revisiting the issues. Corporations are pulling back from fostering white male bashing. Some corporations even believe that diversity issues are a thing of the past. They believe they have successfully incorporated the spirit of those programs into the fabric of everyday operations. They are mistaken. The quiet we are sensing in the workplace is simply a re-grouping of all parties. As seen by the recent incidents at Texaco and in the Armed Forces, the battlefields have moved from the workplace to the courtrooms and the national forum.

Some corporations rightfully have moved beyond the old-type diversity training programs which we now know were doomed from the start. Venting emotions with little solid thinking and direction, promoting victim/oppressor labels, a "you owe me" attitude, and an us-against-them mentality, has not worked! The issue of benefiting from a diverse work force and a democratic society is far from over.

What is needed now is a new beginning. The workplace is central and core to American lives, touching more people than any other institution in our country. For most of us, where we work is the only environment in which we cannot make a decision about the people with whom we want to associate. If we did, we would chose our own kind as we do in our neighborhoods, schools, and places of worship. For these reasons, the workplace is a magnificent—if not the only—laboratory for training Americans to live in a diverse and democratic society. In today's America, corporations have a unique position and a new responsibility. For their own continued success and for the benefit of the country in which they exist, businesses must actively take on this new leadership role.

The term *e pluribus unum* has always fascinated me. Originally, the phrase was used at the beginning of this nation to describe the unification of thirteen different colonies into one united federation. Although they were many colonies, they were united as a country.

That same phrase, that same concept, is applicable to our diverse culture today. As a land of immigrants, we are the only country that continually brings together people from 198 different countries all seeking common goals: freedom, opportunity, and prosperity. The blending of these different cultures has provided the creativity and richness that has made this country so successful. In truth, although we are many different groups—*pluribus*, the whole—*unum*, has been enriched.

Today, many of us in America have trouble seeing that unity, let alone enrichment. Everywhere the emphasis seems to be on individuality, difference, separation, and division. For too long our country and the American workplace has focused mainly on people's differences—the *pluribus*. When one speaks of gender, race, and ethnic background, one speaks of differences. Are differences important? Absolutely! Why do people focus on their differences in America? To remind all of us that "there should be no differences!" What does this mean? In this land of immigrants, many of the citizens born here and those who have newly arrived are steeped in "old world" cultures and behaviors. Many of these old world cultures have historically had a specific race, tribe, clan or group possessing the greatest access to the wealth and power found in their environment.

In America, the white tribe, men, specifically white men, continue to maintain the wealth and power in the "old world" manner and the distinction of classes. Women and those of other tribes or groups, because of their distinctive attributes may not look or act like the "entitled group" and, therefore, are excluded automatically from the opportunities and privileges of that class. Physical attributes of gender and color can be primary indicators of who has major access to the resources and who is left out; who is part of the *in* crowd and who is not.

Yet, in America, in this "new" democratic culture, everyone, regardless of differences, is promised equal access to the resources of this country. However, even a national declaration of civil rights for all Americans did not succeed in looking past differences.

In an effort to show that differences could be important, as well as to encourage group self-esteem and solidarity, women and all kinds of minorities set into motion the movement of "celebrating differences." Now, being different (not being white and male) is not a negative factor. On the contrary, being of another race or gender can be positive, a source of pride, something to celebrate. Although they are not included in the enfranchised clan, women and minorities seem to say that they are just as important. They, too, are worthy of admission into the ranks of those who have access to the resources.

"Celebrating differences" is an important and essential concept, especially in a diverse and democratic society. Such experiences can help the total community to know, learn, appreciate, respect, and benefit from the uniqueness of others. Nevertheless, simply celebrating one's differences has reminded many whites and many males that others are drastically dissimilar and are now flaunting those differences. Many white males conclude that if women and minorities are so different, could they be trusted to the point of being included in a world competing for limited resources?

Furthermore, isn't there something to be proud of and worth celebrating in being white, in being a male, in being a white male? Since there is no celebration of a "male week, "white male week," or a "white culture month," some whites, some males, and some white males view those groups celebrating their color or their sex as saying they are better.

Women and minority groups respond to that by saying "Every day is male day!" "Every month is whitey month!" What do they mean? The "unwritten rules" that govern American society still follow "old world form" (right gender, right clan). To live in a society where whites and males make the rules and have main access to prosperity and power, is to "celebrate" that system daily just by living in that system.

Telling someone over and over how different you are from them, however, doesn't foster the building of trust. Trust is the essential force that brings human beings together. Trust is what holds a family, a group, an organization, a country, together. Trust is built on knowledge and understanding, shared likenesses and values, a sense of commonness and familiarity, and the skills to communicate all that. These are essential elements enhancing human beings' basic need for the feelings of safety and security.

Focusing solely on individual or group differences can make one feel special, unique, worthwhile, and acceptable. Yet, while differences are important, focusing *solely* on differences tends to emphasize dissimilarity. This is a major element that promotes fear and distrust which can lead to separation and exclusion.

In order to keep differences from separating us, we need a context in which to interact and take advantage of these differences. In this context differences would be determined as a means not an end. Differences would be a way to unite and enrich. This context would seek those components that would join us together; elements that we all have in common, regardless of our differences. That commonality is our humanity. That commonness is what every human being, regardless of culture, gender, race, of any differences, share: the need to belong, to feel safe and secure, to be acknowledged and affirmed, to love and be loved, to contribute and receive, to have the opportunity for a good life. To achieve these common human goals, it is vital for all individuals to have an environment, a system, that supports and offers them access to the spiritual and material resources of country and culture. Each of us, however, depending on our uniqueness—race, gender, background—will have different ways to achieve these shared goals. Those ways will be our styles, our methods, our behaviors which might succeed for us as well as enhance the styles, methods, and behaviors of others.

The danger of remaining a collection of separate parts is the subject of Arthur Schlesinger, Jr.'s book *The Disuniting of America*. Schlesinger rightfully warns that to promote separatism of individuals or of groups is to promote destruction of the American workplace, nation, and culture. What Schlesinger writes is logical and sensible, if one stops where he does. One needs to go further. Foreigners like the famous Alexis de Toqueville, who visited our country in its infancy, had a more balanced view. Writing in the early nineteenth century de Toqueville was amazed that our experiment in nation-building could hold together. The French visitor believed our participation as citizens in this new society would benefit all and would bind us together. Yet, he thought that racism was our young nation's greatest pitfall. How right he was! The diversity of citizens in our country can only work if we remain clearly focused on the historic quest for commonality. This commonality—a better life for all citizens—is a bond that can encompass skin tones, ethnic customs, religious beliefs, and gender differences.

The American culture is supported by its economy. The national economy lives and survives in the American workplace. Without this economic base all of our other institutions—home, school, church, government—would have little life. In reality, the workplace has become the center of the American society. It is the chief agent of change in the culture. The American workplace must foster, encourage, sometimes force, other American institutions to change. The need for skilled laborers will ultimately force our educational institutions to keep pace with the changing needs of the workplace. The pursuit of national and international markets, the need for employee and customer protection, the concern and care of this nation's resources will force government involvement at both federal and state levels. The demands and the rewards of the workplace will dramatically affect the lives of the American workers in their families and even in their churches.

Our workplaces are our crucibles for learning how to successfully respond to an endlessly changing world at home and abroad. The technological world, the global village markets, and demanding customers force businesses to remain awake and alert if they are to survive. Conducting business as usual can be comforting and safe. In a competitive world, however, such behavior is tantamount to being in a rut. The difference between a rut and a grave is its depth! Ask the former IBM, or American Express, or even today's AT&T!

In my global travels I have concluded that a country's culture strongly influences how that country best operates for economic success. Most societies tend to be closed cultures. Of course, there is no such thing in our modern world as a truly closed society. Nonetheless, countries do establish territorial, economic, and social boundaries to control external forces and provide an internal environment that is safe and secure. From birth through adulthood, citizens are developed, trained, conditioned in a common style by the institutions of home, school, government, and church to know and live by the country's laws and norms. This is what is called a culture.

The individual is assimilated into a society by following the given cultural rules. In doing so, group harmony and societal order are maintained. In closed cultures, the individual does not have to reflect, to risk, to make choices. Indeed the individual is rewarded for simply following the rules. Severe punishment awaits those who break the rules. In such unity of individuals and institution, there is a national strength.

Sociologists have discovered that a harmonious environment is better attained if a large majority is similar in background and behave in known and predictable ways. This is what is termed *homogeneity.* When that homogeneous national style is brought into the workplace as a work ethnic, great harmony among workers and great focus on a common goal prevails. The workers succeed in production since they have been prepared for this work methodology since birth.

An example of how national culture has made a country an economic success is Japan. Japan is considered a closed culture—very much protected from the outside world; very safe and unchanging. Harmony is essential among a large and growing population of this island country. Orderly distribution of the limited resources necessary to survive can best be accomplished with clear and distinct laws. The laws in Japan are very clear. They tell you what you **can** do (the laws in America tell you what you **cannot** do!). Citizens are assimilated into the culture by following the precious laws, knowing their roles, and behaving appropriately. Order is maintained; harmony provided.

Within homogeneous cultures like Japan, safety, security, lawfulness, discipline, and the citizens thrive. There is a great emphasis on group harmony—family, ancestors, work groups, community, and the nation. The individual's major responsibility is to live a disciplined life in harmony with others. In Japan there is a saying: The nail that stands out gets hammered! In the Japanese culture when an individual disgraces one's family, the individual is disowned. On the other hand, a kamikaze pilot is seen as a hero. He gave up his life to protect the group's harmony.

This emphasis on the rules, living for group unity, using limitations as a positive challenge, fostered a unique quality of life and cultural harmony in Japan. These same aspects of Japanese harmony and concern for a quality life in a limited environment attracted N. Edward Deming, an American statistician.

Professor N. Edward Deming significantly contributed to the Total Quality Management (TQM) movement. The philosophy of TQM is based on the notion that quality of a product or service is fundamental for improving the competitive position of a company. A basic premise of TQM is that any improvement starts with finding the source of failure and removing all errors. This approach benefited greatly by Deming's work which quantified all management behaviors into measured activities.

Deming encouraged the Japanese to apply the principles of their culture to their workplace processes and production. Within the limited space of the material product—say, car size—the harmonious Japanese work teams pursued a harmonious interaction of limited parts in an ordered and error-free operation. The startling result was a quality product! This was a major factor in that country's success in producing high quality hardware. The Deming Prize is Japan's quality award upon which the American Malcolm Baldridge National Quality Awards are based.

There are several advantages to a closed society. One advantage is the safety and security everyone may feel in a known, unchanging environment. Another is group harmony—everything and everyone are in order. Finally, through repetition of the same behaviors, a certain perfection can be achieved.

At the same time, there is a major disadvantage to a closed society— the inability to self-evolve, to be dynamic, and to stay current or alive. The factors essential for an organization to survive and be vital in a constantly changing world are absent. Different points of view, creative tension, freedom to create and examine options, and the ability to change quickly are lacking. All the organization's energy is focused inward to protect the limited and known space and to use the limited and known resources for survival.

For an individual or a country to focus solely inward is to make safety and security the prime value and concern. At best cultural or individual narcissism is promoted; at worst, societal incest. There is no openness to the outside and to the unknown. There is no stimulation for new ways that would allow the system to renew itself, to remain healthy, and to stay alive. To focus outward as an individual or a group is to sacrifice some of the benefits of safety and security for new and creative ways that will ensure continued development and growth.

America is obviously not a homogeneous or closed society. We are a heterogeneous society. We are a land of immigrants, people who come from a number of different cultures, speak a number of different languages, have a number of different customs, styles, and experiences. We are a nation that prizes individuality. A major challenge in America is to forge a constantly changing and dynamic culture that still provides safety and security for individuals and groups. Interfacing these two worlds necessarily creates tension. To make this tension creative and successful requires special skills. These include ongoing education and reflection that creates choices, harmoniously discussing and evaluating different options, and balancing the good of individuals with the needs of the community. At times this process can be troublesome, chaotic, and messy. The rewards, however, are marvelous for individuals, groups, and our nation.

In our 200 years of history we have learned that the assimilation model does not work. To be successful as a nation, we have to *integrate*. Integration is a process of supporting the homogenous safe groups while integrating these same groups into a unified, heterogenous community. The safety and security of individuals in their like or homogeneous groups are protected. The creative and dynamic tension resulting from interfacing of these homogeneous groups can benefit the greater community.

Corporations have been trying assimilation for a generation. This has been less than successful in a fast changing market. When people are asked to drop their differences and assimilate into a dominant culture for the sake of order, a repressive environment is created. Individuals feel unsafe and insecure. Those who are not of their group could be the enemy. This dangerous environment breeds prejudice and discrimination. Individuals survive by withdrawing, avoiding, and going underground. Discrimination moves from overt to covert. Covert discrimination becomes more difficult to identify. In such an environment, tension, anxiety, and hostility flourish.

Men set workplace performance evaluations that ask women to think and act like us, or non-whites to think and act like white. Unknowingly we use such measures to seek order and harmony through a common approach, a united homogeneous group, a known and safe environment. We believe that an ordered group, a well oiled machine, produces more. In so doing, however, we lose the richness of other perspectives. We forfeit the possibility of developing new and creative options that could give us the competitive edge. Asking others to change to fit into one united and static group is to seek our own comfort and decay.

We need the talents of all our people. We need to integrate their differences into unified processes and profitable products. What is so precious in this heterogeneous approach is the ongoing creativity that comes from honoring individual differences. This fundamental creativity has made this country successful and prosperous. Americans have won over 170 Nobel prizes for creative ideas. We have an entrepreneurial and ingenious work force.

Other nations want the success and prosperity that is ours. But they do not want the chaos, confusion, and disharmony that seem to accompany it. To maintain their country's harmony, yet strive for the prosperity that is ours, they send their emissaries to America to reap the benefits of our creative and tension-filled culture. They send their students here to learn the creative techniques of such a diverse culture. They open factories here. They buy American companies with creative American workers. They put money into American research centers.

Interestingly, a growing number of these foreign students decide to stay and work in America. The American lifestyle and work opportunities attract a growing pool of competent workers to this country. They are eager to benefit from this country's freedom and prosperity. They bring the richness of the current styles, views, and experiences of their own cultures.

We need to appreciate and discern among these different customs, talents and styles. Some will fit into our national heritage, some will not. This is *not* a free country. Not every style, custom, or religious behavior supports the American way as stated in the Bill of Rights and the Constitution. To deny citizens the right to practice such anti-American behaviors is *not* to rob them of their rights. Nor is such denial considered discrimination or prejudice. An example of an old world behavior that is unacceptable is the treatment of women as property.

Nor should we try to look past people's differences and treat every-one the same. This is really a dismissal of others. We need to embrace these differences. We need to assist our citizens to develop the skills and behaviors expressive of common respect, mutual understanding, and growing ability to discern and forge those differences for the benefit of the community and nation.

People are at the top of their form when they know they have a stake in the outcome. When they know they are respected, they experience so-ciety and the workplace as valuing who they are. When work respects people, people respect work. Their loyalty is automatic. The more the corporation meets the needs of the individual worker, the greater that worker's productivity.

Consider these two statements: A. In an airline strike many years ago, the president of the company reputedly refused to consider worker in-volvement in management. In his words, "I won't have the monkeys running the zoo." B. An article in the *Harvard Business Review* by R. Roosevelt Thomas, Jr. contains this statement: "What we must do is create an environment where no one is advantaged or disadvantaged, an environment where 'we' is everyone."

It is clear which attitude will get the most cooperative, energetic re-sponse from employees. "Monkeys in a zoo" is a degrading image of the work force. It is designed to diminish and shame those who do not fit. With such a view of the work force, one maintains power by exclu-sion. Excluding those whom you believe are competing with you, you maintain a greater power of access to the resources. And, of course, the more your competitors are not like you, the less you can trust them. People who work in such an atmosphere, whether words are ever spoken or not, do so grudgingly and with a loyalty only to their paycheck.

"'We' is everyone" is a statement of inclusion rather than of exclu-sion. In this context the company is not the property of management to be directed according to its view from the top of the pyramid. It is more an enterprise undertaken by a group of people acting together to add value to the lives of all those involved. It extends outward to enrich the lives of customers. This is what self-organization is all about. In this model everyone's viewpoint on a work team or in a business process is considered. It does not mean everyone's suggestion is followed. In this model the binding force is trust. It is a trust built on fostering common goals and continual growth in understanding all the individual differences brought to those common goals. It is a trust built on the continual development of skills that facilitate working with differences towards a unified goal.

If individuals within an organization realize their potential, then the organization maximizes its personnel in terms of information sharing, problem solving, creativity, and customer responsiveness. Of course, a business may have problems with organization or processes. This may have nothing to do with an empowered work force networked into the company's vision. The good news is that the feedback from such employees will be reliable information about those areas of the business that need fine-tuning or a complete overhaul. Employee ownership means that no member of the organization is any more tolerant of waste or duplicated effort than any other.

Employee ownership is analogous to Stephen Covey's idea of synergy, the sixth of his *Seven Habits of Highly Effective People*. Synergy means that when you bring all of the people together with total respect for their differences, the productive force generated is greater than the sum of the parts. "It means that the relationship which the parts have to each other is a part in and of itself. It is not only a part, but the most catalytic, the most empowering, the most unifying, and the most exciting part," Covey writes. He is talking about energy added to a human situation that makes it different, more creative and productive by an order of magnitude. Perhaps, inadvertently, Covey is talking about authentic diversity. We read on. "The essence of synergy is to value differences—to respect them, to build on strengths, to compensate for weaknesses." The whole is enriched and dependent for its being on each part, as the part is more enriched by being part of the whole. When everyone is fully engaged because each knows he or she is fully valued, the energy generated is memorable.

This does not deny the need for an overriding vision and direction. It does assert that everyone has value and the right to contribute to that vision and to an appropriate reward for profits gained. This is the meaning of employee ownership and ties directly into the idea that "'we' is everyone." It is embedded in management consultant Tom Peters's notion that unless everyone receives some form of bonus in a given year, no one does. Authentic diversity does away with the unspoken Orwellian company policy that says we are all equal, but some of us are more equal than others.

The goals of the organization are miniaturized in the goals of each work team and individual. When workers and the work process are honored the parts of the engine, designed to produce widgets or services and satisfied customers, work smoothly together. Of course, reading the company's strategic plan, one probably assumes that this is the way the company's engine is supposed to operate—smoothly and efficiently.

What is the difference? The difference is the gap between theory and practice—a gap American companies have lived with and written off as an unavoidable expense. It is caused by separation, isolation, and doing things the same comfortable way. To fully benefit from a diverse and democratic culture, one does not accept this view. It alters the human source of that differential, the friction among unequal, unrespected individuals that causes the engine to drag and underperform. Regenerating the work force with respect and equal access gets everyone moving in the same direction again.

The energy spent monitoring, disciplining, and supervising individuals who have the full ability to operate independently is wasted energy. Its price tag is in the billions. The energy individuals spend competing with each other, avoiding work, burying their insights and creativity for fear of stepping out of line is talent wasted and revenue lost. When this atmosphere invades the workplace, competition instead of cooperation results. Secrets, rumors, one-upmanship, and the games people play to survive and get ahead prevail. The dollar value of this lost energy and productivity is beyond calculation.

An enormous amount of work force potential is lost because employees sense that they cannot bring all of themselves to work—their backgrounds, their experiences, their special talents. The fear of being fully human prevents all of a person from showing up for work. This is true when women and minorities suppress their problem-solving styles or their way of focusing on the personal element of a situation because they do not conform to the company's white male culture. When people come to work hiding their feelings, a considerable amount of their energy is expended keeping themselves under wraps.

In this culture white males have been taught to be emotionally restrained. Blacks and Hispanics, for example, frequently find the corporate workplace uncharacteristically subdued and quiet. The white culture has long honored the warrior tradition that values stoic self-denial and personal sacrifice. These values are assets when properly used. These qualities, however, are the unwritten values and the standard of behavior in the American workplace. Others adapt, taking care to reveal only what is acceptable behavior at work, while leaving parts of themselves hidden.

This adaptation has two effects: an overall repression of available energy and a lowering of self-esteem. One response has been the ubiquitous presence in the workplace of coffee, a stimulant that helps workers gain back some of the lost energy. But there is nothing like human energy at its source, and that is what acknowledgement of the diverse backgrounds returns to us. Imagine not being threatened by the differences of others because your differences are respected and seen as an essential part of the creativity and success of the group's goals. Imagine an atmosphere that supports the best of who you are, with common goals and performance the only litmus test of your membership in the group.

"The more authentic you become," Stephen Covey writes, "the more genuine is your expression, particularly regarding personal experiences and even self-doubts, the more people can relate to your expression and the safer it makes them feel to express themselves. That expression, in turn, feeds the other person's spirit, and genuine creative empathy takes place, producing new insights and learnings and a sense of excitement and adventure that keeps the process going." When you allow the personal and the human sides of your co-workers to emerge, you are tapping the real energy of your human resources.

Creativity requires mental and emotional comfort or safety. You have to feel at home, neither judged nor threatened, to let your creative juices flow. The freedom to be foolish and to fail are important. Creativity will be enhanced by the trust engendered when individual and cultural differences are valued. Everyone knows there is no limitation on what creativity can produce and where it can come from in the workplace. Many companies with an open forum for suggestions have recognized this.

Competition has fragmented mass markets, driving even the biggest American companies to downsize and tailor their products or services to specific customer groups. There is a worldwide movement toward specialization and smaller business units. Author Tom Peters in *Thriving on Chaos* quotes a banker friend who advises, "Niche or be niched."

What is a niche market? Besides being a market composed of consumers with specialized interests, it is a market filled with diverse populations. Companies now face a diverse constituency of customers, and when the numbers show a 27 percent return on investment for market segments under $100 million compared to an 11 percent return in larger, less differentiated markets, companies cannot afford to ignore the value such niches represent. A diverse work force coming from those diverse customer populations with an understanding of the corporate products is better equipped to market and sell to their "own kind." A diverse work force is the best access available to the needs of these customers, and it has the best information on how to appeal to them.

Peters gives a good example of niche marketing: Minit-Lube, a successful oil and lube franchise with several hundred units around the country. "Minit-Lube looks nothing like a greasy automotive business. It's clean, painted white, and surrounded by neatly trimmed, lush landscaping," an article in *Forbes* states. "The place should have been named McOil Change. The customer pulls up, is greeted by a smiling employee trained to make eye contact, within 10 minutes the driver is on his way. The bill: $20." Someone at Minit-Lube realized that the days of Dad climbing under the car on Saturday to change the oil are long gone. And what is more, the person behind the wheel is more likely to be Mom.

A diversified work force positions a business to appeal to America's increasingly diverse population. Diversity at home is the stepping stone to interfacing with the diverse global marketplace. Understanding and working with diverse employees and customers at home can be generalized internationally. The Asian American who can tell you what his relatives in Korea want or the Native American who knows the habits of his tribe provide you with remarkable access to the world's variegated population and its consumer habits and desires. The converse is also true. In my work overseas, at the sites of American-owned companies, part of my goal is to assist those workers to articulate their unique cultural characteristics that could benefit and enrich the American international company.

Diversity is America. It is the harvest of differences that has given this country its imagination and versatility. It is what America is and what America will increasingly become. "In a country seeking competitive advantage in a global economy," writes R.R. Thomas, Jr., "the goal of managing diversity is to develop our capacity to accept, incorporate, and empower the diverse human talents of the most diverse nation on earth. It's our reality. We need to make it our strength."

When you seize the diversity advantage, you harness the power of the American dream: all individuals long for opportunity, freedom, and prosperity. It is that longing that unites us all, from custodians to CEOs, all of us different in appearance, talent, and tastes, all of us ultimately alike in our desire for respect and security and the opportunity to express our vitality.

INTERVIEW

John
41
Hispanic
manager
21 years with company
B.A. in business administration

Overall, I'd have to say my career has exceeded my expectations, because I come from a background where there were no professionals. And in the early part of my career I was told Hispanics couldn't do the kind of job I have, which involves scheduling for the production floor. How did I deal with those kinds of remarks? You bite your lip and your prove them wrong; you fight harder. It's still out there. I've heard sly remarks here and there. I'm not on a crusade, but if I can prove someone wrong, I will. I want to show that Hispanic people can do it. I want to open the door for someone else.

I have a daughter who's twenty-two. I've talked to her about what she'll meet in the workplace, just as my mother talked to me. She told me, "This is a white man's society. To function in it, you have to be able to mingle." Oh, it's changing, but I wonder to what degree. I don't know. I advise everybody to take it day by day to do the best you can. After all, it's human nature to be around people you feel comfortable with.

One of the things I had to do to get along in the white man's society was lose my accent. A lot of people feel if you have a Hispanic accent, you're not as intelligent; they'll accept an Oriental accent more than a Hispanic accent. To help us learn how to fit in, my mother wouldn't let us speak Spanish at home.

And we were punished at my public grade school by being spanked or swatted for speaking Spanish. This was in the late '60s. But the irony was, when we went to high school, we were told to take up a foreign language like Spanish. I said, "No way. I just spent eight years getting punished for using it, now I'm supposed to take it up?"

Because of the job I have, the majority of my friends are white. Sometimes that bothers me. And I'm still getting used to seeing more and more female managers. But I usually take their side in meetings, because I know what they're up against.

One thing I see that I wish I didn't is that a lot of the female managers coming up are hard. I wish they would keep their own identities, instead of trying to fit into the male culture. It makes them hard. It's making them change instead of being themselves. They're molding themselves to try to fit in quickly.

A few years ago, our personnel department asked me to set up a Hispanic networking group. I said no because I didn't want to get labeled. I've gone to the black network association meetings at my company, and I didn't like them because they were bitch sessions, and I think you should be proactive instead of bitching about it.

Also, if there have been problems with minorities, I have been asked to take them under my wing. Management has a fear, I think, that if a minority gets reprimanded or something, they'll get sued. But I don't agree with this approach. If a person is a problem employee, just handle it. Don't give him or her to me to take care of just because I'm in the same minority group. But just because I said, "Hey, handle it yourself" doesn't mean I didn't still wind up with the problem! So I'd counsel these people. And sometimes they'd listen to me and sometimes they wouldn't. If they're a bad employee, they're a bad employee.

The way I think you can be the most effective is to be a productive member of the workplace and let people around you see you can do the job. Legislation was a good way to start giving minorities opportunities, but now I think minorities have to get there themselves. Nobody's going to give you anything. You have to get there yourself.

WORKSHOP

1. On a scale of one to ten, with ten being the highest, how would you rank your need to feel emotionally safe and secure in the workplace? Ask two trusted colleagues to rate you on this same safe-scale. What have you learned about yourself from this information?

2. Two things you can do to increase your comfort with differences, risk and change are: a) The next time you are eating out, do not order your usual meal but something that you normally would not order. b) Rather than travel the same route to or from work each day, for a two-week period try a different route every three days.

3. Here are two communication skills that can be used with anyone who is different from you at home, work, or any place: a) Never assume. Many people interpret the American language from their own background. When communication is not working, never assume you understand what the person is saying. b) Ask for clarification. Practice these two skills at work today. On a 3 × 5 card keep track of the times you have practiced these skills, your rate of success, and how you can improve.

4. If you have children what is your method (thoughts, behaviors, skills) for teaching them values? Can you articulate to them the principles and values you consider important? Is what you say and do a good model for them? What are the ways in which you attempt to build character in your children?

Plurality which is not reduced to unity is confusion;
unity which does not depend on plurality is tyranny.
–Blaise Pascal
Pensées

8

SOME LEGS FOR DIVERSITY
TO STAND ON

Turbo-charged affirmative action and quotas—will not, by themselves,
create authentic diversity in the workplace. The motivation behind affir-
mative action and quotas—offering equal access to all—is on target. Yet
the way these policies are carried out is discriminatory. They respond to one
group while discriminating against another. This is not democracy in ac-
tion! Transforming the white male power system that has been operative
in American corporations for generations will create authentic diversity.
It has been a power system that excludes others and requires only newcom-
ers to change—not the established hierarchy. It assumes assimilation and
adaptation of the minority group to the majority group, but as we have
learned from biology, the entire body must change when new elements are
introduced.

Recreating the work force along the lines of authentic diversity principles is not easy. It also is not helpful to simply suggest ways companies
can water down the successful business principles stated in the previous
chapter or provide a short form for superficial results. Most companies
already have some basic programs that foster the creating and developing of a diverse work force. However, many times companies simply
have the rhetoric of diversity. They have a veneer of political correctness
that can pass muster at company gatherings. They also have the deeper
currents of discontent, the internal frictions, and turnover rates that go
with doing the job halfheartedly. What most companies have is turbo-
charged affirmative action, wanting immediate results with no long-term
consequences. It simply will not do the job.

The American labor force is the most sophisticated in the world—smart people, talented people. Old-style diversity—counting numbers, special formulas favoring those historically discriminated against—gets employees in the door with a promise. Once inside they soon realize the practice will not live up to its promise. These workers are denied information, excluded from power meetings, and are seen as lesser-than and, therefore, not accepted or rewarded. How can we expect women and minorities to react to unkept promises, to a "dream deferred" one more time, to the continued burdens of exclusion? How can we expect those who are white, those who are male, to react when they are held responsible and penalized for the societal sins of their historical fathers and mothers?

Such superficial programs set companies up for what we called in the 1960s "a revolution of rising expectations." Most people expect life in the workplace to respect differences and foster real equality. That is the American promise—the American law. There will be equal access to job opportunities. What they find is mainly talk spiced with an occasional meeting or a failed program. They become confused, disillusioned, resentful, angry, and perhaps enraged. Better the promise was never made.

White males must change if the workplace is to break through to a more authentic diversity movement where individuals are respected for their contributions to the common goals. Unless the cultural norms that govern the workplace change, no authentic change can occur. Who created the workplace norms? Who set the standards used for performance evaluations? Who set up the organizational rules and regulations? The white men who started and still direct most of America's businesses and large organizations, whether in education, government, religion, the courts, or the media. The white males who founded this country centuries ago did what males have done in almost all societies and cultures; as resource producers and defenders, they were expected to set up the rules determining how those resources were to be distributed. Most often, however, the rules benefited the rulemakers.

The weak point for diversity initiatives has been that only the newcomers in the already rule-laden culture have been expected to change. To survive, to partake of the benefits of the workplace, those entering had to accommodate themselves to the written and unwritten standards of the organization—in short, to be assimilated. But as Arthur Schlesinger points out in *The Disuniting of America,* the assimilation model has disintegrated into one of separatism in America. Since the power group excludes them, making complete assimilation impossible, to maintain a sense of dignity the excluded group creates its own world in which they are the power group.

As noted earlier, in America the assimilation model cannot work. First of all, those groups already maintaining control over the wealth and resources are reluctant to incorporate more numbers when the wealth and resources appear limited. Second, the group in power would have to incorporate those who are not like them, and those who, therefore, cannot be trusted. Third, the price paid by those being assimilated appears nothing short of a diminishing of who they are as human beings—their talents, their styles, and their differences.

To create a climate that respects differences and empowers all individuals, change must be shared by all. White males, who daily become fewer and fewer in the workplace, must be brought into the change process. White females, who inherit some of the same advantages as white males, also must play a significant role in changing the established rules that not only have to do with gender roles, but with race.

Implementing a process that affords equal access to economic opportunity is a three-stage process. First, the common goals of the organization must be articulated, clarified, and agreed upon. Old habits, although known and comfortable, must be eliminated if they now are debilitating the achievement of the organization's common purposes. Second, old practices that still are worthwhile must be reaffirmed. New practices must be created, tried, tested, and implemented. Third, workers need ongoing education and training as they develop skills and experiences that will give them a firm foundation during implementation.

Such a three-stage process needs to respect those homogeneous groups based on sex, race, ethnicity, age, and position. These groups offer their members safety and security based on likeness. Besides offering a comfortable setting, the homogeneous group needs to clarify its common goals shared and sought by other groups. Each unique homogeneous group contributes its talents and efforts to gain a greater end which could not be accomplished solely by one homogeneous group.

The authors of *Workforce America!*, Marilyn Loden and Judy Rosener, call this view of diversity an apparent paradox. "While today's managers must focus on the importance of valuing human differences in order to succeed, it is also true that they require a set of universal principles to help coalesce, coordinate, and direct the actions of all employees. In other words, there is the simultaneous need for greater differentiation and greater common ground."

What is "common ground"? These authors define it as "a shared set of assumptions that provide the basis for all cooperative action." They say establishing common ground is "a simple yet important first step that can often help allay fears of change."

The American work force does not immediately have to make all the changes it is being called upon to make. In fact, it cannot. Change must be effected knowingly, deliberately, and incrementally. As a bare minimuma, a two-year commitment may be necessary. Some think a generation will not be enough time to effect these changes. Still others believe that such a process would have to evolve through its own rhythm to be successful. There is no "quick fix."

To let go of some of the unhealthy aspects of corporate culture—the ones holding employees back from the full expression of their talents, skills, and contributions—the following principles and practices offer a starting point.

1. Get out of the melting pot mentality. Let go of the assimilation model—that we all are equal or alike. Search for a more realistic model.

We all have similarities that we share as human beings. We also have differences that promote unique styles of achieving those goals we have as human beings. Abandon the idea that the dark skin, the breasts, the earrings, the African-American hairstyles, the paralyzed legs, the tattoos, the Spanish inflections, the attraction to lovers of the same sex are not really there or do not really count for much. They do! Respecting differences means acknowledging that differences are present and do count. As long as these differences do not detract, are not inappropriate for the workplace environment, do not prevent others from achieving common goals, and work for the common good of all, they can be acceptable. They should be encouraged for the individual as well as for the group.

Most people have been operating under the assumption that if we ignore our human variations, they will go away. Or at least they will become inconsequential. In the initial phases of their struggle for equality, women tried to convince everyone that they were the same as men, reports an article in *Management Review*. This tactic probably served to increase the male denial of the presence of sex discrimination. Along with obvious physiological differences, however, women do think, communicate, and act very differently from men. If women were to be seen as equal to men, most men concluded that these women should be held to the same rules which these men create and follow—like workplace performance evaluations. Why should men change then? They were already where the women wanted to be!

An article in *Business Week*, however, asserts that most men are resentful when women in the workplace act like them. They frequently label them "aggressive bitches." Yet, when women act the way men would like them to act, most men resort to thinking of them as wives, mothers, or lovers rather than as business colleagues or management material. Men then reject them as being too soft and easy for this "tough man's world!" Caught in this dilemma, women discover that they are damned if they do and damned if they don't!

Working styles of men and women are different. Encouraged by their historical cultural roles, most men like to act first and think later. Most women like to think things through and make sure the course of action is fair. "To Harvard psychologist Carol Gilligan, this is evidence of women's 'moral development;' but to men it's the kind of hemming and hawing that (they feel) doesn't belong in the office," states the *Business Week* article.

Sometimes ignoring our differences is just plain dumb. An article in *Personnel* points this out: "A highly popular training film for managers shows an Asian employee being publicly rewarded for his contribution with a lot of loud and silly commotion. Many Asians and American Indians prefer rewards that are less public and more personal."

We must give up the unspoken assumption that the white male norm is the only correct, successful, and ideal norm. Any deviations from that norm are seen as deficiencies or weaknesses. Those judgments come from the dominator or warrior model in which all males are taught to rank themselves and others according to perceived standards of power.

One of the reasons we try to ignore the differences of others is a kind of uneasy politeness. To acknowledge differences from the powerful image norm could imply weaknesses of that individual who is different from the norm. To acknowledge differences in the warrior and in an hierarchical tradition is to consider that different individual as less-than, not good enough to be part of the trusted band.

We mistakenly believe that ignoring differences, being "colorblind" or "genderblind," is an attractive virtue. There is a grain of truth in this. To treat all human beings, regardless of color, with respect is noble. But to treat everyone the same is to deny the uniqueness of the individual and submerge the elements that make the person so special.

The reality is that differences are valuable and should be sought after, especially in the global marketplace. In her book *The Female Advantage* Sally Helgesen suggests that with most women's particular instincts, they "may be the new Japanese." A study by the recruitment firm Russell Reynolds Associates claims that "leadership traits are more common in executive women than in executive men." One can understand this comment when one reflects on the traits many women seem to have developed in most cultures: collaboration regardless of differences, group focus, persuasion skills. These are the important skills that are highly regarded in a competitive and international workplace. Management consultant Tom Peters says the time has come "for men on the move to learn to play women's games." A better approach would be for men and women to learn from each other those positive skills that would unite them in their efforts to be more strong, competitive, and successful.

We also must give up the notion that those who are not white males are eager to surrender their identities and join the dominant, successful white male group, or that they should want to. That we all yearned for a world modeled after the show "Life with Father" was a basic premise of assimilation in the white cultural world. There was plenty of collusion as we tried to convince each other that such a paternalistic model was desirable and achievable for everyone.

Many women and minorities do model themselves after the white male. Some of this imitating can be good—loyalty, goal-orientation, commitment, and self-sacrificing. However, many women and minorities frequently take on the entire white male model. After all those behaviors are the ones rewarded in the workplace. "Despite their best efforts to learn new behaviors and modify their approaches," reports *Workforce America!*, "many women, differently-abled employees, people of color, and members of other diverse groups discover that a perceived performance gap still remains. Try as they may, they can never quite develop what it takes for full membership in the dominant culture."

Lastly, give up the idea that white males are all-powerful, resilient, and damage-proof. White males need to be understood. The idea of white male power disavows any connection to vulnerability. As Jan Halper in *Quiet Desperation* and others report, white males, too, are wounded. A study of more than 1,700 workers at two Fortune 100 companies, published in *The Harvard Business Review*, found the impact of diversity on white males is often negative. The white males interviewed said they became less attached and committed as the workplace became more diverse. Often their absenteeism went up, and their commitment and self-esteem went down. "If we want to diversify successfully, we must help not only minorities but also white males with their adjustment to a diverse workplace," says Charles O'Reilly of Stanford. "If we don't, white males will disengage." Beneath the stereotype of armored invulnerability, white males are entirely human with feelings of confusion, fear, frustration, and anger. They too, as human beings, need to be understood and respected.

2. Replace some of the self-destructive values in the corporate mythology with life-giving programs and behaviors.

First, this means giving up the idea that the corporation is a family with a wise father at the head of the table, dispensing truth and justice as he may be expected to do in the home. In today's world and increasingly in the world of tomorrow, competent women and minorities will sit at the head of the table. Unless this happens, corporate America will suffer a hemorrhage of talent. *Business Week* published an article on "The Best Companies for Women" and reported that before a diversity turnaround at Corning, from 1980 to 1987, women were leaving the company at more than twice the rate of men (13.1 percent compared to 7.8 percent). The loss of talent was undeniable and unacceptable.

Similarly, a *Newsweek* story in November 1993 spoke of the anger and confusion high-achieving black professionals feel faced with the barriers they confront. Quoting Ellis Cose in *Rage of the Privileged, Newsweek* reported the "dozen demons" African Americans must cope with, including lack of respect and an inability to fit in. "Executives almost instinctively screened minority candidates according to criteria they did not apply to whites." Faint praise was offered to African Americans. When given, the praise often had the undercurrent that the successful black is the big exception and a rarity. Because of the belief that "whites don't want you to be angry," many blacks pretend that circumstances don't bother them so they won't be labeled troublemakers. This results in their silence and self-censorship. Collective guilt was induced since the race gets defined by the black criminal element.

The idea that the white male is the sole leader of family, school, church, government, and workplace needs immediate and critical evaluation. In the past most cultures automatically gave males the dominant role of rule-maker, of institutional leader, simply because of their inborn characteristic of physical strength. In a world of technology, information, and intelligence, this no longer can be the case.

Second, we need to replace the hollow public image of how things are supposed to be with admitting the way things are. Diversity consultant R.R. Thomas describes this conversation: "I asked a white male middle manager how promotions were handled in his company. He said, 'You need leadership capability, bottom-line results, the ability to work with people, and compassion.' Then he paused and smiled. 'That's what they say. But down the hall there's a guy we call Captain Kickass. He's ruthless, mean-spirited, and he steps on people. That's the behavior they really value. Forget what they say.'" And, as Thomas notes, the majority culture does not readily condone the kickass standard from minority members or anyone outside of the group.

Sometimes double standards are built into the system, knowingly and unknowingly. This double standard approach frequently is not a racial issue; nor is it a gender or group issue. It is a power issue. To keep competing parties out of the running and to maintain control of power positions, fluid standards are maintained, and vital and accurate information is frequently withheld.

Every cultural system, through race or gender, in government or school, in church or family, uses double standards. They are tools for control and power. The way to respond to this tactic is to match the words spoken with the behaviors exhibited. View the situation in the total context of the person or the group's general behavior to see how it fits to form a pattern. Does this standard appear in all situations, in some situations, with all or certain people?

The ethical standards of an individual will determine whether success comes by supporting the rules, by going around, or bending them. Most individuals, most white males, view themselves as being ethical human beings. Yet, many of us admit to practicing unethical behaviors because "those are the rules of the game" you play to survive. We are not the behaviors we exhibit. Practicing the principles of authentic diversity means that we admit we often hold up one rule, but live by another.

Through daily reflection and continual effort, we need to bring into line what we say with what we do.

Third, we need to reexamine, reaffirm, readjust, or replace all of our assumptions regarding the success of people in the workplace. Confronting living mythologies is difficult because their invisibility is what makes them effective. One example Thomas gives is the common cultural notion that the cream rises to the top. He writes, "In most companies, what passes for cream rising to the top is actually cream being pulled or pushed to the top by an informal system of mentoring and sponsorship."

The adage "It is not what you know but *who* you know" should be replaced by the more accurate "It is not what you know, but are you trustworthy." Trust is a key element in the scheme of power for males. When new managers move into their positions, they frequently bring with them all those colleagues with whom they have worked previously and who have proven their professional and personal dependability—those who are trustworthy.

3. We need to recognize that old world ways—where gender and tribe were entitlements to power and riches—must evolve to new world ways—where all are respected and have equal access to the riches of this land.

How to best redress that historical imbalance of citizens in our society has not been resolved. Equal employment opportunity legislation, affirmative action, and quotas have been attempts. Nevertheless, to discriminate against one group for the benefit of another—whatever the historical context has been—does not further the cause of honoring the principles of diversity and democracy in this country. One cannot promote new world concepts—equal access to the riches of this land by using old world methods—creating another favored class. In the new democratic world to replace one gender—a male, even a white male—with a female is discriminatory. To replace one clan—even the white clan—with another clan is also discriminatory.

We need to honor all individuals, all groups, offering them equal access to the resources, to the jobs, without discriminating against anyone. How is this new world principle achieved in a new world way? It will be through the corporations and businesses actively exhibiting their new leadership role as change agents in today's society.

As we saw earlier, the work place is the laboratory to learn how to productively live in a diverse and democratic society. The work place must provide mandatory training programs that foster an understanding and appreciation of a diverse culture as it impacts on the work force. These new training programs would focus on clear thinking, enriching discussions, meaningful organizational applications, and worthwhile skill formation.

The training programs would address a variety of issues from different disciplines as they impact the business world: anthropology (how cultures are different but the same), sociology (individuals in groups, traditional values, and historical behaviors), psychology (identity issues, gender roles, and communications skills), political science (how one lives and works in a democratic and diverse society), business (a diverse work force is the way Americans do business), philosophy (the impact of values, ethics, and motivation), theology (the place of a supreme being as expressed in the religions of the world).

Unfortunately many of our educational institutions have been remiss in fully educating our citizens. Many Americans are schooled in their special career fields and technical skills. They are not educated about themselves, people, and the world around them. No wonder we have individuals who are extremely successful in the workplace but whose personal lives are hollow and whose world views are narrow.

Whatever happened to our educational institutions' Liberal Arts programs? Liberal Arts programs include a variety of courses from the disciplines mentioned above. The purpose of these courses is to offer exposure, respect, understanding, and appreciation of their lives and experiences in the context of humankind. Without such serious study and education, we will behave in shallow and pragmatic ways. Simple and quick old world answers—like passing a law or satisfying diversity needs by counting numbers—will always be seductive but short-sighted.

To those businesses providing these special training programs government would award tax credits. Until educational institutions update their programs, government would provide scholarships for workers in these corporate training programs. If small businesses could not afford to create their own training programs, government grants would be available to assist them in developing joint ventures with other businesses or educational institutions.

This educational background will lead us to the next step. America needs a national policy that governs the workplace in a new world way offering equal access to job opportunity. There is a national policy for elections offering citizens the opportunity to participate in the running of the government. There is a national policy for public education offering citizens the opportunity to develop and train themselves. The country is now ready for a national policy offering all citizens the opportunity to work.

To offer job access to all without discriminating against any individual or group can be accomplished with a national law. This law would state that all companies employing five or more workers can only require a forty-five hour work week of their employees. Ideally this would be nine hours a day, five days a week. Working nine hours a day is a concept strongly supported for a long time by industrial psychologists for promoting greater worker effectiveness. With this new national policy there would be no need for overtime. Instead, good hourly wages would be paid. Those on salaries would have the opportunity by negotiation to determine what could be accomplished in their forty-five hour work week. Most other workplace procedures would remain the same—evaluations, bonuses, merit pay, raises, and promotions.

To maintain this new national policy safeguards would be needed. Those working more than forty-five hours would have their wages docked by the time-and-a-half principle—just the opposite of the present rule of reward. Beepers and phones would contain special chips that would make them inoperable once an individual leaves the workplace. Work computers would be programmed for forty-five hour time limits to ward off home computer usage beyond those restrictions.

The results of such a national law would be overwhelming! Companies currently operating around-the-clock now would have numerous job openings. Millions would move from welfare programs into training programs required by jobs now waiting for them. The need for additional employees would be dramatic. Companies would not consider gender, color, or age. Businesses would be looking for anyone who is trainable.

Affirmative action programs in universities would be a thing of the past! Companies would demand that all educational institutions find ways to educate and train any citizen who is capable with the necessary skills to fill all the jobs. What is more, having an increased diverse work force could step-up the urgency of learning how to deal with and benefit from the variety of talents and styles in a democratic and diverse society.

I am certain management will question the financial costs of such a national policy and the mandatory training programs to support that policy. To me, that question seems easy to answer. The amount of money presently lost on lack of employee productivity is in the billions. The literature continually has shown that most employees are not working to their capacity because of pressures at home and work. These pressures frequently result in general physical and emotional fatigue. Businesses have been handling this fatigue by propping up their employees with Employee Assistance Programs that include drug and alcohol counselling, stress management and burnout procedures, and personal and family counselling. These programs cost billions of dollars annually. Yet the literature is showing that employee loyalty and productivity increases in those companies who actively promote a better balance of family and work. Companies supporting the nine-hour day would truly be family friendly. Less pressured employees would increase productivity, which, in turn, would increase profit. Billions of dollars would be saved by decreasing the number of EAP programs. Whatever money businesses would spend in additional wages would be easily balanced by their savings and profits.

In my presentations I tested this concept of a forty-five hour work week. I was not surprised to find that mostly men were opposed to the idea of a national work policy. As one white male engineer said to me: "I work ten to twelve hours a day, six days a week, and on Sundays I check my e-mail. What would I do with all of the time I would have on my hands?" When I replied that he could spend this time with his wife and three children and for himself, his face went blank. He started to make all sorts of excuses that such a policy would not work for him.

The truth of the matter is that most men who have defined their manhood by work are often uncomfortable to be by themselves or in a relational environment. It is precisely because of this absence of the world of relations—with themselves and others—that many men are experiencing a sense of isolation and a lack of purpose in their lives. It is obvious to me for such a national work plan to succeed, then, parallel programs must be offered that would teach men how to redefine their manhood, and learn the necessary relational skills. Training and counseling programs should be offered to assist their partners and families to better adjust to the "re-entry" of men into their lives.

In this new national work policy, businesses easily could promote many workplace practices that honor and foster a better balance between work and home. Businesses would, indeed, be family-friendly with the availability of additional workers. Programs such as flex-time, child care, and care for the elderly could be better facilitated. Technology will be a major vehicle to promote the new "agrarian" environment. Computers will enable more men and women to work out of their homes, to be physically present in the same space with their partners and family. Individual and community needs would be better satisfied. In this environment a greater sense of wholeness would be experienced by men and women. In this altered living arrangement, hopefully, a greater degree of contentment would be found.

Earlier we stated that special training classes promoting relational skills for men should be held. In reality, these classes need to be available for *all* workers. No matter how many family-friendly programs are offered by corporations and businesses, if employees do not find their home lives satisfying they will not want to spend time there.

We are all aware of the difficulties facing our families today. It seems to me that many families have been drifting since the '60s revolution. At that time, we attempted to discard out-of-date behaviors that supported an old world system—right gender, right clan. We failed to replace many of these old world behaviors with behaviors that would be more meaningful in a contemporary, democratic society. In many cases we even disposed of the traditional values expressed by those historical behaviors; job training replaced an education; individual worship supplanted a community setting; permanency and commitment in relationships was forgotten.

With family relationships and support systems lacking some Americans have found workplace relationships less threatening, easier to handle, and seemingly more satisfying. The structures of the workplace can promote sage and secure personal relationships on a superficial level. We present to these "friends" information about our personal lives outside of work that places us in a favorable light and elicits reaffirmation and support. If we find we are not getting along with a "friend" in this department, we seek a transfer to another department and search for a new "friend." If our "friend" is having a bad day, hold on for a few hours and we can leave each other. So satisfying can workplace "friendships" become for some and so difficult are the permanent, on-going relationships at home, that work has become home and home has become work. The ultimate result, however, is that neither world truly satisfies, and we remain empty.

In this societal renewal corporations and businesses would be a model of an American institution practicing new world behaviors. Businesses would enjoy greater access to the riches of this land, increasing their profitability as in the old world mentality. In this new world way, corporations and businesses would be giving back to the country by respecting and promoting the well being of all their workers.

4. We have to replace the need to feel totally comfortable and safe with the ability and skills to live with the uncomfortable ambiguity that is part of a dynamic society.

We need to give up attempting to control or contain a diverse world because it feels threatening or unpredictable. A certain amount of instability always is present with change. Take reasonable instability and the accompanying pain as a good sign, a sign the organization is alive, dynamic, and trying to become better. Something new is being born, and we are part of the creative flux.

"Most all creative endeavors are somewhat unpredictable," writes consultant Stephen Covey. "They often seem ambiguous, hit-or-miss, trial and error. And, unless people have a high tolerance for ambiguity and get their security from their integrity to principles and inner values, they find it unnerving and unpleasant to be involved in highly creative enterprises. Their need for structure, certainty, and predictability is too high."

Most people are not comfortable with change even though they intellectually know it is good and the reason for its occurrence. Trying new things can trigger a sense of losing control, of feeling insecure. Change frequently sets off an emotional feeling of fear. People do not know how being part of something new will feel. The emotional needs of those involved in an unstable process have to be addressed through acknowledgement and clarification, compassion and understanding, and the learning and practicing of new coping skills.

When the process of change induces fear and anxiety, many people will want to regress to old habits whose familiarity will bring them comfort. We need to be constantly on guard during these unsettling times not to collude with others in supporting a return to old ways of acting. Most human beings have been, and are, guilty of collusion. "Within organizations that value homogeneity, collusion helps to preserve the status quo and to derail efforts aimed at culture change. We define collusion as cooperating with others knowingly or unknowingly to reinforce stereotypical attitudes, prevailing values, behaviors, and/or norms," say the authors of *Workforce America!*

Collusion can be defined as actively going along with certain patterns of thought and behavior because confronting these patterns would be too upsetting. Collusion can also be defined as passively going along with a policy or rule, a way of thinking or behaving, because one has not seriously reflected on those patterns or behaviors and their consequences. In either case, frequently the reason one might collude passively or actively is to preserve a sense of safety, security, comfort, or acceptance.

Collusion is a survival strategy many of us learned as children and still employ as adults. How much and how consciously we use it as adults are the important questions. Conforming to adult patterns and expectations is the way children learn to behave. Some children may suppress their desires—whether those desires are justified or not—simply to gain approval. Behavior that brings approval can keep children safe as they learn the ground rules to survive in the world around them. It minimizes risk. It avoids confrontation.

In the adult world seeking the approval of another adult or an authority figure is no different. Fear of confrontation, fear of losing something, inability to handle the consequences that may result from our behavior, frequently forces us to conform. In turn, we may blame other individuals or groups for why we behave that way and not as we would like.

The unconscious quality of collusion is the most harmful aspect. If you do not express your true thoughts or feelings in a meeting or personal interaction, you are not fully present at that time. If you withhold consistently and unknowingly in other areas—at home, at church, at school, in public office—you are not fully present in your own life or the lives of others. This behavior results in frustration and discontentment.

Workforce America! describes three ways in which collusion is supported: silence, denial, and active cooperation. The authors interviewed a Native American woman in a high-tech company who resigned her position after more than ten years because she could not remain silent. "Last year we launched a major diversity campaign in the company," she told Loden and Rosener. "There was training for all the managers, and everyone was told they needed to become more sensitive to cultural differences. Because of my cultural heritage, I was already sensitized to the way ethnic jokes put people down. I didn't like them, and I let people know it. But that didn't stop some of my peers from making inappropriate remarks.

"After my manager attended a high-impact workshop, I had hopes that some things would change in the department. I thought he'd stop tolerating insensitive remarks and ethnic jokes in our team meetings. I thought he'd be out there more—calling people on their inappropriate behavior. But instead, he acted like he didn't see what was going on. If I confronted someone in the group, he'd stay out of the discussion and act like he wasn't a part of it. Frankly, I got tired of being the social conscience for the whole department. I felt like the diversity thing was just a lot of 'lip service.' There was no attempt to change the team's norms, which in my view, were racist, sexist, and homophobic."

Collusion through denial is described in an article by diversity consultant Leonard Copeland in *Personnel.* The assumption is often made that we all know the rules of the game, denying the fact that some of us do not. "Many whites and men fail to realize that these rules are not obvious to all or they simply don't know how to teach them to others," Copeland writes. "For many white men, playing the game has become second nature—so that they have all but forgotten that the rules exist." Denying or forgetting that there are "rules of the game" is the best way to keep others from playing.

Colluding with practices that oppose principles of diversity can involve making "others" aware of their outsider status. Examples of active colluding include men using sports jargon and military terms in the presence of women who may not be familiar with them, or referring to meetings or information to which others have not had access. Women and minorities are just as guilty. Their excluding behaviors can reinforce the principle of exclusion in the white male power system. The use of insider language by anyone clearly defines who is in and who is out; who is part of the team and who is not; who can be trusted and who cannot.

To fight back, those excluded may form their own cliques and use their group talk to exclude the excluders even to the point of creating their own worlds of thought, language, and behavior. Without knowing it those excluded also may collude through avoidance and silence, appearing not to be injured or offended. These are clearly lose/lose scenarios that promote greater separation and further misunderstanding.

In their attempts to survive in or out of the workplace, women and minorities may collude with white males in power as easily, perhaps more easily, if they feel threatened. This is especially true when they accept a situation in one circumstance that they would not tolerate in another. Silence about these and other inequities only reinforces one's sense of victimization. Hiding what we think or feel protects who we are but is harmful to our self-worth. It is an admission that something is wrong with us. We are not good enough to act on our own behalf, strong enough to stand up for our beliefs, or our beliefs are not worth defending.

5. Diversity benefits are NOT simply a workplace concept nor employee benefits.

The privileges and responsibilities of benefiting from a diverse and democratic society are guaranteed by the interpretation of this government's founding documents. The principles of diversity and democracy should be operative in *all* parts of our American lives. Diversity principles seem to be used by women and minorities only to gain the ultimate unfair advantage over white males in obtaining the greater share of workplace rewards. How can the white male compete with sex or color? Often white males are accused of double standards and changing societal rules to benefit themselves. Women and minorities may use double standards too. They call upon their color or sex when it benefits them. As we saw earlier, women and minorities seem to chose when and where they are responsible for living the principles of equality. Yet, white males believe that they are being held responsible for practicing equality standards consistently in their lives and in every institution in society.

To make a diverse culture beneficial to all, the dynamics of operating by principles of equality cannot be selective. We cannot pick and choose where or when we want to live the responsibilities of a diverse culture. Life in a diverse culture is not like going through a cafeteria line: I will work for diversity and equality issues in my workplace, but not in my church; I want the benefits of a diverse culture from the government, but I will not promote those benefits in my home life. Living a life guided by the principles of diversity and democracy is more like a family meal: you eat everything on your plate or go to your room without anything!

Too many of our American citizens continue to support institutional behaviors that uphold "old world, male-dominated, top clan" power systems. For institutions to say they support traditional human values but demand historic and out-dated behaviors creates unnecessary societal tension. Furthermore, it diminishes respect for those institutions and the people who support them.

As employees in the workplace continue clarifying, experiencing, developing, and benefiting from a diverse environment, they will be demanding the same respect and opportunities in other societal institutions. For example, a woman may now be responsible for running a company or a corporate division worth billions of dollars. To be told by her church and to believe that her gender makes her incapable to carry out certain functions, or that she is denied access or feels unworthy to seek access to leadership positions because she is a woman, is ludicrous. No wonder a great number of our religious establishments are seen as irrelevant. With exclusion frequently comes disrespect; with disrespect, comes disengagement.

INTERVIEW

Carol
33
Black
engineer
13 years with company
B.S. degree

You have to realize you're talking to a feminist here. I think women in the workplace have a long way to go, although it is true more women are going for technical degrees. But we still have a long way to go to get equal pay for equal work and equal acknowledgement from our male peers.

It is a double whammy being female and black. There have been instances in my career where a female of my educational background who was white had it easier. I had to prove myself a lot more, with more reports, staying late and being seen staying late, reading extra material, being twice as knowledgeable, and so on. Racial differences are parallel to gender differences, I think, although I can't speak for my male counterparts. I'm sure they have a whole different story to tell.

Since most of my experience has been on the East Coast, I can only speak of that area, where there's a covert atmosphere of racism. You feel it intuitively, especially when you discover you're getting misinformation or no information at all.

I'll give you an example. I was in a conference room with five people, where I was the only black but one of two females. One of our planners came in (a white male) with his customer, another white male. He introduced everyone except me. Now, I'm about 5'9" tall and very dark skinned. I'm hard to miss.

I wanted to make sure I was correct in my thinking before I approached this man, so I went to everyone separately after the meeting and asked if he or she had been introduced. Each had. I took about a day to think about how to approach the man before I went to him. I asked him how he'd feel if he was the only male in an all-female high school and if he was ignored or subjected to derogatory remarks. His office mate told me he was screwed up the rest of that day, so I knew he wasn't a racist. He was just ignorant of what he was doing.

I often think that people like to come off as liberal, but really, it's true that people feel more comfortable with their own. I grew up in Roman Catholic private schools, with mostly white kids, so I feel comfortable with both races, but I'll admit I'm more at home with blacks I can relate to.

Racial differences aren't the only ones. Since I've moved away from the East Coast people remark on how "hyper" I am.

I think everyone can bring value to the workplace, whether they're a CEO or a clerk typist, because they all have different perspectives on getting the job done. Sometimes when you have more of one kind of person who thinks a certain way, they might hear but not necessarily listen.

It always helps when people have been to awareness classes. If you're a minority you appreciate that people at least know what's going on.

In a utopian workplace I'd look for everyone being able to bring something to the table without any comment that would be derogatory or degrading. I'd wish to get rid of cockiness. And I'd wish that the myths of EEO [Equal Employment Opportunity] policy would be dispelled. A lot of people have skewed vision of what quotas are all about. They think that I got my job because I'm a black woman. They assume I'm not qualified. I constantly have to live with and work with that perception. But it's not true. The only reason I am where I am is that I am qualified.

I think the quota system is good because without it we wouldn't have the numbers of women and minorities in management jobs that we have. But it is not marketed well. What's touted is always the numbers, not the qualifications required for promotions.

I was raised by a feminist. I believe in family and a life outside work as well as work. I think everything is important, and I want to make everything a part of my life. My mother used to always say to me, "Don't let your husband or your significant other be your whole world. Other people can give to you and you can give to others besides him." I try to live by that philosophy, so if I lost my husband, for instance, I wouldn't be lost.

My mother is a great influence in my life. I try to take her advice.

I think change happens if it's not too drastic, not too confrontational, if it's enjoyable, and if upper management supports it. That's real key.

As long as people carry baggage from previous years and centuries, there's going to be a level of mistrust. I don't expect to see equal opportunity in my lifetime.

WORKSHOP

1. List each one of your family values with one or two behaviors that you use to express those values.

2. List three examples of what you say or do that are NOT congruent with what you really believe. Examine why you say or do those things. What does that examination tell you about your true motivations in those situations? What one or two things can you do to get your behaviors more in line with your beliefs?

3. Have you ever been guilty of active or passive collusion at home or at work? Why did you collude? How can you avoid collusion in future similar situations?

4. Suppose your company decreed that everyone would have a forty-five hour work week with good pay. How would you feel about it? What would you do with the time you would have? What would your home life look like? What skills would you need to learn to make all that time worthwhile? Assuming you agree with the idea, what can you personally do to bring about a forty-five hour work week in your workplace?

Culture is simply how one lives
and is connected to history by habit.
–Amira Baraka
The Legacy of Malcolm X

9

BECOMING AN AGENT FOR CHANGE

To create and take advantage of an authentic, diverse workplace white males will have to join women and minorities as change agents. They will have to join diverse work groups as empowerers, facilitators, and co-workers, learning from others as much as sharing their own experience. White males will have to confront their own hidden prejudices as well as others' prejudices. A unified effort needs to focus on scripting new corporate scenarios that reaffirm the best of the past while incorporating new ideas that fit the future.

The change in the workplace that most of us seek begins with ourselves. At whatever level of the organization we work, we lead with our example. We must embody the vision and the direction. We must embrace the concept of richness in differences. We must develop and practice the necessary skills needed for the implementation of what we want to achieve. We cannot separate the message from the messenger. The medium truly is the message.

In these times the intellectual conceptualization of change or the delegation of the process of change is no longer sufficient. "In the end, the manager's minute-to-minute actions provide a living model of his or her strategic vision," says management consultant Tom Peters. "'Modeling,' the behavioral scientists tell us with rare accord," he continues, "is the chief way people learn. This is true in general, but now more than ever, when the search for themes by people beset with uncertainty and fear is at an unprecedented level." This means that if we want co-workers (and every manager will be a co-worker in the twenty-first century) who are interactive and cooperative in their dealings with each other, we cannot be autocratic and dismissive. If we want people to listen to one another, we cannot be talking at them all the time. It is that simple and that difficult.

The first lesson for the twenty-first century diverse work force is not to undertake diversity training and consciousness raising programs:

- unless we have studied what a diverse workplace means
- unless we believe in the principles and values of a diverse work force
- unless we see the diversity movement as essential to the success and survival of your enterprise
- unless we are willing to make a diverse work force a business issue and not simply a social issue.

Let us not deny it. We are not sure what a diverse culture and a diverse work force look like. We need our best skills—reflection, discussion, trial and error methods, re-evaluations, and new starts. We are talking about risk. We are talking about danger and uncertainty. Feelings of fear and doubt will understandably arise. These can be perilous times. These, too, can be times of excitement, enthusiasm, and opportunity. Leaders, managers, and workers are all on courageous courses. Neither doubt nor fear is a reason to abandon such promise.

Recognize that all of us are pioneers in this world of understanding and implementing the principles of democracy and diversity. Never in the history of the world have men and women attempted to execute a model of social cooperation among different groups that diversity movements represent. Diversity makes unique differences safe for individuals when they are supported by a homogeneous group or community. Our heritage as a nation was formed by immigrants living in common neighborhoods. Maintaining the richness and support of these homogeneous groups while transcending the obvious differences of ethnicity and appearance of other groups is the challenge. This process requires clarity, respect, appreciation, and interdependence. This is the challenge for this nation of the one and the many—*e pluribus unum*: to find the richness of our national unity in our multicultural pluralism. This is the challenge worldwide.

Continually developing an environment that benefits from a diverse population is not a cross to bear but an ongoing pioneering effort in social reorganization. How important is such an environment for a successful corporation? It is essential. Managers must "develop insight into a different mindset," writes Audrey Edwards in *Working Woman*. Not only managers at every level but everyone in the organization must get to know the unique talents, styles, strengths, and liabilities of others. At the same time, everyone in the organization must understand and contribute to the common corporate goal.

Here are some helpful guidelines about interfacing with differences culled from recent thinking by those studying male-female communication, cross-cultural interaction, leadership styles, and several other workplace issues.

1. People need to be a major consideration.

"You can divide the world into two communication styles," writes consultant Myrtle Parnell. "One is a style that connects people through doing things together and revolves around task, structure, and time. This tends to be the Anglo-American approach to work. In Hispanic and African-American cultures, the relationship is what's important. There is a need to have some idea of who that other person is in order to work together—what's your common ground?"

With the increasing number of women, minorities, and foreign nationals in the American work force a new direction is emerging in managing human resources. For many women and for people of many cultures the person is a dominant focus. Attention is placed on the individual's past and present. Credence is given the cyclical process of human interaction which undergoes change as the individuals continually change.

Developing a product or service frequently requires a linear process, step-by-step operational functions. Creating an understanding of the different styles in human interaction before beginning a work program can make production more creative and infinitely easier. Respecting and involving the talents and traits of the individual in the development of the product or service can gain the worker's interest, enthusiasm, commitment, and dedication. Emphasizing the human element in the equation for corporate success can work nicely in America as well as globally. Interfacing common individual needs with corporate products brings balance: humans with objects, linear with cyclical, processes with products, individuals with groups.

Placing more focus on the individual can be foreign to the American emphasis on objects and goods. Interacting with people as human beings rather than as objects may be most difficult for males, especially white males. Through conditioning, training, and skill development many white males have learned that the classically successful male puts aside all human considerations in pursuit of his goals. Women and foreign nationals, talking about the importance of human interaction in the workplace, can place the white male in an unfamiliar environment for which he has little understanding and fewer skills necessary to survive. Most males need a tremendous amount of time and energy to focus on getting the job done. To ask them now to make an additional investment of time and energy on human interaction appears incomprehensible. Besides, this new emphasis on human interaction would change the system and rules for achieving success that many males have been taught since childhood. The white male can see himself as being robbed of his advantage. And if success is out of reach, achieving his very manhood is out of reach!

2. Realize that men, women, and people of other cultures communicate differently.

In *Theorizing Language and Masculinity*, Sally Johnson emphatically notes: "there is no such thing as 'men's language'. This does not mean that the notion of 'difference' has no part to play in the study of language and gender. But it would undoubtedly be more appropriate, as Deborah Cameron has argued, to shift the emphasis from 'gender difference' to 'the difference gender makes'.

Some communication specialists believe that 60 percent to 70 percent of what is communicated conversationally is verbal. A gesture, tone, inflection, posture, or eye contact may enhance or negate the content of a message, even a verbal message.

Communication styles differ by race, culture, ethnicity, and gender. Studies suggest that most women and minorities, for instance, use and read nonverbal cues better than most white males, who seem to focus on words. Historically you could trust a man if he gave you his word. When you asked a man if he was listening, he frequently would repeat every word said. In contracts or in laws, men carefully examine every word.

Some examples of the different emphasis on communication styles: When white males listen to a speaker, they make eye contact with the speaker about 80 percent of the time. When speaking to others, they tend to look away about 50 percent of the time. However, if the white male wants to intimidate another, he increases eye contact. Most blacks, on the other hand, make greater eye contact when speaking as a method of bonding, of respecting the speaker. Yet African Americans make infrequent eye contact when listening as a way of considering what is being said.

Silence is also approached differently by each culture. The English and the Arabs use it for privacy; the Russians, the French, and the Spanish read it as agreement among parties. In Asian culture silence is a sign of respect for elders.

Rappin' and woofin' are two aspects of communication peculiar to the American black culture. Rappin' originated as a dialogue between a man and a woman in which the intent was to win the admiration of the woman. Imaginative statements, rhythmic speech, and creativity aimed at generating the woman's interest are parts of this courtship ritual, according to Herbert L. Foster in *Ribbin', Jivin', and Playin' the Dozens.*

Woofin' is verbal banter which involves an exchange of threats and challenges to fight. Woofin' is thought to have roots in the history of slavery. Woofin', anthropologists tell us, trains those who use it in self-control, in managing their anger and hostility in the face of constant racism. It allows the establishment of hierarchy without violence.

In a multicultural, democratic, and diverse society we must continually study and celebrate the different languages and styles that Americans of different backgrounds use. Ideally as Americans we need to become multilingual citizens, learning a variety of languages and styles while maintaining a common language—American-English—that unites all Americans.

Verbal and non-verbal communication, the written word, even dance, are all expressions of an individual's thought processes and feelings. How people perceive, formulate, categorize, and evolve information into matter that makes sense and is meaningful can be uniquely individual. These patterns of thinking and feeling are influenced by the culture in which one lives.

Cultural differences of intelligence and learning patterns can be explosive issues, as the publication of *The Bell Curve* illustrates. Some educators think the way we define and measure intelligence in America excludes other forms of intelligence. Harvard psychologist Howard Gardner has catalogued seven different intelligences many of which do not conform to standard testing or teaching methods in America. Gardner suggests that the IQ movement is "blindly empirical." "It is based on tests with some predictive power about success in school and, only marginally, on a theory of how the mind works." His seven intelligences are: linguistic, musical, logical, mathematical, spatial, kinesthetic, and personal.

Working in different cultures has taught me a great deal about the commonality of people even though there is a variety of their styles of living. When I worked in Africa, a large black dropout from the educational system did not exist. When I worked in Spain and Puerto Rico, I did not see a large Hispanic dropout from educational institutions. Determining what is intelligence will determine the style of teaching and educating. Course content—information—is important too. The environment of a child—home and community—can support or discourage education. In America, the definition of intelligence and the method of teaching appear to be geared for the culture of white males, not even white Americans! Family and community support the great emphasis on schooling and training for one's job future. Moreover, research has shown that all levels of the school system are geared to favor white males.

Perhaps one reason for the dismal failure of our public schools is that we are approaching education in a white male mode. The classic gender role of a male focuses on the material world of the resource producer. We force everyone to act and think in the patterns of a white male. It is no wonder that our school systems are overwhelmingly focused on preparing and training students for careers and jobs. Little emphasis is placed on understanding the spiritual world of self-knowledge, feelings and emotions, relationships, the role of community, and the richness of the histories of cultures. This is the field of Liberal Arts education. Without this spiritual aspect our institutions will simply *school* our children. We will not *educate* them. We must expose and develop our children to an appreciation of this spiritual meaning of life. If not, they are destined to be as the white male finds himself today: disengaged, empty, lonely, and without purpose.

Maybe the American school system needs to integrate different understandings of intelligence with different styles of teaching and different types of schools that would benefit diverse groups. One way to achieve this variety of schools and methods of teaching is by the establishment of an educational document stating the basic and essential principles and information content of what is perceived as a fine education—not just schooling: the accumulation of information—for America today. Fundamental to these principles would be an understanding of what it means to live in a diverse and democratic society. Such a document would be produced with the collaboration of government, community, educators, and parents. Monitoring and evaluating the implementation would be an ongoing process.

Once these fundamental principles are in place, allow guided free enterprise with its competitive spirit to take its course. With the assistance of vouchers, parents would have the freedom to select the schools that offer the national common educational program presented in an environment and manner that responds to their specific group needs. Our public and private schools, then, would be forced into the mainstream of a democratic and diverse society.

For too long our public schools have held a monopoly on the education of the majority in this country. As they are now, most public schools are run very much in old world ways: complete control by a "clan"—teachers and administrators, hierarchical in governing, autonomous in their operations, accountable to no one, benefiting not the students but unions, and expecting unquestioning citizen obedience, support, and money. Today's public schools are the last of old-world public institutions in our democratic society where citizens cannot exercise free choice. Parents are the consumers and the customers. Why shouldn't they be allowed to chose what method of education they want by utilizing their voting privilege through a voucher system? Such a process would place schools in competition with each other for students. Such healthy American competition would promote the best schools, get rid of mediocre schools, and offer quality education at competitive prices.

3. Continually update attitudes and behaviors to fit the changing times and to accommodate others' growth and change.

How each cultural group sees itself in relation to other groups is frequently not explicable. As Ellis Cose in *Rage of the Privileged*, says: "To those inclined to see black and white racism as different sides of the same coin, the implications should be obvious. While any stereotype is bad, all stereotypes are not the same, either in their conception or in their consequences. A stereotype that casts a group as superior is very different from one that renders a group inferior. To recognize that is to realize that white racism and black racism and anti-semitism are all evil things, they do not lead to the same place or spring from the same stream."

As complex as it may be, Americans must seriously, deliberately, and continually examine their perception and interactions with regard to different groups in our country, especially those of race and ethnicity. "It is wrong, however, to assume that the solution is simply to urge people to go along, or somehow to mix members of one camp in with the other?" asks Cose. "For even if racial peace is maintained, the web of stereotypes is left untouched, and those stereotypes, as already noted, are particularly destructive to blacks. They not only encourage whites to treat blacks as inferiors but also encourage blacks to see themselves as many whites would have them be."

A 1995 survey discovered that most of those questioned, regardless of race, greatly overestimated the number of minority Americans in the United States. The sharpest divisions occurred in the way blacks and whites view the world. A majority of whites say that blacks have achieved equity with whites on the basic issues that were the impetus for the civil rights movement over thirty years ago. Most blacks, on the other hand, believe that discrimination and racism have been on the rise.

The state of affairs described above seems to clearly identify African Americans, more than most other racial or ethnic groups, as the most excluded from the wealth and power of the United States. Yet African Americans are the largest racial minority in America with 12 percent of the population. Racism is a serious problem and appears to be getting worse. Peter Drucker calls it "America's oldest and least tractable problem." Drucker notes the fact that blacks were the only racial group to suffer a net decline in jobs as a result of the 1990-91 recession. Consider the startling fact that one third of black men are in jail or on probation. Even today educational trends indicated in the 1990 census seem to continue; only 13 percent of African Americans in the work force are college educated, compared to 24.6 percent of whites and 38.6 percent of Asians.

African American women, who have to contend with being women as well as being black, remain near the bottom of the ladder of success. On the whole they are more educated than African American men. Nevertheless, their wages still lag behind those of men by 14 percent. Still, the decade between 1982 and 1992 saw a dramatic rise in the numbers of African American women entering the professions, at the rate of 125 percent.

Obviously many Americans do misunderstand the make-up of this country and what is happening to white males, women, and minority groups. This lack of information may well affect the way people think of themselves, of others, and their country. Government statistics show whites on average earn 60 percent more than blacks. The problem is that although African Americans have made some major income gains in the past twenty years, nearly all of that gain has come in industrial and unskilled jobs—jobs America is shedding at a rapid rate.

Moreover, when minorities and women do enter the work force they are unable to enter the upper levels of management where increased wealth and power reside. When you look at the racial groups who have made it in white male institutions, you see that the likeness factor determines who gains entrance. Boards of directors, top executives, and managers seem to follow a "pecking order" based on homogeneity. In America the white Anglo-Saxon Protestant male is on top since his group set the rules in the founding of this country. Even among white males, however, there is a pecking order: the closer you mirror the top individuals, the better your chances of being trusted and included. Thus, nationality, religion, education, even physical characteristics play a part in determining which white males will be trusted and invited into top positions. The formula of acceptance seems to be: if you look, act, sound, and think like me, the more I will trust you. All homogeneous groups tend to trust their own.

In the normal evolution of cultures, gender and skin color are strong signs of likeness and can promote natural bonding. Following all white males in the line of power are light-skinned males. It is not race but skin color that matters. For example, look who have broken the barriers of race in politics: the Andrew Youngs, the Coleman Youngs, the Dikinses, the Wilders, the Colin Powells. Light Hispanics, such as Henry Cisneros and Frederico Peña, also seem to be included easier. All are light-skinned, thin-lipped and male. This group frequently is followed by those males who are darker-skinned and even less like the rule-makers.

Even so, for the most part white males recognize a solidarity with other males. In most cultures, regardless of color, it still is a man's world with similar rules. With more in common one can trust more. Men, whatever their racial or ethnic groups, are pretty much the same. Deep down they are warriors; they are competitive. It is this competitive nature that makes men cautious when they are around each other. Males always are guarded with other males whatever their differences. Can another male be trusted, especially a male not of your race or tribe? To discover that answer takes a great deal of time in association. Males of another color who have been thoroughly tried, tested, and proven trustworthy are the ones who move into the upper echelons of the white male power system.

Next in order of ascending the white male power system are white women. Gender differences sometimes present insurmountable obstacles to trusting. Nevertheless, when you are surrounded by other racial groups, women who are white are most familiar and offer a sense of solidarity to the white male power group. Next come light-skinned women. Near the bottom, because they are most unlike white males, are dark-skinned females. Besides their gender, you do not trust them because of drastically different racial and ethnic backgrounds.

Finally, at the very bottom of the power system are known homosexuals whatever their gender, race, or ethnicity. Most men, women, and minority groups seem to be united in opposition to this group. They seem to be the most *unlike* to the vast majority of heterosexuals.

But there is one caveat in this normal pecking order. The past couple of years have not been normal times. White males are experiencing social, legal, and governmental pressures to rapidly implement the principles of diversity and democracy in upper levels of management. There is now a variation to the "look like, act like, sound like, think like" formula for inclusion.

Trusting a female of the same race, although having its gender pitfalls, is less threatening. White women have been brought up in the same culture. Chances are they unconsciously have been trained to defer to males of the tribe. As noted earlier, with all races, if color issues threaten most whites will pull together. Contrary to the solidarity of males whatever their race, white women are being invited more rapidly to share power positions with white males. Furthermore, incorporating women into the power structure shows the world that the white male seems to believe in the principles of gender equality.

In these times of social pressure the next group to move into the trusted body of white male power is women of color. Again, since they are women, most of them have been raised in their cultures to see males as dominant. This female submissiveness to males seems to be the norm for whites, Hispanics, Native Americans, Asians, and those of mixed races. This norm fits African and Jamaican women but not African American women. Because of the tragedy of slavery most black women had to provide and protect their families assuming many of the cultural roles normally assigned to men. Given our history in the last 130 years this same dominant role for African American women continues even today. African American women, then, have had over three hundred years of strong women models who have been resource producers, resource protectors, and resource directors.

African American women come into today's workplace independent, direct, and self-confident. Because it is unusual that women act this way in almost all cultures, their behaviors frequently are misinterpreted as being aggressive, strong, and radical. They frighten women of other races as well as men of all races.

As with all racial and ethnic groups in America, this factor of women's role is where the African American culture carries its share of "not walking the talk." During times of slavery, white plantation owners purposely forbade black slaves from maintaining any institutional structures that would unite and support them. In the absence of such internal support, and with the exclusion from external white institutions, blacks were easily dominated and controlled. The only strong "institutional" support for black slaves was religion. Negro spirituals were not only religious hymns but political rallying cries in response to bondage, both spiritual and in this world. To this day the major unifying and political force in the African American community is the church. The church is the only African American institution where women are not numerous in positions of leadership. Men continue to dominate. It is understandable, therefore, that major African American political leaders continue to be men of the church: Reverend Martin Luther King Jr., Reverend Jesse Jackson, and Reverend Louis Farrakhan.

4. Examine how you were raised, how you were conditioned and trained from childhood.

Even though our culture and subcultures are changing, research continues to show that for the most part American males and females are raised the way they always were. Most boys are raised to work and most girls are raised to have families and be responsible for relationships. In spite of the efforts of women's and men's movements over the past thirty years, not enough has changed in the development and affirmation of new roles of men and women.

Many institutions in our country, especially outside of the work force, continue to support the dominance of the male and the dominance of the white clan. However, when men and women of different races and groups come together in the American workplace, they surprisingly discover a set of rules different from the way they have been raised. There now are laws stating that men and women of different backgrounds are to have equal access to the resources in the workplace. We work in one world; we live in another. Confusion abounds for everyone.

In childhood most boys exist in a hierarchical environment. You are either one up or one down. Life is a journey in the struggle to be Number One and to remain there. You are only as good as your last game, your last success. Most girls, on the other hand, live in a network of social connections: bonding, collaborating, compromising. Anthropologist Marjorie Goodwin learned from her studies that boys give orders and make power plays in order to gain rank. Among girls the play is egalitarian; suggestions, not orders, are the mode of discourse. The punishment among girls is ostracism for those "who stand out or seem better than others." Ostracism is the perfect sanction for any homogeneous group that defines itself by a network of connections. But what happens when those girls become women trying to climb the corporate ladder?

Sociolinguist Deborah Tannen believes that ostracism for trying to be better is directly related to women's fear of success. In two recent books, *You Just Don't Understand* and *Talking from 9 to 5*, she helps us better appreciate the critical differences between men's and women's communication styles that may add to that fear. "For males conversation is the way you negotiate your status in the group and keep people from pushing you around; you use talk to preserve your independence. Females, on the other hand, use conversation to negotiate closeness and intimacy; talk is the essence of intimacy, so being best friends means sitting and talking. For boys, activities, doing things together, are central. Just sitting and talking is not an essential part of friendship. They are friends with the boys they do things with."

Tannen explains how such childhood training affects women at work. "The skills girls are more likely to have learned, such as linking one's comments to those of others, waiting to be recognized rather than speaking out, making suggestions rather than demands, supporting others' remarks rather than making all one's comments sound original, are very constructive when everyone at the meeting is observing those rituals. But they may not help a speaker stand out or even get the floor at a meeting. And there are good reasons why speaking up and being the center of attention in a group, especially a group that includes men, is a more difficult and complicated matter for women, since so much of their socialization has taught them not to attract attention. All these patterns make meetings more congenial for men more than women."

When men don't share information with women, "[women] see it as a big rejection because for women, intimacy is telling secrets, and if you withhold something, you're not as intimate as they'd like," explains Tannen. For men disclosing information gives the competition an advantage. Disclosure requires more trust than many men can muster whether in business relationships or personal relationships. Since most men find women less of a threat in a personal context they disclose more about their private selves even though they are less friendly with those women. Most men disclose very little about themselves to other men in personal or business contexts, even if they have known those men a very long time.

Men and women trust differently. Because of their cultural role most women have greater confidence in human interaction. It is a confidence that results from having accumulated information about people and extended experience in relationships. Women are comfortable entering new relationships telling all: "Hello. How are you? Here is my whole life." When women find that the information they disclosed is used against them, then they tend to "subtract": I will never say that again; I never will do that in front of so-and-so.

Most men have learned from childhood to enter all relationships, business or personal, with a great deal of caution and little trust. Only after others have proven their loyalty time and time again will men disclose more. Men disclose or "add" more information about themselves as they feel more safe. Even as they give more information, men will watch to see how that information is used. They are always on guard. Your friend today can be your enemy tomorrow. This defensive behavior also keeps many men in a state of isolation and self-imposed loneliness.

Tannen and others have created a useful catalogue for understanding differences in communication styles between genders:

- Women are perceived as "too nice" in conversations, whereas men are viewed as verbally aggressive.
- Women use a linking strategy to respond to the remarks made by previous speakers. Men will ignore preceding comments to regain control of the conversation.
- Women tend to discuss issues and give advice; men see this attempt at discussion as a request for a solution, which they willingly

provide. However, a woman is often just seeking input from various sources with the intention of making her own decision after she has gathered sufficient information. A man will view his solution as the logical choice and may not understand why a woman won't take his advice.

- Women encourage others with questions which men view as direct requests for solutions.
- Women employ side comments as a normal contribution to conversation and view conversational topics in a broader sense than do men. Men view side comments as the other person's attempts to take control of the conversation or as a lack of focus.
- Women use taglines, which, to men, imply weakness, lack of directness, and ineffectiveness. A tagline is usually a question added to the end of a sentence, as in "I'll have the report in Tuesday, okay, Bob?"
- Women use hypercorrect grammar, which conveys uncertainty to men because of the convoluted sentence structure and sentence length. For example, going to great lengths to avoid ending a sentence with a preposition.
- Women operate on a "socioemotional or affiliative level and men on an instrumental or task-oriented level."
- Men are less likely to ask questions in a public situation if they feel those questions might expose their lack of knowledge or inadequacy.
- Men downplay their doubts and women downplay their certainty. Women are reluctant to boast about their successes. Men are eager to boast of their successes.
- Women often are misunderstood when they say, "I'm sorry." Typically, they use the expression not to apologize but to indicate understanding and caring for the other person's situation. Men see "I'm sorry" as an apology, a weakness, an admission of the other's greater status or strength.
- In mixed groups females—whether adults or children—tend to adapt their styles to reflect the presence of men. Women may be quiet and let the males dominate. Or women's tendency will be to become more like men, raising their voices, interrupting, and thus acting more aggressive. Women, in a submission mode, may agree more, smile more, and talk less in mixed groups.

- Women frequently "save face" for one another. A woman may take a one-down position temporarily because she trusts that the ritual will be returned in kind by the other woman at a later date. For men one-up-manship is a sign of position and strength.

Tannen says communication problems can be particularly frustrating because words have specific meanings and "we expect language to be clearcut." "We want language to be firm so we can feel in control of our messages: This means that, period." Tannen cites another confusion in the way women mix business and personal talk. Women might begin a business meeting with a personal chat to create a comfortable environment. Men are likely to reserve chatting for after the meeting, after the "battle." Men may resent personal questions as intrusive. If women do ask personal questions they may even be misconstrued as a sign of romantic interest.

A male colleague of Tannen's studied women's and men's presentation skills at a conference. The woman presents her thoughts with the aim of being understood, he says, but the man is thinking about something quite different. "He's concerned that no one in the audience will be able to stand up and put him down once he stops talking. He's 'covering his ass.' Whether or not people understand what he's talking about is way down on his list of priorities." Tannen contends that "men live in a world where people are in fact trying to put them down, so that perspective makes sense to them."

The way men and women use the same language is obviously different. Because of this some men see women as making no sense, of "being crazy." Some women see men as "not getting it!" Many authors have described clearly this confusion but few have told us why it exists or how to make sense of it. One of the best rules-of-thumb to help clarify the confusion is to see the words used by men and women in light of their classic roles in most cultures. Most men's roles have to do with objects, work place, order, and achieving goals. Most women's roles have to do with people, relationships, feelings, and on-going processes. For example, men's use of the word "help," may not mean the same as women's. For a male who has been conditioned to focus on the workplace, "help" means to assist the one in charge, to wait for orders, to avoid stepping on anyone's toes. For a female who has been conditioned to negotiate relationships, "help" means to assist the other, to collaborate, to instigate, to take charge. A major skill needed to clarify possible confusion between men and women is: Never assume! Always ask for clarification!

5. Understand that men and women engage in gender politics to control their own destinies.

What Barbara Gutek has called "sex role spillover" will need to be continually addressed in the workplace. Although we come to work to work, sexuality is too deeply embedded to be left at home. Women, who are much more sophisticated in the field of relationships, can easily categorize relationships with men to fit the situation: another human being, a work buddy, a romantic liaison. Most men, with much less relationship experience, have fewer categories of friends: men are work buddies or sports buddies; women are romantic buddies. Most men and some women believe that flirting and dating behaviors naturally go on between men and women even at work. For most men this behavior could be an indicator of manhood. Men and women need to clarify the different roles they may be involved with in each situation. They need to make sure that verbal and nonverbal messages are not misleading, crossing-over from business to social, or mixing one role with another.

From business researcher Lynn Renee Cohen here are some common behaviors that can lead to miscommunication cues:

- Personal space: Men maintain more personal space around them than do women. Women allow even strangers of either sex to come closer to them than do men. Thus a woman manager who allows a male subordinate to stand a bit closer than she prefers is seen as having diminished power. Or, she is viewed as having a romantic interest in him.

- Body size: Men tend to sit in sprawled out positions and stand with hands on hips, elbows out to the side (all power positions). Women keep their limbs close to their bodies. "Habitually making the body appear smaller leaves women open to quasi-courting behaviors and to misinterpretations of their status and power," says Cohen.

- Backing off: Observing an average urban sidewalk on a busy day, researchers found that "females back out of the way of males more often than males back out of the way of females. It has also been shown that the individual with less power and status tends to back out of the way of the person with higher status and power unless the higher status person deliberately allows the opposite to happen

as a gracious gesture. This still indicates that the higher status person is in control."
- Touching: Men touch women twice as much as women touch men in conversations among acquaintances. This shows that the toucher generally has greater power and status than the receiver. Touches also are a primary form of sexual inquiry, something both genders must be keenly aware of.
- Smiling: Women smile and laugh more often during a conversation. Rather than expressive, this can be considered frivolous by men.
- Eye contact: Out of respect for the other, women maintain eye contact for a longer period of time during conversation than do men. For men prolonged eye contact could be a courting cue or a sign of power. The one who breaks eye contact first usually holds the position of greater power since it can be a gesture of control and dismissal.

This brief trip through verbal and nonverbal styles gives some insight into how differently most men and women behave. No action or behavior is automatically good or bad. We are different. In some respects men are from Mars and women are from Venus as John Gray's book of that title suggests. For much of history, the genders and races have treated each other as aliens, with our biologies and our behaviors dividing us as much as if we really came from other planets.

6. Make an organizational commitment to practical and continual change.

Ongoing training of all employees in the understanding and practice of principles and behaviors of diversity is one of business's best investments in a vital and efficient work force. Recognizing and using the different talents and styles of people can promote greater productivity and greater customer understanding. Such training is too important to be left to chance. Corporations must dedicate company time, space, money and personnel during the work week for groups to meet, to learn, to share experiences. Employees will see clearly that the company supports and values their participation in building a diverse work force.

While building awareness and respect for the concepts and principles of diversity, businesses might consider creating two groups for each employee: one composed of People Like Us (PLU) and one composed of white males, women, and minorities.

The PLU group is a homogeneous pod, safe and secure, in which people can air their attitudes about those with whom they do not feel comfortable. Each group of people has its own prejudices and sense of superiority or inferiority to others. Each group has its positive and negative experiences with others. Prejudices can be aired and processed in this environment. The facilitators at these meetings must be skilled in dealing with human differences, human emotions, and skill-building techniques.

After a period of time these homogeneous groups should evolve naturally into support circles. Participants will assist one another to gain a sense of inclusion rather than exclusion. They, too, will be able to explore how their uniqueness can better assist the entire corporation in achieving its goals.

The second group is a diverse group. This group is a heterogeneous pod, a microcosm of the organization in which the members work. From the start this pod needs to explore individual differences as values and resources. Exercises developing trust will be important as group members emerge in their uniqueness while supporting a common goal. Some of the initial interaction will be challenging and rife with conflict. Opportunities naturally will occur when members can learn listening and interactive communication skills, conflict management techniques, and team building processes. Some groups may grow in their unity and be far in advance of the current organizational climate. Facilitators must carefully guide these groups back into the company mainstream. These groups must work always toward the day when the inclusive climate found in their individual groups will prevail throughout the entire company. When trust levels are high enough, these heterogeneous groups can evolve as internal advocacy groups for a diverse workplace.

Each of these groups should be small (six to ten), guided by a trained in-house or external facilitator. Participation should be mandatory and should occur about two hours per week, over a four month period for each employee. Periodic renewal sessions need to be held. Such an investment can be recorded as part of the required employee training program if the participant wants to be considered for raises and promotions.

Company diversity councils can be created from among these small groups representing a cross-section of individuals, jobs, and levels of power in the organization. The role of the council would be to examine and implement suggested individual and organizational changes for the corporation. This is where the authentically diverse workplace will take shape and structure.

Over the years the persons appointed to the role of coordinator or director of diversity programs in an organization surprisingly have been given a unique role in the white male power system. Frequently, the director is a women or a person from another racial group. Appointed by white males they are assumed to have a better understanding of the issues of being a minority in the white male system. Nevertheless, some white male managers believe they have to be on guard while interfacing with "those minority activists" because they are different. On the other hand, placing a white male as director of diversity training may put most white male managers at ease, but might be cause for great concern and suspicion among women and minorities. At this time, what I propose is a joint directorship with a white male and a woman and/or a racial minority. Such a formation would respond to the issue of trust with all parties. Above all, such a group would be a working example of the goals of a diversity program.

Initiatives fostering diversity in the company might be of several sorts: a day when everyone in the company eats lunch with someone outside his or her PLU; a plan to repaint the company hallways in mural art that respects the multicultural traditions of the diverse work force; a day serving ethnic cuisine in the company cafeteria. Ideas must emerge from employees and employee groups. Care needs to be taken that changes are not imposed on employees, breeding resentment and a return to the old authoritarian organizational model. All these activities need to be identified as ways of respecting diverse individuals working together for common goals.

Since there are few proven plans for the operation of diversity programs, the company as a whole must be as flexible as possible. As ideas emerge from the diversity councils and other groups, they can be implemented and evaluated company-wide.

7. Top management's commitment to the principles of diversity must be stated clearly and consistently.

Those in the top levels of management must be active participants in the process of incorporating the values and principles of a diverse work force. Management sets the standards of behavior individually and in the corporate structure. Many times white males are good loyal soldiers. They will follow orders even if they do not totally understand or believe in them. This response may be sufficient at first and as a point for further growth.

Members of upper management need to be models to their employees by being members of a homogeneous support group and a heterogeneous interactive group. Upper management must hold employees reporting to them accountable for practicing those individual skills that speak of a diverse environment. In turn, upper management should expect to be held accountable by their employees. Moreover, upper management should hold each other accountable for behaviors promoting the benefits of diversity.

Performance evaluations, promotions, bonuses, and merit pay should consider the employee's diversity efforts and behaviors. These measurable behaviors are much more than simply the number of women and minorities in that employee's department, in succession planning programs, and management positions. Although numbers are one of the important indicators of a diverse work force, other more subtle, quantifiable behaviors need to be examined. These behaviors include: mentoring of women and minorities to prepare them for more responsible positions; including women and minorities in meetings, both formal and informal; giving them access to information so necessary to survive in the workplace; encouraging women and minorities to actively participate in everyday group meetings; understanding the cultures and communication patterns of women and minorities; and using inclusive language in all communications.

Of course, a way to produce an environment that encourages multicultural benefits is to continue hiring qualified diverse employees. In the high tech industry, frequently the excuse offered is that there are not enough professional women or minorities who are educated in technical fields. Although we might blame society for this problem, corporations—for their own survival—need to spearhead societal efforts to increase the number of women and minority professionals. For example, corporations could redirect much of the money they now give to established engineering schools dominated by men to all women's colleges. These women's colleges provide a strong female environment that could impact the content of the field with another style and way of approaching the world of engineering. The staff would include the best engineering teachers, male and females. A pipeline could be created with programs that would encourage young girls, starting at elementary levels, to enter the math and science fields.

Once your employees have sufficient understanding and have developed the skills necessary to take advantage of the breadth and scope of a diverse environment, actively seek from them suggestions for other ways to increase the positive aspects of a diverse work force.

As the concepts, behaviors, and skills of managing a diverse work force are woven into the fibre of the organization, it will become a breeder reactor, an ongoing process nurturing positive change. Plans, programs, and changes will come not only by deliberate thought but by intuition and "feel." Of course there will be some "trial and error" efforts. Programmed professional evaluation and assessment must continually monitor the system. Be prepared for the unexpected. Be prepared for a different look than one was used to or had anticipated. Be prepared to start over and make continuous change a part of your operating practice. There can be no such thing as failure—only learning from failure. To quote Tom Peters the only "failure today is failure to change."

INTERVIEW

Joan
27
White
software engineer
3 years with company
B.S. in computer science

When I got into my field, there weren't that many women graduating in computer science. I expected a very male-dominant society, and it is. The men I've worked with have reacted well to my presence for the most part. When I got pregnant and had my child, there were a few who did not receive me well. They were upset that I wasn't going to stay home and take care of my baby, that I didn't want to continue my career. That was frustrating for me—that it was okay that I was in the workplace until I had a family. Then it wasn't okay that I was in the workplace anymore.

I came back to work after eight weeks, even though I know there's a big trend to stay home now. It's amazing to me how many women are staying home with their children. In ways I feel guilty because I chose my career. I could stay home, financially, but I don't want to risk my career. If I wait four or five years until my daughter is in school and then try to come back, they're going to laugh me out of the office. I would lose all the technical edge I've got. Another frustrating part is, even if I stayed technically sharp the whole time I was home, I still couldn't get back in, because I would have left to stay with my family for awhile. If I did leave, the perception would be that I'm not serious enough about my career and my job, so why should they even look at hiring me back? It's ironic, isn't it?

I'm not the only one who has this perception in the workplace. I get the same perception from comments people make—especially upper management. When I asked to go part time to begin with, I was pretty much told, "not a chance—don't even ask, because you won't get it."

Things have changed here since then. Our H.R. department has changed, and the mindset is shifting. I've just started an alternative work schedule, which is great for me, because I get to spend every other Friday with my daughter. I work eighty hours in nine days. It's called a compressed work week. And there are other schedules available now besides the one I'm working. Three women and one man are piloting new work schedules. The man is doing telecommuting.

It's frustrating to be playing in a man's world, even though I knew I'd be playing in a man's world, even in high school. The conditioning thing is so true. If you're smarter than the boys, they don't like you. I didn't date until I got into college for that reason. I'm blonde, so I portrayed the dumb blonde role. I don't have to play it anymore.

I know I have to play the men's game, but sometimes it makes me really angry that they expect different things of women. You know that old adage, "Women have to work twice as hard as men to get the same respect in the workplace?" It's not as bad at my present company, but in the last two jobs I've had it was definitely true. I got that feeling from comments from my manager like, "This guy over here works late hours. Why don't you?" My manager there was a chauvinist. He didn't like women in the workplace. It wasn't so much what he said or did. It was a feeling I got. If you did something really well and really fast, that was the only way to get approval.

I don't care for the good old boys network. Upper management in my group has a buddy that he likes to go out with, to have a beer and party. It's always men that do this. Even if he's not giving them preferential treatment. It's perceived that way even by men. These guys are extremely intelligent, but they like to party. They're totally career focused. Their wives stay home. They're older than I am.

I feel excluded. One time I needed a person at a meeting I had scheduled. We couldn't continue without him. And he had gone out with his buddies for lunch and decided not to show up. I didn't handle it very well. I was so angry I ended up leaving work. I couldn't get anything done. The next day he came to me and apologized. He realized he did wrong. But I'm leery of him now, very distrustful of him.

For the most part, though, things are working out fine at my job. It fits, because I was prepared for it. I grew up with three brothers. I'm the technical lead in my group. Every once in a while I'll be talking to some guys and I'll say, "Don't you get it?" I'll realize later I didn't actually say what I meant, but I knew if I were talking to a woman, she'd get it. I'm learning to be more specific. I'll say, "This is what I want done or what we need to do." I can't say, "We probably ought to try something like this," even though that's what I would say naturally, trying to present an idea in such a way that it doesn't come off as totally mine. The guys ignore me when I say something like that.

I'm having to learn to be much more direct, to say exactly what I mean and not offer choices when I really don't want there to be a choice. I found I have to do this with my husband too. I don't say I don't care anymore when I really do.

In the evening I get a little stressed because it has normally been a very long day and my husband comes from a traditional background. Although he helps out a lot, the case where he doesn't is when it comes to making dinner. He goes and sits down and reads the paper while I'm trying to fix dinner and spend time with our daughter. We have fights over that. I say, "Why don't you put the paper down and play with her." By the time we're done eating we have an hour to play before she goes to bed. I get so frustrated that my husband doesn't see what has to be done. I expect my husband to see everything that I see, but he doesn't.

We just bought the house I've always wanted. I'm hoping it's our last house. It's on a lot of land so we can have horses. I attribute our realization of the American dream to our education. My family was not educated. I made a choice of education and both my spouse and me make a good living for. We scrimp on a lot of things to get what we want.

I value my family first and my career next. I value quality time at both, that when I'm with my family my body's not just there but my mind too. When I'm at work I like to be devoted to work and not wondering about my daughter. I like to work at work and be with my family when I'm home. The alternative work schedule has helped me a lot. It's made me more focused at work because I know I have to get the same amount done in one less day a week even though I have the same hours. It's a mental thing. Telecommuting wasn't for me, because I like the separation of the two worlds.

WORKSHOP

1. When was the last time your read a book or article, listened to a tape, or attended a presentation on the topic of diversity in the workplace? Can you program into your schedule once a quarter a new seminar,

reading, etc. that will increase your knowledge and skills of diversity issues?

2. Examine the gender or racial behaviors of your family and those around you during your early years of childhood. What were they? Do you see any similarities or differences in your behaviors? What three changes can you make as an adult in your family to affirm the positive behaviors or change the negative behaviors regarding those different from you?

3. In the workplace are there people like you (PLU) with whom you discuss common interests and issues? Have you ever discussed how differences (race, gender, age) can help the organization better succeed? Are there colleagues in the workplace who are different from you in race and gender with whom you have discussed your differences and how they fit in the workplace? How did you feel during that discussion? What did you learn about yourself, about others?

If . . . we always trust in the difficult,
then what now appears to us as the most alien
will become our most intimate and trusted experience.
–Rainer Maria Rilke
Letters to a Young Poet

10

TRUST—A NEW WAY OF DOING BUSINESS

The old model of the workplace has gone the way of the Model T Ford. The new model, while still maintaining the quality of the old, now must incorporate relationships—customers, communities, governments, employees. The old model was founded in patriarchy, rules, and unquestioned obedience. The new workplace requires partnership, process, and trust. Partnership demands at least two new behaviors from men and women in the workplace: a level of trust that white males have a hard time finding in their storehouse of manly skills and a new risk-taking behavior by women and minorities.

Two industry leaders call to mind the distance that management in America has traveled in the last seventy-five years. In 1922 Henry Ford wrote, "[A business] is a collection of people to do work and not to write letters to one another. It is not necessary for any one department to know what any other department is doing." "It is not necessary to have meetings to establish good feeling between individuals and departments. It is not necessary for people to love each other in order to work together."

This approach of "getting the job done," focusing solely on production, fitted the workplace of that era. In fact, this approach fitted the way most institutions in America—schools, churches, governments—were run. The life of the structural organizations was more important than the people. Emphasis was placed on following the organizational rules and not on the good of individuals. Individuals existed for the benefit of the organization.

In 1997 Henry Ford's ideas could not be more outdated. The reengineering of business as a lateral process between employee and customer calls for continuous communication. Technology—fax machines, telephones, e-mail—and the speed of travel have made such communication possible on a grand and intricate scale. Many other forces in society (education, travel, media) also have blurred the boundary lines between individuals and organizations, work and home, product and process, objects and people, profit and satisfaction.

The warrior notion of dividing life into distinct battles or neat categories to better focus and to better conquer is being redefined. Most women and a growing number of men in the workplace are refusing to separate their work lives from their home lives. An increasing number of employees are sadly discovering the emptiness in their lives and the effect that emptiness has on the lives of those around them. They are beginning to say their families are the important part of their lives although they continue to spend the best of their time, talent, and energy at work.

In *My Life and Work,* Ford described a workplace driven by rules. Sixty years later Lee Iacocca describes a workplace driven by human interaction, a climate in which communication is the fertilizer that makes things grow. Iacocca has gained a reputation for being a famous innovative manager. The key word he uses is "motivate." His assumption is that rules and a paycheck at the end of the month are no longer sufficient as motivation. This is especially so in a constantly changing atmosphere that requires an abundance of dedication, emotional strength, and energy.

When you perceive yourself to be valued and important in your organization—in a word, to be trusted—the power of your attitude and motivation is immeasurable. You will do whatever it takes for that organization, including sometimes working yourself to exhaustion. The organization's success and your success are synonymous. When you perceive your talent to be a replaceable tool that easily can be undervalued, and your advancement to be hindered by factors you can not control—and, you are not trusted—you separate your success from the success of the organization. Your own self-interest and survival become the core of your motivation. You begin to focus on the game of personal survival *in* the organization rather than the success *of* that organization.

When one's talents and contributions are excluded, employees work to the best of their ability. In today's climate of rampant downsizing there is an increase of the workload on those who remain. This sends a message warning workers to protect themselves at all costs and trust no one. "Nothing kills employees' work ethic more than the belief that the organization does not care about their well-being," concluded a 1992 survey by the Public Agenda Foundation.

The challenge today is knowing how to incorporate the necessary organizational rules with a greater appreciation of the unique talents and abilities that different people bring into the workplace. Many workers may not be aware that the human element is significant. Yet a few companies are making attempts to see that the humanity of their employees is an essential element in the success of their businesses. In his autobiography, Lee Iacocca describes work as a much more human process than did Ford: "The only way you can motivate people is to communicate with them." "A good manager needs to listen at least as much as he needs to talk. Too many people fail to realize that real communication goes in both directions." "The reason they're following you is not because you're providing some mysterious leadership. It's because you're following them."

One of the major ways of discounting the talents of individuals in the organization is by excluding them from the higher levels of power and influence. Because of the fear of losing control, power, and success, most organizations have excluded those employees not trusted by making invisible rules that act as barriers.

Let us look at how the dynamics of trust play out in the male power system. Every group—family, school, church, workplace—has a culture or personality. The infrastructure that gives form and direction to each of these groups is very much the same. Why does the organization exist? Why did these people come together? For the corporate world, that is the "mission" of the organization. In a capitalistic society, the mission is profit.

When two companies have the same goals or vision, they are distinguished by how they achieve their mission. What are those unique processes and procedures they incorporate to achieve their goals? In a word, what are those special rules they follow to succeed?

Many males cling to the arena of rules, the laws, and the concrete structures for order. When all those in the group follow the same rules, a sense of order and safety is available. Personality, gender, color, or any other difference is not important. In fact, they become distractions from maintaining order. Everyone acts and is treated alike. Justice and fairness prevail. Structure and rules are essential for group effectiveness. They gain more credibility and power if by following them a history of success is attained.

In a hierarchical structure rules are what makes the structure work. Upper management creates the vision and the goals for the organization. Middle management promotes that vision through a series of programs, rules, and regulations. Lower management implements those programs, rules, and regulations. From middle management up is the realm of ideas and programs that will spell success for the organization. From lower management down is the realm of implementation—by following the rules the job is accomplished by the employees. Team building efforts are a mix of these levels in ways that create interfacing and interaction, resulting in finer processes and procedures, bringing greater productivity and profit.

Approximately 80 percent of the rules of lower management are written down and made public. These concrete rules can include: the time the workday begins and ends, the dates when budgets are due, the process for requisitioning information or personnel, forms to be used for employee benefits, and the steps followed in technical manuals. The other 20 percent, although not public, are understood as "the way things are done." For example, to be seen as dedicated, you have to spend ten to twelve hours physically present at work each day. Everyone learns these formal and informal rules. Within each employee's competency—job skills and function—these rules are obeyed. Each employee is held accountable and is rewarded for following the rules. This system is called the Formal Organization.

In middle and upper management, sometimes called the Informal Organization, although there are some traces of these concrete rules, approximately 80 percent of the rules are unwritten. These private rules are divided into two main categories. The first contains emerging information on future plans and changes which leadership is discussing. They have not settled their plans to the point of making that information public. If you are privy to this flow of information before it is made public, you have the advantage of knowing about future job openings or closings and future projections for certain departments or sectors. When this information is finally made public, it becomes a part of the Formal Organization and open to all.

The second category contains what I call the "art of management." Lower management and the everyday employee have the "science of management"—the body of publicly known rules and regulations. The "art of management" is the political system that has to do with people— their personalities, their interactions, their goals and their methods. This political system breathes life into the organizational structures and rules. Knowing the political system is knowing the heart of the organization where the core power resides. The "art of management" is knowing who is in, who is out; who has the boss's ear; whose support you need to get things done; who really makes the decision; whom you should have on your side to survive.

Those who do not understand how upper management operates can hit what has been mistakenly called a "glass ceiling." While there appears to be an effect similar to a ceiling, it certainly is not glass! Women and minorities frequently believe that the entire organization, from bottom to top, is formalized with public rules and procedures. They are aware of pockets of informal "good ole boys" clubs. However, they believe the organization as a whole is run in the same formal manner and by the same formal rules. You keep working hard and follow the rules and you automatically will be rewarded and promoted. Not so!

Women and minorities are entering the work force. They gradually are moving through the lower ranks by knowing and following the rules of the organization. Any movement into upper management is difficult, if not impossible. The 1991 Department of Labor (DOL) study concluded that "the glass ceiling exists at a much lower level than first thought."

Don't women and minorities measure up? A poll of *Fortune* 1000 CEOs found that 80 percent of almost all male respondents said there were identifiable barriers that kept women from the top. A Catalyst survey, reported in *Fortune*, concluded, "Women do not lack the technical skills to make it. After all, they have been going to the same schools as their male counterparts and now represent over half of all college students, 37% of graduate business students, and roughly 40% of law students. The problems, said an astonishing 81% of the CEOs who acknowledged the existence of barriers, are stereotyping and preconceptions."

The phenomenon of a so-called glass ceiling is such an egregious example of confusion and perceived unfairness in corporate America that the Department of Labor launched a "Glass Ceiling Initiative." It conducted ninety-four reviews of *Fortune* 1,000 companies and published its findings in 1991. Six years later not much has changed.

- Of 147,179 employees at these companies, women comprise 37.2 per cent and minorities, 15.5 percent.
- Of the 147,179 employees, 31,184 were in levels of management ranging from the CEO to the head of the clerical pool. Of these, 5,278, or 16.9 percent, were women and 1,885, or 6 percent, minorities.
- Of the 4,491 managers at the executive level (assistant vice president and higher rank), 6.6 percent were women and 2.6 percent, minorities.

"Just wait, was the old excuse," said a *Fortune* article: "A decade ago, even women's staunchest male advocates said time had to pass; women lacked the seasoning and seniority to run the show. Today that explanation rings increasingly hollow. Women have gained access to virtually every line of work and are bulging in the pipeline. . . . But only a minuscule number of women have top jobs at America's major companies, and not many more are in the zone for promotion to those jobs anytime soon."

Titled "Why Women Still Don't Hit the Top," the article also noted that women managers on average earn 64 percent of what male managers do, and that most women do not leave their jobs for family reasons (a common stereotype) but rather, to find greater career satisfaction.

Unfortunately, while the Department of Labor reported such bad news for women and worse for minorities, it failed to give the reasons behind the so-called glass ceilings. Their report of March 1991 did little to clarify or explain the phenomenon. As stated in my explanation of the "glass ceiling," an understanding of the historical cultural roles of men and women, male psychology, organizational theory, and male power systems would have benefited their report.

Since the Industrial Revolution, when men moved from the home to the factory, they lost a direct and daily connection with their families and communities. They lost the purpose for their lives, the soul of their being. Having lost direct contact with their families, most males now believe that their time and talent in the workplace still benefit their families, but indirectly. The means used to contribute to their families and achieving their manhood—being resource producers, protectors, and directors—now has become their end. The cultural role of man now is fulfilled in the organizational workplace and not in the home.

The classical definition today of male success is: moving up the corporate ladder and gaining more titles (the old world resource director); gaining more financial rewards (the old world resource producer); and achieving more prestigious fringe benefits as recognition for being the best (the old world resource protector). In reality, the definition of workplace success which men offer women and minorities is very much the definition of manhood. No wonder women frequently state they feel they are losing their femininity in the workplace. They are!

If one buys this definition of workplace success and does not continue to move up, gaining increased signs of success, one's career is said to stall or to plateau. Feelings of inadequacy and failure may result. Over the years, white males have called this plateauing "career dead ends" or "job plateauing." Women and minorities have called this stalling a "glass ceiling." Everything looks the same in the upper levels, but you cannot move up any further. Ceiling it is; glass, it is not.

When most women and minorities—and men, also—hit this ceiling, they usually say, "Maybe I'm not doing enough. Maybe I need to do more to move up: work more hours, work more days, take on more projects, show more success." They mistakenly believe that the upper levels of management follow the Formal Organization approach of public rules and regulations. Increased effort is the male's approach to capturing success. You conquer it with more effort and more force. Doing more is not the way to break through these management barriers and ceilings.

Hurdles have always been present to protect power positions. After all, these positions give easy access to the limited wealth or increased control in an organization. Such hidden barriers exist in the organization from bottom to top. Many individuals pass through the lower level barriers without even knowing it. One becomes more aware of these check-points at the upper levels of the organization where one nears the power positions that control and govern the total organization.

This check-point phenomenon is part of the invisible world of male power. As a "rite of passage" it determines who gets through and is rewarded and who does not. This system is most operative especially at middle management and above. Earlier we called this the Informal Organization. It is not objective-based as in the formal organization of lower management. It is subjective-based. You prove at the lower levels of the organization that you are talented, hard-working, dedicated, committed, loyal, and successful. To move into the invisible and highly selective world of power—middle and upper management—you must exhibit loyalty and trustworthiness. It is not what you know, how much you succeed, or how competent you are, although that certainly is a part of it. It is who you know that can identify you as loyal and reliable. You are worthy to be included in the powerful inner circle.

Trust is a key factor for those in upper management. The environment at the top is actually the opposite of what most people think. It is not an easy and cushiony place. It is the arena for the "professionals," the "gladiators." It is the environment where the "best of the best" proves who really is the greatest of all men! In this circle the supreme risk to one's power and control is found. A great many of those individuals who have made it to that level of the organization have thoroughly bought the classic definition of being a successful male: the more powerful, the greater the success. The very top is where the most power lies, where ultimate success is reached. As in any battle or sports game there is high risk and stiff competition. As you climb the corporate ladder there are fewer top jobs. Failure to increase corporate profits could cost you that limited position. Those above you maintain their positions by the increased productivity of those reporting to them. If you are not doing the job, you easily can be replaced by many others who are waiting in line, hungry to prove themselves and be rewarded. Furthermore, if your behavior does not remain supportive to others in that environment, you might threaten the delicate security of the group. When you do not follow the rules, you are no longer considered loyal or trustworthy. This, too, can cost you your position.

This upper level of management, therefore, is filled with high anxiety. The classic male definition of success, of manhood, is under constant siege. Top salaries and constant public recognition are the rewards for withstanding this psychological onslaught. You use the corporate jet. You are quoted in *The Wall Street Journal.* You finally have reached the pinnacle of success. You have achieved full manhood!

For continued challenges and risks, for an even greater sense of power, excitement, and thrill, you seek leadership roles in other corporations—especially those corporations which are considered failing. At this point in your career you have entered the level of a very, very few individuals in this country, in the world. You have entered the realm of SUPERmen!

If burnout does not claim these magnificent gladiators, age and retirement will. The *real* test of life is now to be met. Having devoted all their time and energy to corporate battles, they frequently have had little time for family and relationships. Without the daily excitement and adventure of the corporate world, they are left with little else of substance. They often find their families and relationships in disarray due to the years of neglect. Few, if any, in the business world now seek their advice and counsel. Retirement becomes boring, dull, empty, and lonely. It is no wonder that Lee Iacocca admitted in a *Fortune* cover story that he had flunked retirement.

Given this intense environment and competition for ultimate success, whom do you trust? This is where the "good ole boys" club fits. When one views the organizational environment as competitive, threatening, and hostile, one seeks safety in likeness and numbers. All organizations—schools, churches, governments, workplaces—have a "good ole boys" network. Most people's first encounter with "good ole boys" groups was in middle school. There was the "in group" usually made up of the athletes, or the cheerleaders, or the most popular students.

In religious organizations, for example, the "good ole boys" club is called the hierarchy, the elders, or, the prophets. In the Roman Catholic Church every time the Pope names a new group of bishops, you know he is naming new members to his "good ole boys" club. Cardinals, in the Roman Catholic Church, are the "good ole boys" of the "good ole boys" club. One way you can tell they are part of this select group is that they all dress alike, think alike, speak alike, and act alike. Remember, there is safety from outside harm and preservation of your power from attack when all are united and present an undivided front.

This special network of individuals informally shares all of the unpublished information at the power core of the organization. This is done constantly and most often in informal settings: over lunch, in the company parking lot, over a cup of coffee, in the elevator, in the executive bathrooms—not just on the golf course. Women have thought that if they played golf they would have much more access to the inner workings of the organization. Not so. As soon as men discover that women are picking up information, men will find new and protected settings, like auto racing or riding motorcycles together. Effective networking has much more to do with safety and trust than with any particular setting.

As noted in the Catholic hierarchy, there are even "good ole boys" clubs in "good ole boys" clubs! At every level of the organization there always are a chosen few that the top executive trusts even more. A short time ago, I was consultant at meetings of a Fortune 500 company's senior vice presidents and their CEO. After an hour and a half of observing their interaction, I knew who were the "good ole boys" in this high-level group and who were not. Frequently the CEO would call on three of his senior vice presidents when things got sticky. He would look to these same three for support and reaffirmation. During the breaks in the meeting these same three vice presidents and the CEO frequently would chat informally. This is another example of the "good ole boys" club.

This need to remain included, to be trusted, to maintain your job keeps many of those in upper management on red alert. In order to survive this uncertainty, many of these managers employ a philosophy called CYA—cover your ass! The meaning of this graphic slang is clear. When one is seated—as most executives are—what do the buttocks do for the body? They give the body a solid base, position, and a stable foundation. What gives the male in the culture his position, a solid basis, and stability? It is his role as resource producer. To cover one's ass is to cover, to protect one's job.

What better way to cover and protect one's job from uncertainty than to have the rules at this level unwritten, unpublished, and unknown. You cannot play this game unless you know the rules. You can change those rules whenever you want and to your advantage. Finally, if no one knows the rules, you can never be held accountable.

Another part of this conspiracy of silence stems from most men's conditioned response to trust no one. Most men have learned in sports and in war that disclosing one's plans could give your competitor the advantage. Disclosing his feelings or his thoughts is to disclose a man's level of courage. One's weaknesses easily could surface, placing you at a disadvantage with your competitors. You could be killed or lose the game. The same strategies work in the competitive corporate world. You can be fired or let go.

In the early 1960s Sidney Jourard, in *The Transparent Self*, published his study which explored how men trust. Although this publication is almost forty years old, it is a classic study on men's self-disclosure and well-being. I learned in reading his work that men trust people who look, act, sound, and think like themselves. Men are no different from all humankind. All of us tend to trust those with whom we have the most in common, with whom we feel safe.

Sooner or later, however, men discover that, even among their own, they cannot hold the power they get from their positions. Someone can always find a way around positional power, discover a damning imperfection, or produce a better way to do your job. As a result, men often trust neither the person nor the position, but the function. Men put aside all personal and professional issues to bond together as a team of functions in support of a common goal. This is what is called *duty*. A sense of safety and trust comes from knowing that each team member is committed to doing his job, performing his function, or doing his duty. Collective security is achieved when everyone is following the same rules and supporting each team member as they seek a common goal. This commitment to the group, to the attainment of the common goal, is called loyalty. Knowing that the other is loyal and can be counted on promotes trust.

Most men seem to subscribe to two procedures that are paramount for survival in corporations: work for the success of the company and work for their own survival. They trust only insofar as they succeed in reaching corporate goals and securing their share of the spoils for such success. They operate much as a sports team operates. You buy and sell players. You buy and sell loyalties. If any one team member gets too big a head, other team members may not hand him the ball. They might refuse to cover for him as he carries the ball. The team has its own internal checks and balances.

Mentoring in corporations is the ultimate expression of checks and balances. I call mentoring the *male reproductive system for passing on power*. You reproduce those who are mirror images of you. You pass on power to those whom you trust. Whom do white males typically mentor? As noted in the previous chapter, other white males—PLU. That is one of the major reasons women and minorities are kept out of the upper levels of management. They are unlike the white male. Their ways may be unfamiliar. They may be a threat to the white male's security and safety. They may be a contender to the white male's power. They are not trustworthy.

In the process of mentoring, the mentor gives to the protege—a man whom he sees as already professionally successful, and whom he has grown to personally trust—the cloak of creditability, access to the inside information, and to the powerful people. In turn, a good subordinate re-inforces his mentor by supporting and reaffirming his power. He serves as his mentor's liaison to the underground information network at lower levels. A good subordinate frequently takes on all the "dirty work" for the mentor: drawing up time-consuming reports, securing information, doing jobs and errands that the mentor may not have the time nor the interest to do. All this interaction is accomplished in informal settings.

Since the mentoring process is carried on in informal settings, the im-plications of gender and race are of major importance. The social condi-tioning of people by the culture continues to be present in the corpora-tion. To be seen frequently with someone of the opposite sex can lead to office gossip about an affair. The American culture has few models of women in institutional power positions or in informal business relation-ships. The American culture has not experienced the interfacing of dif-ferent races at such sensitive levels of power. To be seen frequently with someone of another race can trigger suspicion, anxiety, curiosity, and questions of trust and group loyalty. To be seen frequently with some-one who is different in any way can lead others to believe you are "one of them and not one of us."

Those who are not white males and who are seen frequently associat-ing with upper management—the power system—are often treated un-kindly by their own groups. When some white men see other men in these associations, they say the male is not "covering ass," but "kissing ass," or "brown-nosing." (Interestingly, when a white male behaves in the same manner, he sees himself as "playing politics" or "playing the game"—doing what you have to do to get ahead.)

Some women call those women associating with upper management "sluts." They may say she is making it up the corporate ladder by sleep-ing with her bosses. Some African Americans refer to other African Americans, who frequently associate with white male upper manage-ment, as sell-outs, Uncle Toms, or "oreos"—brown on the outside, white on the inside. To Hispanics they are "coconuts"—brown on the outside, white on the inside. Some Asians call them "bananas"—yellow on the outside, white on the inside. Some Native Americans call them "apples"—red on the outside, white on the inside.

Many times men, women, and minorities are not aware of how the mentoring process and the white male power system works. Those who are not white males and who informally associate with upper management unknowingly place themselves in limbo. They are not fully accepted by any group. They are being scrutinized by the white male to see if they really can be trusted. They are avoided by their own group because they are seen as betraying the trust of their own kind. Caught in the middle, these individuals can experience a great deal of emotional pressure and stress since they make enormous efforts to keep themselves acceptable to both sides. Yet, other women and minorities who see themselves being denied access to upper levels of power continue to berate white males for excluding them.

Sometimes women and minorities who are in upper management are afraid to mentor members of their own group. There are several reasons. First, a great deal of time and energy is needed to remain politically current when you are not really a trusted part of the informal power network. You do not have the time or stamina to mentor. Second, knowing that the system can handle only a few deviants, you question the wisdom of sharing the unwritten rules and information with others who are like you, deviant. The white male may replace you with another deviant who may be seen as—professionally or politically—better than you. Finally, with so little power afforded women and minorities in the white male system, you may tend to fight among members of your own group for a greater share of the limited power available to "deviants." To maintain their positions, sometimes women and minorities will not only refrain from helping their own, but will actively work against their own.

Outside of the workplace most women, however, exercise power and operate a team differently. The male power system is competitive, individualistic, and quantitative. It is respectful of *how much* you do. A team for men is a collection of functions working towards a common goal. The female power system trusts the person not the function. The female power system is group oriented, collaborative, and qualitative. It is respectful of *who you are*. How you do something is as important as how much of something you do. A team for women is a collection of individuals working for a common goal. As we have seen, the upper echelons of white male corporate structures are dependent on relationships—who you know. Because of their own conditioning, many women are better equipped to build and maintain relationships. Ambitious and competent women who have those relational skills and the necessary leadership abilities can be a real threat to traditional white males at the top.

Yet as aware of this invisible world of power as many women, minorities, and even some white males are, this world is unseen by most white males who are in it. In one of my seminars for a group of top managers, after we had finished discussing how the white male power system works, one of the white male vice-presidents said out loud: "Holy hell! There is my whole life in twenty-four minutes. I never knew!" Was he being honest? The answer is yes and no. At some level he had to know how the system works in order to move up the ladder to his present position. At another level he was unaware that what he was doing was part of a system that could be defined and labeled. Living and surviving in that system had tremendous implications for himself and those around him. It is the world of special inclusion. It is part of the fishbowl phenomena—invisible to those inside. It is a world totally surrounding the white male, a world in which he lives and breaths yet does not see.

Acceptance at upper levels of the male power system reflects the military/sports mindset: Are you friend or foe? Can I trust you to support me, to back me up? Will you cover for me? Will you be loyal? In an article on men and women as colleagues in *Management Education and Development*, authors Helen Solomons and Audrey Cramer rightfully argue that breaking through invisible barriers has everything to do with "comfort zones." They write, "As women, just by virtue of our physical differences, we create discomfort in most corporations. While it is true that we can't eliminate that problem, we can be aware of it and strategic about what we do."

The question of power boils down to how we distribute the resources—material and human, and who makes the decisions that affect that distribution. White male power arises from control of the resources. To better benefit from a diverse and democratic society requires sharing that control with trusted, qualified, individuals outside the traditional PLU group, who may not look, sound, think, or act like "one of the boys." Successful businesses of the '90s at home and abroad are increasingly open to better understand and trust everyone who shares the common goal of helping the business to be profitable. By including others and the variety of styles and talents they offer, the power system can become even more powerful. Power that is exclusive is incestuous. Turning in on itself, it drains what energy is left defending itself from outside enemies. Power that is inclusive can become expansive, enriched, multiplied, and life-giving. The more power you share the more powerful you become.

As long as there are human beings—whatever their gender or race—there will always be power systems. There are even power systems in families. The more we know about power systems the better the chances are that we can adjust, change, or reaffirm positive parts of that system. Some of the components of power systems can be positive: growing relationships can lead to a greater sense of trust opening up to greater delegation and involvement; greater understanding and unity among those on top; a greater opportunity to focus group efforts; a greater clarity of vision resulting in a smoother operation of the entire organization.

I spoke about collusion with the power system in an earlier chapter. W. T. Greer, a black male who is vice president at Motorola's Semiconductor Products Sector, describes the invisible, many times unconscious ways many women have colluded in their own disenfranchment. "I think women, specifically white women, have had within their grasp the power to make changes much more so than minorities because of their proximity to power: You marry white men, you go to school with them; you grow up with them. Finally, women are understanding this, waking up, and applying pressure. [What can keep women from being powerful] has been their desire to be protected—as a wife, a mother, a girlfriend. They're learning they don't need men to protect them. They're saying, 'Just pay me [for my work] and I'll protect myself.'"

Shattering the so-called corporate glass ceiling, those hidden barriers, has to be a total team effort. How did the women who have made it shatter the glass ceiling? *Fortune* writer Jaclyn Fierman offers a variety of examples: "America's most successful businesswomen wave not the feminist banner but the corporate one. 'I've never particularly thought of myself as a woman in business, so I've never let it get in my way,' says Kathryn Braun, senior vice president of Western Digital in Irvine, California.

'Yes, there are awkward moments,' says Edith Martin, who was a deputy under secretary of defense under President Ronald Reagan and is now a Boeing vice president. 'You can either walk off with a hot head or laugh it off. But after you have a couple of drinks and everyone laughs it off, it brings you closer.' 'The moral,' says Fierman: 'Greet the wrong gesture with the right attitude.'

'You have to prove you're a leader. You have to show you're willing to steal second base. Women don't project that ability well,' says Mary Rudie Barneby, who built from scratch a $3 billion corporate retirement-plan business for Merrill Lynch."

Successful businesswomen usually have several of these stories. "Ambitious women would do well to choose employers whose expectations are compatible with their own. Banking has always been fertile ground, perhaps because women have been paying their dues for years and now represent 91% of tellers. High-tech companies and small startup ventures too bent on survival to be exclusionary are also women-friendly," says Fierman. "'There is no old boy network in my industry, because it's too new,' says Western Digital's Braun. 'So women rise more easily through the ranks.'" "Our best hope for the future are women who don't see the ceiling but the sky," says Claudia Goldin, the first woman tenured economics professor at Harvard. Fierman's final advice to women: "Look like a lady; act like a man; work like a dog."

These are some success stories, but remember that they represent a fraction of one percent of the women working today. There must be a concerted effort by white males, women, and minorities to work together to eradicate the obstacles preventing freer access to positions in upper management. If not, there will remain only three ways to break these barriers. First way: one can break through into upper management by buying two-thirds of the stock of the company and taking over major control of the organization. The second way is to be the son or daughter of the founder, owner, or CEO of the organization. Most often you can trust family. Royalty always has maintained power through family succession. In Chinese organizations everyone in power positions from middle management and above is family. Family trust still is part of the American success dream of a male: to move up the organizational ladder, marry the boss's daughter!

If you do not have the money or the blood, the third way is to imitate the behaviors of those who have reached the top. You go to the right schools; belong to the right fraternities; make the right contacts; drink Bud Light if your boss does; support the same sport teams as your boss does; belong to the same country club; be of the same religious denomination; and, if you have a boss whose spouse does not work out of the home, you follow suit. In a word, you become a mirror image of your boss. You now can be trusted.

We need to move towards a more rapid change of these age-old ways of attaining power positions. We need to develop other definitions of a resource producer and resource director other than those the culture and history have bestowed on males. We can use the cultural talents and styles normally ascribed to women as an additional opportunity to increase our success. Other cultures also have creative talents and styles that can contribute to the common goal of greater corporate success.

Often, however, men and women, whatever their background, pay the same price extracted of white men who wish to move into upper management. They work long hours apart from family and friends. They achieve immediate gains of wealth and position. They suffer long-range consequences of fatigue, burnout, and loneliness. Should one have to pay that price? Is this the ticket for admission to power positions in upper management? Knowing this, how many talented people refuse to enter this arena?

In a democratic and diverse culture, as in business, we have more choices. In order to exercise those choices and benefit from them, we need to redefine what true success means. We need to reconfigure power as a better balancing of both outer and inner forces. The power that comes from producing and enjoying the wealth and prosperity of this land is not enough. We must combine that with the power of being in touch with the real meaning of being human: enjoying the richness of feeling and connecting with those people who are part of our lives. The material power of success in the workplace must merge with the spiritual power that comes from family, friends, and community. Personal power comes from being united with others, while still maintaining the power of being an individual. Only in this ambiguous, ongoing, and delicate balancing of these worlds of power can each of us have the realization of who we are and not just fragments of what might have been.

INTERVIEW

Keith
28
Black
production supervisor
2 years with company
B.A. in English

I got my present job when I was hired to be full time during a tempo-rary position after I graduated from college. There's very little connec-tion between my education and what I'm doing now, but I'm hoping to move up. They'll need people to move up who have an education. I've reached as far as I can go on the production floor.

What I've learned since I've been here is that it's more a networking thing to get promoted than a matter of your work or your education. You have to find out who the people are where you want to go and go over and talk to them. There's no way to just move up. The reason I think it takes networking is that I know a lot of people with education who aren't getting the jobs, and I know people without education who are getting the jobs. To me, that means it's got to be a networking thing.

I work at night, so I have a chance to go to school during the day, and I'm enrolling in a community college to get more courses in marketing and computer science and some of the other things I'll need to get promoted.

I have big goals for myself. I want to be flexible, so I can go where they might need people in the company. My first step is to get into tech-nical writing because of my background in English.

As I said, I've noticed the bias is toward hiring friends, or, as Dr. Ipsaro says, PLUs. I feel as though everyone should be treated the same and given the same chances. Being a black person, obviously it's harder for me to network. The jobs aren't as open to me as they are to other people.

I think it's unfair, especially so because other people don't understand the frustration that I have. They feel it's just "the system" and you should be able to work with it. They don't understand that it's harder for me to work within the system because I'm not a PLU.

Yeah, I have anger. But I can't do anything with my anger at work be-cause there's a stereotype about black people and anger. If I showed my anger at work, they'd look down on me. So I can't show it. For survival, I have to put up with certain things to be able to work. I can't just say, "I'm not going to put up with them." I can't do that. What do I have to put up with? I've been called several names in passing by people I see every day.

You know there's a power structure within the power structure, right? In the production area, there are certain people who have that power to manipulate people. They can be racist and not have to worry about it because they might have a friend they've networked with who is over the person they're being racist toward.

When that happens, I just remain calm. What really makes people upset is if I come back in the next day happy. They get really frustrated with that. They're really making themselves angry as far as I'm concerned.

Another thing I've had to do to get along in the workplace is adjust my dress. I like to dress well anyway, but I have to make sure I dress very well here. People tend to connect me with another black person, a stereotype, and that's not right. Also, I have to make sure my language is clean because I don't want to say sexist things or racist things.

I have a long drive away from work and I relax and let my anger out on the drive. I'm married. I have three children under five years old. I think about them and just relax. My wife doesn't work outside the home. She doesn't want to send our two month old to day care.

What do I want out of life and work? Well, my wife says all I care about is my job, but what I want is to develop my family and have fun with them and make life better for them. I want us to get into a house. I want to get an education for my kids. I'd like to help out my initial family. I'm the youngest one of six kids. They all have an education, but I'm already at their level, money-wise, even though I'm younger. I have a better chance of making more money then they do.

I want to represent my race as best I can. I think what I contribute to the workplace is a fairness and my difference. I developed a mentor program that ended up being a promotion program. In it, people who are standouts in their work and have education do well and have a chance to go to other departments and get some mentoring. I feel that's a better way to get positions than the networking process. It's more fair that way. If you stand out because of your work, then people say, "Let's give him a chance."

WORKSHOP

1. What do you see as your unique talents, aside from your professional competency? Do you believe these talents are used in your organization? If so, how? If not, how could they be utilized?

2. How do you see your gender, race, ethnicity, sexual orientation, any other unique part of you helping the corporation better succeed in making a profit?

3. Have you ever been part of the "in group" in high school, college, neighborhood, at work, or in any group or organization? If you were, how did it feel? If you were not, how did it feel?

4. Are you developing a networking system to benefit you and the company? Who are your mentors? What specifically are you learning from them? What are you offering them?

Where love rules, there is no will to power;
and where power predominates, there love is lacking.
The one is the shadow of the other.
—Carl Jung

11

THE NEW FRONTIER
FOR WHITE MALES

*Although traditional values still hold, many of the old behaviors that men
and women use to express those values will not work anymore. Holding on
to traditional values while not expressing those values in comfortable but
outdated ways can be confusing. The problem with looking backward for solutions and behaviors is that the past holds no vision for the uncertain future of our technological world. Cultural vision for the twenty-first century
has to embrace not simply our past, but our present, and our future. Our
vision has to embrace national and international multiculturalism, the
expansion of the roles of men and women, the diverse styles of workers in the
workplace, the better harmonizing of life at work and home, the comple-
mentary aspects of masculine and feminine, object and people, product
and process. These apparently different environments are more complemen-
tary than one might expect. The twenty-first century workplace demands
that these seemingly opposed views become more of a continuum in which
boundaries blend together.*

As long as we men maintain the old definition of manhood—resource
producer, resource protector, resource director—for its own sake, we
will not change our behaviors in our personal lives or work lives. As long
as we maintain the old view that men rule a culture because of physical
strength as in the animal world, and our human intelligence and the impact of the technological world are to be ignored, we will not change
our behaviors. Neither new developments in the world of technology,
nor statistical information regarding international customers, nor the
growth of minority groups in America, or the changing role of women,
will convince most of us men to change. Most men will not change be-

cause we should. To remove the historically dominant role of men without replacing that role with a new description of manhood is impossible. Men need a place and status that will be important in a culture. Men need an identity that gives new meaning and new power to their masculinity. They need a purpose for their lives. Men will change because the old role is too confusing and too confrontational. It hurts too much not to make adjustments. We will change because we will finally feel what Lee Atwater articulated on his deathbed. We will change when we feel in our gut what Atwater felt: "the spiritual vacuum at the heart of American society, this tumor of the soul." We will know that the old definition of being a man has left us frustrated, tired, restless, bored, and empty. We will change because we want better relationships with people both at home and at work. The restlessness, boredom, and emptiness we feel finally will be labeled correctly. We will know it as loneliness— the result of years of disconnection from all those people whom we say are important in our lives.

Surprisingly we will discover we can learn from women what has given them success in the world of relationships. Women can learn from us those cultural skills that have made men successful in their world. Such an interchange of understandings and skills can set many men and women on the road to a greater balance between work life and personal life. It is a balance between the world of objects and the world of people, between doing and being.

Focusing on their personal and relational lives will give men a sense of renewed purpose. Men will see that their warrior spirit of competition can now be reframed. Men will see themselves as defending and protecting those people who are important in their lives, not only physically but emotionally.

The entrance of more women into the economic world, combined with the interfacing of different cultures both at home and abroad, will challenge men to change. Men will change because they will have evolved a new meaning to their historical role of being a resource producer. We will change to improve the economic world for everyone. Respecting the lives and talents of employees, we will work smarter rather than longer. The recognition of the boundaryless global workplace will call for new processing skills and fewer hierarchical attitudes.

There is a comfortable feeling that comes with continually living out the historical behaviors expected of men. This is more safe than reflecting and discovering new behaviors that can be more productive. When daily habits become routine and have no meaning, life becomes fragmented. We are not living but simply acting. We endlessly repeat patterns because their familiarity makes us comfortable. The repetition of a certain behavior makes us feel secure and in control.

In their obsession with work and material prosperity, men are becoming more and more hollow and sad. They have lost touch with their true purposes and sacred obligations in the culture. Men have been the cultural caretakers. They have used their physical strength to maintain an environment that promotes the well-being of those in the community. They have provided protection and the material resources to nurture those in the community. Men's roles provided a formula in which they could live out their lives, obtaining the fullness of being human. Manhood, in a word, was the seedbed of community.

For women the historical role of the female has been the bearing and nurturing of the young. Women ensured the physical and emotional health of children. Men ensured the preservation of social values through structures and institutions. Together men and women ensured the future of the total community. That is why men have started 99 percent of all the world's religions. This is the reason most philosophers, the debaters of values, have been men. This is the reason men have occupied the political arena, the practical wing of philosophy and ethics.

Historically, men have infused the life of the community with meaning through religion and ritual. Initiation rituals were the usual way to bond young men to those values and to their critical role as community caretakers. Once the agricultural age moved into the industrial age, meaningful initiation of the male as caretaker was dead. In general, although present for the family as provider, protector, and rule-maker, the male as a nurturing, caretaker father has been absent for over 200 years.

Women now seem to rule most families. Men continue to rule the cultural context that surrounds the family. This division of roles worked because it appeared as common sense and practical. If it has worked, why change it? Why are women in the workplace? Why are they blurring such clear definitions of roles and causing such societal confusion? Why are they trying to be supermoms? First of all, women are working because they are often the single parent supporting children. Working for them is not a choice. Secondly, the goals set up by some families require that both father and mother work to financially achieve their ambitions.

Thirdly, for a great many women the workplace brings them into a world of adult interaction and the satisfaction a successful career can bring.

Women know that balance and cultural sanity need restoration. Intimately involved in childrearing, many women see firsthand the crisis in families. Historically women were grounded in relationships. They see more clearly than most men the utter destruction, chaos, and confusion that many relationships, families, and communities suffer. Men still believe they can stop the cultural drift into valueless chaos by focusing even more intensely on accumulating greater material wealth and increasing political power and legislation.

Many times in a fast-changing society made up of unreflective and non-thinking people there is a widespread interest in back-to-basics, to fundamental and simplistic ideas. This search for the right and sure way to live in a confusing world has even affected the defining of the roles of men and women. Many men are hungry to discover what their role is in this confusing world. As we noted earlier with the "Promise Keepers," some men are turning to the basic tenets of the Bible. In ancient times men were seen in the family as husbands and fathers, dispensing wisdom and controlling their flocks. There is great clarity and little anxiety when one is told that your role as a man has been the same for more than 2000 years and has God's approval!

Fundamentalism whether religious, political, educational, or economic is always attractive. Simplistic, tried-and-tested ways, and what seems like common sense, can be seductive. Yet fundamentalism calls us to the past, to what we know worked in a previous world. The problem with such an image of ourselves is that it lacks vision. Cultural vision for the twenty-first century embraces who we were and who we are now. It encompasses the diversity of choices, styles, opportunities, and the variety of talents people have. It values the past, recognizes the importance of the present, and hopes for the future.

The distinction between values and behaviors again is essential. Traditional values—honor, respect, love, family, sense of belonging, spirituality—are ageless. The richness of our customs—historical expressions of values—can nourish us. But historical behaviors are the habits of a past we no longer inhabit. They are inappropriate to who men and women of all races have become and are becoming. These historical behaviors are inappropriate in today's world. Historically, cultures had time to deliberate and meditate and discuss values, policies, and behaviors. Technology has contracted time and made us the servants of the machines meant to serve us. The speed of society's movement has robbed men and women of the time to think, discuss, read, reflect, and evaluate what behaviors are most fitting in this time to express traditional human values.

Men need a vision of themselves that will recover the experience of time and the clarity of values. Men need to revive their place in the family and community. We require a vision of ourselves that will be human at work and productive at home and vice versa. We need a vision that includes masculine and feminine values, that combines actions with feelings, that blends the human values of relationships with the productive values of the workplace. We crave a new vision of what it means to be a man.

We need that vision now. It is a vision that includes authentic diversity—the recognition, appreciation, and sharing of the variety of gifts and styles that each man and woman contributes to the welfare of the general community. We need more mature men to help shape this new vision. White men are the people who have the power to change this American culture towards this new vision. This is the reason I have emphasized white males in this book. With proper use of that power everyone can profit.

Yet white males, as previous warriors, have been the ones who have been overrun by their own competitive and self-centered urges. They have been seduced into believing that raw power, control, and more material goods are always better for them. At the same time, women and minorities, blinded by their frustration and rage, have ignored and attacked white men. They are denying that white men, as insensitive as they may seem, continue to hold the key to changing this society.

Over the centuries white males—because of their talents, initiatives, opportunities, and advancements—have become synonymous with power, wealth, position, and success. Achievement has come to them justly, and sometimes not so justly. In many cases white males have gathered this wealth and power for themselves often at the expense of others. Men must transcend selfish acquisition and consumption. It is now time for men to return themselves, their talents, and their successes at the service of the community. In doing so, men can attain full manhood. In his compelling book *Manhood*, Stephen Shapiro addresses this concern in depth. "One powerful play in recent seasons is Peter Shaffer's *Good*. It is about a man, an intellectual, a professor, who is hollow. He is flattered and seduced into becoming a Nazi. There is no value for which he is willing to sacrifice—not friendship, not humanity, not love. This refusal to sacrifice and actively seek the common good is the core of the soul of the male who fails to achieve manhood. The refusal to be vulnerable to our kin and to the needs of our friends opens the way to personal despair, social disintegration, and dictatorship.

"Manhood, democratic manhood, is precisely the barrier to autocracy. The American democratic cultural tradition, from Jefferson to Thoreau to Saul Bellow, is an effort to activate democratic models of self-respecting manhood. It calls for men who will defend values they are responsible for to people they are responsible to. It is a corrupt tradition, corrupted by violence, the murder of Indians and blacks, racism, sexism, inequality, and militarism, but it is the tradition of our fathers, and we must look to it for guidance, as well as transform it."

Like Robert Moore, Shapiro calls for a return to male heroism in its full sense of service to a community. Simultaneously, this brings the male access to his inner resources and to the meaning of his life. It is by the misguided pursuit of simplistic and old behaviors that fundamentalists believe they will gain this inner strength and peace.

Shapiro writes, "The crucial questions for a man are: Can I stand up and speak for what I believe? Can I bridge this gap between people? Can I halt the spread of panic and violence? Can my love or care hold these people together? Heroic manhood has been held so precious because it is the foundation of the meaningful social world."

My work with individual men and groups of men clearly shows me that most men are capable of swift and important change when they understand and see their course clearly. Much of their past formation as a man allows them to focus, marshall up all their resources, gather their courage and wisdom to achieve whatever they hold dear.

In committing so much of their lives to attaining success in the workplace, many men are misdirecting those energies that will bring them to the full dimensions of their manhood. Juliet Schor, in her insightful book *The Overworked American*, offers a female perspective that provides well-thought-out alternatives to our present course. She argues that "the market system tends to create work" and reduce leisure and that the preceding "medieval economy" was not, as we have been led to believe, a time of continuous toil.

"The medieval economy also provided ample opportunities for leisure within the year. And the medieval period appears not to have been exceptional, at least in western history. Leisure time in ancient Greece and Rome was also plentiful. Athenians had 50 to 60 holidays annually, while in Tarentum they apparently had half the year. In the old Roman calendar, 109 of 355 days were designated *nefasti*, or 'unlawful for judicial and political business.' By the mid-4th century, the number of *feriae publicae* (public festival days) reached 175."

Schor says that a short-term comparison between 1850 and the present fosters the illusion that we are working less today than ever before. That has been our conventional wisdom and the continuing argument for advancements in techology. She contends that in the mid-nineteenth century men worked between 3,150 and 3,650 hours annually, more than ever before or since in human history.

"Since 1948," Schor continues, "U.S. productivity has failed to rise in only five years. The level of productivity of the U.S. worker has more than doubled. In other words, we could now produce our 1948 standard of living (measured in terms of marketed goods and services) in less than half the time it took in that year. We actually could have chosen the four-hour day. Or, a working year of six months. Or, every worker in the United States could now be taking every other year off from work—with pay. Incredible as it may sound, this is just the simple arithmetic of productivity growth in operation.

"But between 1948 and the present we did not use any of the productivity dividend to reduce hours. . . . Hours have risen steadily for two decades. In 1990, the average American owns and consumes more than twice as much as he or she did in 1948, but also has less free time."

The loss in time has been paralleled by a gain in income. The average American's annual income of $22,000 is sixty-five times the average of half the world's population, Schor tells us. Today European industrial workers in West Germany or France work over two months less than their American counterparts—320 fewer hours.

The Industrial Revolution may only have accelerated tendencies that were already at work in European culture—for example, the kind of synchronism Max Weber pointed out in the dynamic that fused Protestantism and capitalism. The effect on the male was to partition him from the home. It eliminated the time he had for leisure reflection on his experience. The Industrial Revolution was the birth of work as obsession. Workaholism became men's addiction of choice. The Industrial Revolution marked the devastation of men's inner life, particularly a serious spiritual life. The rise of industrialism also marked the social decline of religious belief.

It is instructive to remember again that men and women are socialized differently. Women mature in relationship to a *person* their mothers. Men mature adapting to a *code* of masculinity—what Joseph Pleck has called the fraud of "male sex role identity." This has been true since the eighteenth century. The father, as the role model for the boy, either followed in the footsteps of his father's work or left the home to go away to work.

Small alterations in the masculine code produced big changes in adult males. Men construct their identities around such alterations. For women the story is different. In spite of child labor, girls continued to model themselves in relation to their mothers. Boys had an absent, overworked, and sometimes stressed father. The birth of industrial work created a mentality of product orientation—achieving a goal on a massive scale. Father worked long hours. Father was exhausted and irritable. Father had to shield his family from the work worries and pain by keeping his emotions and feelings to himself. The model of manhood—absent physically and emotionally—was born. Aloofness, remoteness, distance, isolation, and insensitivity became manly virtues!

The partition that separates the lives of men and women has increased dramatically in our time. This lack of experience in the art of relating is the heritage that continues to frustrate many men. In their present-day attempts many men cannot communicate and share their lives in relationships. In fact, ironically, it is considered to be more masculine when lacking the finer skills of interacting.

The Industrial Revolution also was the period that destroyed trust as the bond between men. The handshake that sealed an agreement was replaced by the contract. Legal stipulations ensured compliance between competing strangers rather than honor. Suspicion replaced trust. Competition replaced friendship. Men developed a sense of isolation from other men by not sharing any information about themselves that might be used against them in a highly competitive world. Pseudo loyalty became something you practiced if the circumstances at the present moment benefited you. Furthermore, by isolating themselves from other men, men lost a forum in which to share, to learn, to be affirmed, and to be challenged by another caring male. In fact, the culture applauded the man who was the loner, the rough and tumble guy, the John Wayne type, as the man's man. This distance between men has grown so wide over the centuries that we suspect the manliness of any man who has any close relationships with other men. This gives a deeper meaning to homophobia. Having already isolated themselves from relationships with women, men have added another level of isolation from their own sex. It is no wonder, then, that most men today feel *totally* isolated and lonely.

This schism of the worlds of objects and people is played out so clearly along cultural gender lines. Social theorists speak of the male and the female culture and refer to their different ways of seeing and communicating. Psychologically, the individual is divided by such partitioning. Each person has access to only part of what he or she would have if a full complement of human qualities were nurtured. By being divided, one is less able to have access to the fullness of oneself, is less at ease, less content, becomes less productive, and is less powerful.

Western culture today festers from the toxic residues of that loss of the male's spiritual, feeling, responsive side. It represents a cultural and psychological split in the psyche of the male. The male, as the dominant power in the culture, has brought this split to his world by separating his work from his home. Material gain and competitive action rules in one; connectedness and feeling in the other. Each world requires a different set of skills.

Most men and women fail to recognize that the rules of relationships/intimacy and the rules of today's business/success are diametrically opposed. Intimacy requires collaboration, disclosure, and commonality. Success in work requires individuality, distance, and competition. The skills necessary for a successful relationship are diametrically opposed to the skills necessary for success in the workplace. This is the reason most men find it difficult to maintain both a successful marriage or relationship and a successful worklife.

Most men see their lives as a series of discrete steps with discrete goals to attain full manhood. You first direct your attention to rationally gaining an education and winning a job in your career field. After succeeding in those endeavors, you turn off that rational part of your life and turn on the emotional side. Disclosing your emotions and your weaknesses in courting is what wins a woman, leads to marriage, and an opportunity for a family. Once those personal goals are attained, you turn off the emotions to return with full-court-press energy to the work world where you now prove your love for your family by becoming the best "resource producer."

For most men this switch from the emotional world of personal relationships back to the work world comes between the ages of twenty-eight to thirty-four. By the time they have reached the top of their career ladder and attained "manly success," they are about forty-five to fifty-five. At this point they frequently discover that being a "successful" male has not given them the contentment and happiness they now seek. They become restless and bored. They feel empty and hollow. They are disconnected and isolated. They are sad and lonely.

What some men do when they experience these empty feelings is to start on the road to successful manhood all over. Maybe they missed something along the way. Maybe if they go through the steps again, they will succeed this time. Following this pattern of reasoning, these men usually physically disengage from the wives and children of an earlier marriage. These present relationships seem irreparable anyway. Besides, these broken relationships are constant reminders of the failure to have done it right the first time. These men quickly seek distance. They seek a divorce. At some level, since they have devoted so much time and energy to their jobs and not to their relationships, many men feel guilty and inadequate. They partially blame themselves for the break-up. This is the reason that in divorce proceedings some men, out of guilt, offer their wives overly generous financial and material compensation. At the same time, many women feel so betrayed and angry, they feel justified in taking whatever assets are available. Coming out of these emotionally bruising situations, men search for relationships that make them feel better. They want to prove again their success and competency in relating to a woman. These men frequently are attracted to women who will readily respond to their pain and hurt and any unfulfilled emotional needs. Many times these men are emotionally stuck at age twenty-eight to thirty-four, the age they tuned-out their personal relations to climb the corporate ladder. It is understandable that they now search for women who are emotionally and physically where they left off—age twenty-eight to thirty-four.

By the same token many of these women have the need to be needed. They immaturely define their womanhood in being attractive to men and taking care of them. Other women may need to emotionally control men. Others may need a father-figure. Many of these younger women especially are attracted to these older, successful, wealthy, powerful men. They feel great pride in being chosen at their age to share the acquired success of these males. These women become the instant beneficiaries of wealth, position, status, and power. They need not work or sacrifice. They have achieved fulfillment easily and quickly. They feel successful as a woman. In turn, the male has achieved another one of his goals—being successful in relationships. He now has his trophy wife or woman to prove his success.

Complicating such relationships is the fact that frequently a woman twenty-eight to thirty-four wants children. The fifty or sixty-year-old male agrees to satisfy the woman as part of her decision to marry him. At the same time he sees new children as another chance to fulfill the dream of being a "successful" father—another experience he missed the first time around. We now have a fifty-five year old man interacting with a baby. When that child is in the midst of adolescence and a responsive father is essential, dad could be in his mid-seventies, impatient and weary. Nature has reasons—physical stamina and emotional agility—for the youth of childbearing years. Frequently in such life-reconstruction, men focus solely on fulfilling their own needs and dreams. Little thought is given to the children's present or future needs. Some men speak negatively about women trying to have it all. What about some of us trying in our own ways to have it all?

The dilemma faced by men today is to balance their work lives with their home lives. Since some women are behaving more as men, they share similar problems. Balancing home and work seems sometimes impossible. How do you blend the world of product and process, of present gains and future rewards, of objects and people, of power and intimacy? To succeed in balancing these two seemingly different arenas one needs first to reach the heart of both worlds. The key to a satisfying, relational, intimate life is the disclosure and expression of feelings, thoughts, desires, and vulnerabilities. Intimacy, in the full sense of the term, means being psychologically naked before the other. Disclosure and expressiveness generate a trust bond—the essential element for intimacy.

In the business world you cannot afford to be naked or transparent. You do not disclose, express, or trust. A business will trust your expertise and performance not your feelings, emotions, or vulnerabilities. Many corporations will ask you to check your personal life at the door. Trust in the workplace is replaced by respect. I may not trust you, but I do respect your ability to perform successfully. You may respect me if we have worked side by side with good results on several projects. But trusting me is something else.

Earlier I mentioned Barbara Gutek's term "sex role spillover" for the sexual dynamics that occur in the workplace. Clearly in our off-hours men, and now women, have "work role spillover" as well. The work ethic is embedded in the male core. This is a learned behavior that is too central to many men's identities to be checked with guns and tools at the doors of their homes. Many men return from work or war with the cluster of behaviors that has made them winners. When these successful behaviors do not bring about winning results at home, many men feel like visitors or strangers in their own homes.

How do we bring men home when home is such a foreign place, an area of constant failure? How do we bring them home to successful and fulfilling intimate relationships? How do we bring men home to themselves? Conversely, how do we bring women to work so they do not unconsciously seek intimate relationships in an environment that presently is combatant? How do we assist women to enrich the workplace by some of the relational experiences many of them have had? Diversity—the infusion of different styles and experiences, the blending of the best of both worlds—provides the way. Diversity includes a certain amount of disclosure and a certain amount of holding back. Supporting the principles of diversity provides the atmosphere for learning about each other, learning from each other's experiences, and thus valuing the unique differences of the other. For men diversity enables them to give notice to the values and attention to the feelings of co-workers, seeing them as individuals not only as producers. For women diversity means gaining the goal orientation and positive competitiveness that make them effective and successful colleagues. For women and men diversity means transforming home and work into environments that welcome both relationship and productivity.

To create a new model in which these two worlds blend requires adjustment and change. Change is a process. Most men are unfamiliar with process. Men are comfortable with maps and formulas that take them to a known destination or goal. Unfortunately most individuals and groups, even corporations, only change when there is a crisis. In the computer world change is rapid, continual, unending. Change is a way of life. The worst crisis happens when you do not change.

Men and their world of business need to search for additional ways to respond and benefit from such a changing environment. The patterns and skills of women down through history may be one place to look for these new ways. In most cultures women, in powerless positions, always have had to adapt to uncontrollable change in their lives, in the development of their children, and in their communities. Viewed as second class and physically weaker, women have had to read the surrounding environment to anticipate what changes might happen before they occur. In today's workplace reading the environment before the fact, predicting the future, is an element of marketing. In a changing workplace, reading the customers before even the customers know what they want and need is the key to business survival and success.

Down through history women have learned to live with constant change. Over some of those changes women have had little or no control. Forced to go along does not mean, as some men have believed, that women have no goals. Most women do not go around aimlessly waiting for men to direct them. Women do have definite goals. Sometimes due to uncontrollable circumstances, women are forced to be open to a variety of ways to achieve their goals. Many times women have had to be creative and inventive. Furthermore, most women are quicker than most men to change in midstream. Men will work the same plan but try harder. Women will try a plan, and if the original plan does not work, they will look for different options. Women have gifts for men in this area of change—the ability to explore options, to be flexible, and to change quickly.

Learning about other cultures can sensitize white men to read existing signs in the process of change. Cultures that have depended on the earth for their survival have learned to read the signs of nature and adapt to nature's extraordinary gifts, sense of timing, immeasurable power, and unpredictable changes. Not only have these cultures adapted, but they have been enriched by nature's assets and strengths.

My belief has always been that the global community is on an international search for the benefits of differences and similarities. We in America know this concept as *E pluribus unum*. Today, in a democratic and diverse culture, we attempt to integrate differences for the betterment of the whole. Each culture, each citizen, has talents, ways, styles, and experiences that are in themselves unique and beneficial. Over the centuries unique environments and historical situations have refined and polished these styles. When this wealth of thought and experience is brought together, wouldn't it seem that the whole becomes greater than its parts?

The Western world is a world focused on action, performance, material. The Eastern world always has been seen as more passive, meditative, and spiritual. These worlds are at opposite ends of a continuum. The blending of these two worlds can bring greater wholeness to individuals, communities, institutions, and corporations throughout the world. With increased access afforded by travel, instant communication, and global television, sharing and interdependence on all levels of cultures are rapidly hastening the reality of a global village.

Receiving these diverse gifts from others is not a skill readily taught to the American white male warrior. White males see themselves as winners. Real men are supposed to be all-knowing and all-powerful. American men have only to look around the world to see that they have created a culture that is strong, prosperous, and dynamic. The best of a material world and prosperous life can be found in America. Moreover, white males see males of other cultures not only wanting to emulate them but wanting to join with them in the white man's methods of achieving instant wealth, power, and success.

Given this history of success, can the white male learn from men—let alone women—who come from other cultures? Asking white men to listen and receive is unplugging them from the male identity of warrior and performer. Reflecting, negotiating, accepting, and giving are seen by a warrior mentality as passive and weak. In most cultures, women are the ones who are passive, who wait, reflect, negotiate, accept, and receive. And, women are seen as weak.

I try to show men that I do not want them to give up everything they have learned about manhood and masculinity. I want them to retain the good qualities of resource producer, protector, and director: goal orientation, the sophisticated ability of working with objects, team strength, loyalty, self-sacrifice, and courage. Intensification of these qualities does not guarantee being a better man. Pushing loyalty to the extremes can result in aggressive, reckless, and insensitive behavior. Men must complement the fine qualities of manhood with compassion, collaboration, sophisticated ability in working with people, individual dignity, and understanding. With the blend of these two worlds men will discover even greater strength, enormous resources and wealth, a deeper quality of life, and a new understanding of what it means to be powerful.

Unfortunately, we have few models of men who exhibit a blend of these two worlds. Many of our institutions, even religious ones where you would expect an appreciation of the spiritual life, still promote the male-dominated, warrior-triumphant behaviors of primitive and ancient times. Institutions, like people, fear change. Change can be seen as a loss of power or a sign of weakness. Change may be considered even *morally* wrong. But change of behaviors—not values—is inevitable! It is a necessary part of life for people and institutions. History has shown that many times people often change faster than institutions.

Institutions have the responsibility to be the community's historical deposit and guardian of traditional values. Individuals and societies experience and experiment with new behavioral expressions of those traditional values. The role of the institution is to guide, support, challenge, and lead the community to more authentic behavioral expression. Avoiding change can be a distinct sign of institutional atrophy. To remain dynamic and alive, all things must change and evolve—nature, societies, institutions, organizations, individuals.

In this book, I hope to help men to see that changing from one behavior to another does not mean they have lost their significance. When men realize that they cannot know everything and never can be perfect, another level of inadequacy may arise. If men were adequate, *they* would have recognized the need to change. Additional feelings of inadequacy can be triggered by not knowing the required skills to implement change.

In the process of change, I attempt to teach men some effective skills, including a map to carry them through the territory of change. Men seem to gain some confidence by having a format. My map, however, is not a step-by-step procedure but one that gives clear destinations (product) with a few strong road markers (process).

In this ongoing process of changing and redefining, men need others. With few models and mentors in the process of redefining manhood, men need other men. Many men, who have come to the realization that they must change, believe they can make these changes themselves. They see no need for help. Unfortunately, they soon become confused and frustrated, regress and remain isolated. While these men fumble around trying to change their lives in their own time and way, those around them continue to suffer.

In order to avoid such frustration, I frequently direct men to individual counseling with another male who is advanced in his process of redefinition. I also encourage men to join men's developmental groups where they can compare and learn from the experience of others. They can receive support, challenge, and encouragement for their ideas and behaviors. In this safe and caring environment the layers of old defenses can be peeled away. In this openness, especially in the presence of other males, a man becomes vulnerable. This is a new and very frightening experience to the fully-armored male warrior. In acknowledging vulnerability, a man comes to see himself as he truly is. Now he can rediscover his assets of loyalty, courage, intelligence, and strength. He can find his hidden strengths of sensitivity, feelings, compassion, tenderness, and his need for others.

In finding this need for community, a male discovers more about who he is and what he needs to be a more complete person. In learning about others, he learns more about himself and how important his talents and experiences are for others. It is only in interacting and connecting with other people that a man gains a greater sense of contentment and well-being; his sense of loneliness is diminished.

Men's groups teach process from a male perspective. Process is not as foreign to men as they may think; they call it problem-solving. But problem-solving for men is a process with a goal in mind—to create or use material objects. The new learning for men is that the process is as important as the goal. On-going, interactive, and developing life with people in relationships is a process. The end of this process, however, is also its means. The ultimate goal of this process is the movement toward being a person who shares with others in relationships for greater satisfaction and growth. Seen in this light, even a men's group is nothing more than males coming together in process.

At some point in individual counseling or in men's groups, men must face their homophobia. Sharing more and more of yourself with this other man or men may result in an emotional feeling and connection. These feelings may trigger some anxiety because most men have simplistic views of emotional connections. Any emotional connection to a male may cause men to think of themselves as latent homosexuals or, perhaps, bisexual.

Most men are novices in the arena of relationships and friendships. Women are much more sophisticated in having all sorts of friends with whom they share their lives in varying degrees and around varying topics. Given a limited background in relationships, most men see any sort of sharing of thoughts, feelings, and ideas as a means to an end. A man shares these parts of himself with a woman so that he can proceed to his goal. His destination is connection—frequently expressed in sexual activity. Men seldom realize that they can share feelings and thoughts at different levels and with different goals. This sharing may lead to sex or just to some level of friendship.

When a man feels close to another man, discussing these feelings with a male mentor helps him to gain insight, understanding, and the skills to handle this part of the relationship. Often men in such a situation will terminate the relationship. They are frightened by the feelings and the thought that they may be or may be seen as homosexual. The sad part is that these men are left wondering if they are homosexual. Homophobia is most men's worst burden. Homophobia is more than an aversion to same-sex activities. Connell in *Masculinities* reminds us: "Homophobia is not just an attitude. Straight men's hostility to gay men involves real social practice, ranging from job discrimination through media verification to imprisonment and sometimes murder. . . . [the purpose of these practices is] to draw social boundaries, defining 'real' masculinity by its distance from the rejected."

Frightened, then, by their misunderstanding of homosexuality, men avoid close male relationships. They avoid showing any feelings and affection. They keep their conversations on very safe levels: work and sports. In isolation, then, men deny themselves their full manhood. They remain little boys, at best adolescents, frightened of disclosure and fearful of feelings and emotions. They behave immaturely in relationships—even with women. Because of their ambivalence and insecurity they often fear any sort of permanency or commitment. Connection with women is an essential element for men to experience their manhood. However, to feel truly whole—to feel their manhood completely—men also must connect with men on deeper, more personal levels.

Sometimes the path to our deepest desires, our fondest hopes and wishes is right in front of us. We experience this blindness individually and as a community. The American culture is a culture that must continually re-invent itself: maintaining traditional values but updating historical behaviors. American businesses must continually seek new structures and methods to take advantage of the cultural changes that will ensure them continued economical success. So, too, American males must seek new masculinities to reinvent their manhood.

We need to open ourselves to others—white males, males of other races and ethnic groups, females of all cultures, men and women of different backgrounds, points of view, and experiences. From these diverse and rich sources we will continually become better men. We will share with these diverse groups those manly virtues and valuable experiences which have been our special gifts as men. We will better live the heritage that is ours: *E pluribus unum*—although we are many, we are one; from the gifts of many, each one will be enriched.

INTERVIEW

Bob
37
White
technical staff
four years with company
ten prior years as entrepreneur
M.S. degree

The corporate world is very different from the entrepreneurial world. The number one difference is it's easier for people in the corporate world to push aside the really tough questions. When you're involved with something that is really difficult, it seems easier to put that in the parking lot, so to speak, and not get back to it. Whereas when you are in the entrepreneurial world, you want to spend your time doing the things that have the greatest impact, whether they are the hardest or not.

In the entrepreneurial world, you feel the effects of all your actions directly in your pocketbook. In the corporate world it seems that although we're encouraged to find the real items that have the greatest impact, and to work on them, the processes that are set up make it difficult to get involved with the really tough issues.

By corporate processes I mean, for instance, the way we budget resources. There's always a limited amount of time you have to work on a project. If you identify something that's a real major issue, you might not have enough time allocated to tackle that issue. So you document it for the future, but you don't pursue it.

The corporate processes are set up so that sometimes you're not looking long-term. It may takes six months to succeed on what your are working because of the fragmentation of the work into many different hands, many different budgeting cycles, many different planning cycles. So you have no guarantee that the work budgeted this year will continue next year. If I know there is a chance that a project won't be continued long-term, I am forced to tie it up in a nice bundle before I can complete it.

In the corporate world, there is a great deal of management job hopping. When I was an owner-operator of my business, I was forced to focus on the same bottom line during all my years in the business.

But I decided to leave the business I was in because I was getting worn out, and I wanted to get married. Nobody else would have judged me as being worn out, but I could feel that if I continued for another thirty years the way I was going, it would get worse. For two years before I met my wife I was looking to get out. After I met her, she helped me make that decision and take my chances.

I think I treat my work and my home life 50-50. I do not prioritized my home life over work, but I do look for opportunities to get away from work. That's new for me. When I was in my own business I was always on call.

Even though I think I balance my life 50-50, I still spend more time on my career than I do at home. The reason is I am studying for another degree. But I think I have it under control. What is different for me now is, is that I am at home studying. I am paying myself first. I put my personal interests first, not my company's.

My wife is still building her career. She is working on her MBA. We are thinking about having children, but we're not certain. Right now we are more concerned with our lives and our careers. I guess what I get out of my career is a feeling of achievement, of doing a good job. I like being effective and excelling. I want to study for a Ph.D. I figure as I gain experience and more education, I'll be able to do a tremendous amount of more work in less the time. One of my goals that I want to reach in ten years is to be able to produce more in less time so that I can have more time for family and leisure.

I guess I consider myself a liberal when it comes to diversity. I think the skills that help a male relate to a female and one race to another are the same skills that help you relate to your own race and gender. I think diversity training leads to an openness to think differently. I don't think people usually implement radical ideas because they don't feel safe. People are avoid risks in their work. The big problems are never tackled. You want only to be able to demonstrate your successes. Doing a fair job on an unbelievably hard project is not nearly as rewarded by your bosses as doing an excellent job on a fairly easy project.

From past experiences I have an opinion regarding change. You facilitate change when you make the obvious decisions immediately. When something is proposed, tested, and there is evidence it is the right thing to do, you need to do it quickly. This gives people the opportunity to see there has been a change and an improvement that was based on analysis and good decision-making. Once the decision to change is made, the change needs to happen quickly. If the change eventually comes, sometimes all the people that worked on the change have moved on and don't see that anything has changed.

In the entrepreneurial world if you have an idea, you try it the next day. You evaluate it the day after that. You can't afford to wait weeks and weeks mulling over how you're going to do something.

If you are looking at the corporate workplace, you will find very little motivation to make changes. If you are looking at society, there is a lot of motivation. So I think white males are more motivated to change outside the workplace. My view is pretty liberal on this. In order to really enjoy your life, you need to grab onto new ways of thinking. The appeal of diversity, new ideas, and new ways of thinking, is not so I can do a better job, but so I can enjoy myself more. I can have more fun at night and on the weekends. I am learning more about the benefits of diversity outside of my workplace.

What diversity is doing is opening my mind to all the different dances there are in the world. It makes me feel more aware, in touch with how big the world is, and how much there is out there to enjoy. I don't think my thoughts are unusual. I am unusual in that I am thinking about this right now. If you freed people up from their daily drudgery and trying to get by, you give them a chance to learn about these things. I think you would be surprised what would happen.

When I was an entrepreneur I operated with a narrowly defined view of diversity: acceptance of other people and other ways of thinking and using their skills. What I have learned since then is the broader definition: helping people feel comfortable in the workplace; helping them not to be scared that they might be stomped on; letting them try to succeed their own way. I've learned about stewardship and delegation. This means creating an environment where people feel comfortable opening up. I think you do that by making them the boss, the owner of their own work.

WORKSHOP

1. When was the last time you reflected on the gender roles of men and women? What is your present definition of manhood? womanhood?

2. Understanding what you know today of masculinity or femininity, what behaviors would express those concepts at home? at work? Are those behaviors different from old historical behaviors?

3. In the words of Stephen Shapiro do you present behaviors that stand up and speak what you believe? Are your behaviors bridging the gap between people and halting the spread of violence and panic? Are your behaviors holding people together in love and concern?

4. What behaviors would you like to have received from your father and your mother that you did not receive? If you have children are you expressing those behaviors to them? For example, are you more openly affectionate, do you spend individual time with them; have you promoted your daughter's academic achievement, your son's expression of feelings?

One man may hit the mark, another blunder;
but heed not these distinctions.
Only from the alliance of the one,
working with and through the other,
are great things born.
–Antoine de Saint-Exupery
The Wisdom of the Sands

12

ORGANIZATIONAL CHANGE AND THE MOTOROLA MODEL

Although every organization has its peculiar history and personality, there are some basic concepts that are common to all for promoting diversity issues. At Motorola's Semiconductor Products Sector (SPS) diversity managers dare to explore cultural change not only in the mirror of affirmative action and parity goals but at the deepest roots of individual and organizational values, attitudes, and behaviors. The process of change has continued for eight years with no end in sight. Diversity has been recognized as a business issue whose payoff will appear in productivity and profits.

The rules that Henry Ford thought would control workplace behavior applied to a melting pot theory of assimilation into a dominant culture that was governed in a paternalistic manner. But the world of the twenty-first century is pluralistic, and there can be more complexity and chaos ruling than compliance. Corporations with people who have differences—whether they be of race, or ethnicity, or organizational function, or level of talent—must learn to use their differences for the company's common goal. As Scotsman Brian Bedford, senior vice president of human resources at Motorola's Semiconductor Products Sector in Phoenix, notes: "It's easier to work with [diversity] issues in the workplace (than in society at large) because you can legislate the workplace, you can set goals, you can demand attitudes."

In America and especially in the workplace, we are beginning to learn how to integrate rather than assimilate differences in a changing work force. We are slowly discovering how to foster the learning that creates attitudinal, behavioral, and organizational change rather than to demand those changes.

Trying to describe how a company simultaneously addresses all the levels needed to take advantage of a diverse work force can be confusing and misleading. Each company has its own personality and structure. Each company has it own history and resources. Each company must create its own process and must write its own story. However, there are some basic ingredients that are essential to developing a workplace that takes advantage of a diverse work force.

Many American companies are forced to practice the principles of diversity and democracy by the outside pressures of law and common social morality. Greater motivation and action is necessary to create a truly diverse workplace. Furthermore, if enforcing the law—civil rights, EEO, affirmative action, quotas—was the major responsibility of businesses, companies would become the national courts of justice. They would be unable to pursue productivity and profit. The obligation of businesses is to uphold the law, not become its primary enforcer. If practicing the principles of diversity and democracy was carried out in businesses simply because it was the right thing to do, companies would take on the role of churches. Law and the common good are part of the ethical reasons for a company to practice diversity. More convincing business reasons are essential.

Practicing democratic and diversity principles must enhance a business's productivity and profit. Diversity must have a business rationale that strongly promotes active involvement in creating and fostering a more diverse workplace. As mentioned throughout the book, and now summarized here, the following points should convince businesses that diversity is *the* competitive edge; diversity is good business; diversity can spell success:

The Talent Pool Factor. We have noted the changing demographics in America. Women and minority groups are a significant part of the work force. What is more, we have seen that the majority of jobs in the technological work force will require employees to have sufficient intellectual skills. Intelligence is blind to differences of gender, race, physical attributes, and sexual orientation. Successful companies will seek out an intelligent work force regardless of their other characteristics.

The Creative Thinking Factor. Any company that wants to remain competitive must continually be innovative. Finding new and better ways of offering new and attractive products or services is the key to continued success. Fostering creativity and innovation is essential! A basic ingredient to creativity is having several options or choices. A diverse work force offers a variety of ways, styles, and alternatives. Creativity is inherent in a diverse work force.

The Customer-Orientation Factor. In today's American marketplace customers come from a number of different demographic groups. Who better knows how to respond to a select population than someone from that group. In matters of product design and marketing, sales representatives from target customer groups must be present. In a diverse America, a diverse work force makes common business sense.

The Global Market Factor. With the world becoming more and more of a global village—a global economy—companies that want to survive need to enter the international marketplace. Practicing the principles of diversity at home can offer companies the comfort, skills, and abilities to become global. Diversity at home is a stepping stone to successfully interfacing with different cultures throughout the world.

The Best Practices Factor. Companies that actively respect the uniqueness of people are attractive for employees, customers, and investors alike. These companies frequently are the most progressive in terms of employee programs and customer business practices. They treat their employees as they would want their employees to treat their customers. Characteristics of these companies are flexibility, responsible risk-taking, and experimentation. These companies are active, innovative, dynamic, and evolving.

The Societal Factor. The workplace is the only institution in which our citizens have little or no choice of people with whom they associate. This environment becomes the laboratory for living in a diverse and democratic America. Businesses, for their own survival and success, must now take on the responsibility for educating their employees to live and work successfully in a diverse workplace. Corporations must take on the societal role of leading, modeling, influencing, pressuring, and convincing all other institutions to strongly support and live by the principles of a diverse, democratic society. The corporation is not a cultural island. Its employees and customers live in and are influenced by other institutions. For their own enduring success, corporations must take on the role of society's key change agent.

Having established a business rationale for benefiting from a diverse work force, we would profit from understanding the overall philosophy of the change process. Three cycles are continually present and interfacing in the evolution of a more diverse culture.

Assimilation. The need for homogeneous groups is essential in a diverse culture. Forming these groups based on gender, race, and sexual orientation is one way. Homogeneous groups can naturally form around jobs—support staff, technical staff, engineers, facilities workers. These groups offer a safe, supportive, and comfortable haven. A major focus would be to help the members gain a greater understanding of their uniqueness and special talents. Another would be an awareness of how their differences can enrich the common goals. Care must be taken that these groups do not become hotbeds for isolationism, for promoting a siege mentality, or encouraging an us-against-them attitude.

Differentiation. Individuals or groups will better understand themselves when they examine who they are and who they are not. This process helps to understand and appreciate one's uniqueness. Furthermore, this process of differentiation can foster clarification and understanding. It can develop those skills needed to see how individual differences can enhance, challenge, and enrich the larger community.

Integration. This cycle is both the means to and the end of a diverse and democratic culture. Individuals and organizational structures promote the skills, opportunities, and environment for attaining the integration of differences that succeed in achieving a common goal. Common goals need to be emphasized so that differences will be channeled properly. Differences will enrich a group rather than fractionalize it. This cycle must stress that integration, and not assimilation, is the goal for the American democratic society. Integration is, therefore, the inherent cultural methodology of how Americans best do their business.

With the above points as a backdrop, let us examine a living example of a company that is actively developing an environment which promotes diversity as good business. We will discover that several key concepts are focused upon:

1. Ongoing adoption of the philosophy of valuing diversity and encouraging greater employee differentiation.
2. Increasing the total work force's awareness of cultural differences and similarities.
3. Redefining relationships between individuals and groups.
4. Acknowledging the limitations of an assimilation strategy and the benefits of greater employee differentiation as the best way to achieve greater productivity.

5. Reducing gender and cultural bias in performance standards and organizational processes.
6. Cultivating collaborative alliances based on similarities and differences, individual and organizational needs, and the tried-and-tested, creative approaches.
7. Harnessing differences for improved productivity, enhanced customer relations, and increased profit.
8. Aligning organizational objectives and structures with the emerging realities of a diverse work force.

A number of corporations are involved in this process of working with diversity. I believe one of them, Motorola, is a fine example of a corporation that is on top of this learning curve. Despite its ups-and-downs over the years Motorola consistently has remained a financially successful organization. It has refused to just stay on the surface in dealing with the diversity question. This corporation is no longer satisfied with simply counting numbers and following the letter of the law. Instead, Motorola has plunged into the depths, analyzing the underlying attitudes and prejudices of workers. They have structured the organization, and "holding the space," as organizational psychologists say, for individuals and groups to change. Let us listen to the employees of Motorola tell their stories of how they made diversity a business issue.

Bobbi Gutman, one of Motorola's ten black vice presidents, explains what motivated Motorola to adopt its unique approach to corporate change: "At most companies I know of," she says, "the diversity issue is addressed by mid-level managers, who are generally women or minorities. It's treated as a human resources issue, but the function of HR is to advise and serve, and putting that function at the forefront of the diversity initiative is not the most effective approach.

"At Motorola it was the triumvirate of our chairman, our COO, and the senior executive vice president who decided we had to address the diversity issue. In the late 1980s they saw some basic trends and realized the importance of assessing what we needed to do to address them as well as the impact if we did not. We knew, for instance, that the black birth rate was four times the white birth rate in America, that the Latino birth rate was seven times the white rate. We knew women were leaving corporations. And the Labor Department was predicting a severe shortage of technically trained people in the United States.

235

"While we knew Motorola would continue to draw the best people, we knew that as these demographic changes became more apparent in the workplace, people of color and women would ask, 'Where are the people who look like me?'"

Formerly one of six female vice presidents at Motorola's Semiconductor Products Sector (SPS) in Advanced Custom Technologies and now vice president and general manager of the Derivative Technologies Division, Julie Shimer proves the point. "Two things are important to me as a woman who usually is at the [glass] ceiling because of my age and ambition: that the organization I am joining develops its women and that there are networking opportunities." Shimer has found both at Motorola, although both are relatively recent developments. She and the other five women vice presidents in the semiconductor division were promoted within the last two years.

To assure women an environment where they can discuss and support each other, the Women's Executive Forum of about fifty members at Motorola Semiconductor and an East Valley Women's Partnership in Phoenix were formed. The forum hosts Saturday morning brunches, where senior women invite junior associates. Shimer hosted monthly "diversity lunches" for her technical staff where "you have to invite someone who is not like yourself. The diversity cuts across educational, racial, gender, age, and functional lines."

Gutman says that back in 1989, "if we had to answer the question, 'Who here looks like me?' we would have lost out to our competitors, companies like Hewlett Packard and Digital. Our focus until 1989 was on compliance, not cultural change, because we were used to doing what was required by the government as government contractors. We hadn't looked at the diverse work force as a bottom-line-oriented issue."

Today Motorola has made diversity a business issue. They have made reaching parity—using 1990 U.S. Census data to measure availability percentages for professional and other positions at various organization levels—a workplace goal for the year 2000. "When we looked at other companies," Gutman says, "we found while everyone was doing training, no one was determining where participants in those training sessions were before the training and what impact the training was having on their attitudes and behaviors in the workplace."

As a result Motorola did not hire trainers to preach the gospel of diversity to the multitudes. Instead, the company decided to focus on its vice-presidential corps first. "We thought it was critical to have those who hired, fired, and transferred people become more diverse, because they would then drive diversity down through the organization with their words and deeds," says Gutman. "We said, 'Every year three women and three people of color will be named to the officer corps of Motorola.' At that time (1988-1989) we had two women and six people of color who were vice presidents. In September 1996 we had thirty-nine women VPs worldwide, of whom six were women of color. We had forty-one people of color who are U.S. based Vice Presidents in addition to others globally. There are over four hundred vice presidents in the company."

For a company to undertake an overall cultural movement to promote diversity, effective leadership must be constantly active and present. Effective leadership in a diverse and democratic organization has the following characteristics:

1. The leadership group concretely articulates a vision, recognizes the values, and models the behaviors that make diversity issues a way of life in the organization.

2. Managers continue to develop in themselves and those who report to them a wide knowledge, a heightened awareness, and the appropriate skills to effectively promote diversity issues.

3. The officers of the corporation maintain an ethical commitment that respects the uniqueness of individuals while working together for common goals; therefore, they will not tolerate discrimination of any kind.

4. Investing in others, directors remain open to suggestions and responses, especially regarding personal bias and blind spots.

5. Supervisors remain active in empowering and mentoring others, especially those who are different from them.

As an engineering company, Motorola had taught its leaders "if there's no metrics, there's no movement." To assess improvement, you have to measure it. But the company has not rested on reaching numerical goals. Across the organization, the effort to integrate women and people of color into all layers of management has taken different forms depending on the subcultures of the company's seven major business groups. As Gutman explains, "We've learned while it's important to tell managers 'what' is required of them (and up to 10 percent of executive staff's compensation is tied to reaching diversity goals), if you tell them 'how,' they take no ownership of the process. If you don't tell them the 'how,' you get the benefit of their own remarkable creativity."

Sometimes something as simple as a phrase can be the beginning of profound change. For Larry Gartin, a white, senior vice president and director of finance at Motorola's Semiconductor Products Sector, the expression was, "Equal treatment of unequal is not equality."

Gartin laughingly describes himself as a person who is so conservative he thinks all rights should be subordinate to property rights, "But, I'm a sucker for catchy lines, and when I heard this and realized giving people equal opportunity who are on an uneven level playing field won't work—you have to reach out and help a person who is disadvantaged—I began to change."

For Gartin's financial group the challenge was not as daunting as for others. "About 50 percent of graduating accounting majors are female," whereas in engineering, female graduates are less than 20 percent. With a qualified talent pool the only reason Gartin could think of for the lack of women in upper management was "the incorrect notion that women have to be more ready than men." "For years," he says, "my managers had said to themselves, 'Let's give [a woman candidate] four more experiences until she's ready.' We didn't want her to fail. But two years ago, we said, 'This is baloney.' Every one of us got put into a job that was way beyond our capabilities, and what made us grow is that every one of us had to over-reach and stretch ourselves."

Two men in Gartin's group devised a career-mapping exercise that Gartin now substitutes for the traditional performance evaluation. A "green zone" shows experience an individual has had. A "red zone" shows experience he or she needs to move to the next level or a lateral level. The experiences include education, training, and on-the-job positions. "It's a five-year road map that I used to track progress among high-potential, female, and minority staff," Gartin says; "but now our entire corporate finance group has adopted it." The mapping technique showed Gartin and his managers what a performance appraisal could not: where an individual stood in a career progression. It helped him track the progress of women and minorities in his group. It assisted all of the individuals who used it "see" where they were in their career progression and why. Patterns of progression emerged. "We realized after doing this mapping," says Gartin, "that it was a commonality among all of us in the group that we had a bachelor's degree in finance, for instance."

For Chuck Thompson, the now-retired, white male, former SPS's senior vice president and director of world marketing, the motivation for change that made sense was obvious: "More than half the customers we deal with are female and minorities; the purchasing profession is heavily dominated by women, and the number of women distributors we deal with has grown from 20 percent to 50 percent in recent years. I am going to lose if I don't have a population that relates to them."

Thompson used a marketing approach to set parity goals. He had breakfast meetings with 300 of his women employees in thirty or forty-person focus groups. He asked them "what changes they would make to make world marketing the finest place in the world for them to work. "To speed the process of creating such a workplace he decided to "overload at the front end" with people with different values from the dominant white male culture at Motorola. "I listed all the women within a grade or two of the levels that were short in my group and made sure they got the training and education they needed to be promoted," he says. Furthermore, he created the full-time, two-year position of a diversity director for his work force.

Tracie Hightower, a black woman and engineer working with Motorola's sales force in Detroit, was one of twenty-two volunteers from throughout the World Marketing Organization who met with Thompson to discuss diversity issues. The main topics the group focused upon were career development, mentorship, and personal/family concerns. As these issues unfolded, diversity concerns, it appeared, were broader than racial and gender differences. Diversity was applied to sexual orientation, parenting, and family styles—functional roles that included the entire gambit of human styles and interaction. "Diversity has to fall in line with the managers and be integrated in all the systems and practices," says Hightower who later became the diversity director for world marketing. Setting a goal for herself, she made a two-year commitment to spread awareness to the sector's sales offices around the country. Hightower says the process has taught her that everybody is not on the same level in their understanding of diversity issues. For her, diversity awareness and skill building have to be integrated with job performance.

Marygrace Ohab, who started as a production operator twenty-five years ago on the manufacturing floor, is the director of diversity for the Semiconductor Products Sector. Under her enthusiastic, insightful, dedicated, and many times behind-the-scenes leadership, the diversity process of change is emerging at the SPS facilities. This process involves individual and group training and skill building, leadership and organizational change. For Ohab diversity initiatives are successful when individual, group, and organizational aspects combine to support and reaffirm employees to focus on the bottom-line profit and success of the sector. Therefore, SPS's diversity training spotlights four areas:

- to provide concise, energetic, business-linked content
- to support team and individual development objectives
- to assure the culture, systems, behavior, and leadership are in place to ensure the business and personal success of *all* employees
- to develop "thirst" for awareness, skills, and overall change

The integral role of diversity in the organization is not a program, as SPS internal organizational consultant Diane McGraw says, "It's a process. The role of the HR department in today's world is one of empowering managers and their staffs to do a lot of the processing that was left to HR traditionally."

Brian Bedford, SPS senior vice president of Human Resources, describes the change in thinking: "Typically, what happens is the manager comes into the company's HR office with a problem and drops it gently on the desk. The HR manager then cleaves it to his breast and works on it until he can take a solution back, neatly gift-wrapped. The trouble with that approach is, when the same problem comes up again, the manager doesn't have a clue how to deal with it. We have been trying to change that process so the managers will use the HR staff as consultants and will take as much ownership of the solution as we do. The reason they will have the time to engage in this new process is technology. A lot of the routine managerial paperwork can be done by employees themselves."

The human resources group that is driving the process of change at the Semiconductor Products Sector isn't the legal or compliance arm of the company. Guiding this drive is the organization and management effectiveness arm, headed by white male vice president and director Richard Wintermantel. Wintermantel brought transformational rather than transactional leadership to the table from his years of experience with General Electric, which also has a strong program for cultural change.

Black vice president and director of advanced technologies for the Logic and Analog Technologies Group, W.T. Greer, says he is more involved than many managers in the diversity initiative because he is black.

"I mentor many of the young minorities," he says. "They want to know what's necessary to be successful in a large corporation. I realize employees are a corporate investment. If you spend money on a person and they leave the organization, you've lost your investment. We try to bridge the gap between minorities' cultural background and the culture at Motorola. After all, you're introducing these people to a strange environment. The socialization of that person will have an impact on his or her productivity. We've learned it's much easier to cross from one culture to another if you can walk on a bridge rather than a tightrope.

"The way to make it easier is to make both sides more aware of people's ethnic and racial differences, by teaching the majority some of the cultural differences of the minorities."

Greer believes both homogeneous and diverse groups are effective in this process. In homogeneous groups people can vent their feelings. "They can say exactly what they want to say in their own language. Not only that, instead of holding back, they're a lot more open. They hold back in a diverse group because they don't know how it will be perceived by the other side. [In homogeneous groups] they can get to the root of their problem. They have no inhibitions about talking about how they're being treated by other individuals or by the company. Sometimes the perceptions are wrong, but perception is reality to the person who's perceiving it."

In diverse groups people learn that reality is not just their perception of it. Information from different perspectives helps enlarge one's viewpoint and understanding of other positions. As white male vice president and director of final manufacturing operations at this group Robert Hill says, "the diverse approach is three-dimensional—individual, like-group, diverse-group—rather than linear."

Brian Bedford has been in the United States only three years after serving many years as director of human resources for the company in Europe. He admits "it has taken me a long time to come to grips with some of the diversity issues, because I've probably been overly simplistic. I was brought up to believe your differences are irrelevant. You relate to people the way they are and get on with it. When I was at university in Edinburgh, we had a diverse population of students, but Europeans don't look at diversity the way you do in America. I was talking about my experiences in a diverse group here at Motorola's Phoenix offices when a black employee in the group said to me, 'You may not be openly prejudiced, but you're prejudiced without knowing it, because you're prejudiced by definition. You're a white male.'"

Bedford agrees with the corporate approach that the way to attack inequities in hiring, firing, and promoting is to make those responsible for the bottom-line businesses accountable. "What we're talking about, after all, is a power shift, isn't it?" he says. "The very concept of parity numbers is a power shift. The management of the organization will shift by definition."

Power shifts do not come without blood, sweat, and tears. This organic and visceral level of change, as Marygrace Ohab describes it, works across all five business groups in the Semiconductor Products Sector. She likes to use a gardening metaphor to describe the work: "We're churning the ground, planting the seeds at the grassroots in parallel to the work at the upper and mid-levels of management." This process is not always a gentle activity; often it feels very painful. As Ohab says, "You're working at the roots of the organization, allowing all the anger and frustration to come out, but you're putting a process around that [venting]. Change is a process, and if we don't put the new roots in place, it's not going to happen. . . and when the growth occurs, you need a lot of gardeners."

Working at the roots of change is a long, painstaking process. Ohab describes the strategy that evolved at SPS: "For years we had been very traditional in our approach with the emphasis on EEO and affirmative action compliance. We basically approached it from a 'numbers' perspective. We hired and trained women and people of color and then they left, because there was nothing for them here. The culture wasn't ready to receive them, because it was still very traditional."

Jim Norling, formerly president of the Semiconductor Products Sector in the early years of the sector's diversity initiatives and now president of Motorola in Europe, the Middle East, and Africa is considered a diversity champion at the company. To underline his concern for diversity, Norling noted in a letter to his staff in 1990: "In the past we have expected 'newcomers' to adapt to the existing workplace culture. As our employees and our customers become increasingly diverse, this 'adaptation' process no longer makes good business sense. Across the U.S., progressive companies are . . . changing values and behaviors to acknowledge that employees (and customers) have different perspectives and achieve results in a variety of ways."

"When I was asked to manage the diversity initiative in 1988," Mary-grace Ohab says, "I was concerned about the whole aspect of change and how to involve people to implement change. The person who preceded me in my new job had just put together a team of high-potential white men, women, and people of color to address the issues, and when he handed me the keys to his office, he said, 'these twenty people are barely speaking to each other anymore.' When I spoke to these team members one-on-one, I realized they felt they were put on the team to improve the "numbers." The numbers had always been a source of frustration and our employees were coming to conclusions based on their functional, gender, and racial differences. The white males were saying that they didn't want to take a stereotypical role, so they wouldn't talk. The women were basically not speaking to each other because they had vast differences of opinions on addressing "being women" in the workplace; the people of color felt that the work would go nowhere and only had the potential for more frustration.

"We started looking at our task and decided that what we really wanted was for people to thrive, to be able to reach their potential and be appreciated for their different contributions to the company. So we looked at how that company culture would feel if we operated out of diverse perspectives rather than the way it worked now. It looked a lot different from just moving the numbers around. We began looking at the process of change, so, over time, there would be a sense that we could support each other's success."

The diversity teams facilitated dialogues with 600 people in focus groups assembled to analyze commonalities of issues that crossed gender and racial boundaries. Each session brought together people from a specific group, i.e. black males, Hispanic females, white males. "It was the first time we gave people permission to be who they were," says Ohab. There were a number of commonalities around career development, mentoring, and work-family issues. Surprisingly, the men were much more willing to bring up these issues than the women. Women were afraid of being stereotyped around certain issues. People were concerned about being excluded from information, about bias, about not knowing how to create support systems.

A scribe at every session pulled the data together. Ohab convened a mini-group again to look at the data in terms of the commonalities by cultural and gender groupings. She gave group generic statements that could be made by anyone. Ohab also gave the group statements about certain issues that would be affected by race or gender. "This was to accelerate their thinking," she says. "Then we expanded that process. We called the original 600 people back into small sessions, but now in mixed groupings and let them see the data before we presented it to anyone else in the company. That laid the groundwork for respect for people, for their feelings, and their contributions to the process." From this data, the diversity team came up with four guiding principles:

1. The process of change would involve everyone, not just women and people of color. White males would be as indispensable to change as the others, because the whole would never be healthy unless all the parts could be integrated. Unless white males transformed their perceptions of what it means to be in the power positions in the culture, the workplace would not change. "When I benchmarked about seventy companies around the country, I found that US West was the only company talking about white males as a significant part of the process. Dr. Ipsaro had created this perceptive initiative for them, and now for us." If white men were not actively removing themselves from the process, they were covertly "backlashing" the diversity emphasis on women and minorities in the workplace.

2. All people would be given the opportunity to influence the change. The strategy was to throw "experiences" in front of people. Some will trip; some will try. Others might say: "Put it on the back burner for a while." While acknowledging these hesitations, SPS established a group of "diversity activity champions" to integrate diversity concepts and dialogue with different task force groups.

3. Change was a process, and it would unfold. "We wouldn't go out and mandate that everyone be doing it in a certain way."

4. Change would be accomplished from the perspective of leading and learning. In other words, the boundaries between managers and workers would come down. All would be partners in the process.

"Some of the managers had the language, but they were still in the tell-sell phase," says Ohab. In 1994, to move the issue forward, Tommy George, then President of SPS, had a discussion with the Executive Women's Forum. Prompted by this meeting, he, his Vice President, Murray Goldman, and seventy-five of the most senior leaders in the Sector—white men, women and ethnic minorities from around the globe— came together for one and a half days to see what this new culture would look like. Later that year, another pivotal experience occurred. The Black Leadership Conference was a driving force in the formation of a sector-wide Multicultural Board for African-American achievement.

This awareness process happened first at the sector-wide level then moved to the Group and Division levels. Different manufacturing organizations now have incorporated a similar change process. Ohab says the focus group process takes one or two months. With the result of this process, the groups take the data and create plans and strategies around their findings. One such organization, lead by Jerry Walton, a white male Vice President of Sector Materials Operations, is doing pioneering work in this area.

From such information you can learn who is promoted and whether people are being pulled from the pipeline or from outside the organization. You can learn how the local, regional, and national community perceives your company's hiring and retention of people different from the majority culture.

"What we're seeing," says Ohab, "is we've looked at this as a change process and allowed it to unfold. Different people have different roles to play as we create the process. If you're the president or a VP, that's one leadership role; if you're professional staff, that's a different set of strategies; if you're in manufacturing operations, there's a different set of responsibilities. Regardless of your functional background we are all responsible to be part of the change. Once you know what the issues are, you can begin to see what things you can do to make shifts in the culture, in the system, in behavior. You begin to see what sponsorship and leadership look like."

What Motorola saw was that the diversity process focused as much on planned implementation as on deliberate training. This implementation translated into small group dialogues with people of difference attending events where they experienced being in the minority. Then came a surprise. "People started to experience other dimensions of themselves that they hadn't experienced before, the men especially," says Ohab. Many men were surprised to discover that you could make the work less tiring and more productive once you knew how to work with people with different talents. The adage "Work smarter, not harder or longer!" became understood.

Motorola is exceptional in that it has dedicated staff, time, and money to this long-term endeavor. For Motorola diversity is not an added organizational concern but a basic business issue involving employees' productivity and customer effectiveness. Motorola mandates that all employees spend forty hours each year updating their technical, managerial, and human resource skills. Diversity issues are included. Many departments mandate diversity training. Carole Rabin, a member of Ohab's diversity staff, has developed a diversity curriculum of over twenty offerings that would give every employee an awareness, an understanding, and the skills to participate in the company's endeavors to make diversity a major factor in the success of the company.

Motorola brings in outside consultants to assist in particular parts of the process. I was brought in, for example, to help address the feelings and responses of white males—as well as others—to the parity goals, affirmative action, and power shifts. More important, my presentations offered an intellectual schema, showing that diversity was not simply an issue for women and minorities but for white males as well. Work force diversity was not simply a business issue but was embedded in the American culture and the very life of this nation. Understanding and learning how to use aspects of diversity is not only good business at home but internationally.

The seminars I offered were attended by women and people of color as well as white men. The women needed to hear from a male that their perceptions about the men weren't "crazy." Many of the people of color who attended had felt, but never analyzed with a white male, the white male power structure.

Once individuals and groups grew in awareness, skill building, and preliminary organizational initiatives, they asked Ohab, "What's the next step?" The next step, she noted, was determining what role individuals would play, how they would do whatever they decided to do, when they would do it, and what outcome they expected from their new awareness. A map of implementation and evaluation was drawn up.

"The next two or three years," says Ohab, "they would take steps forward, then backward. People started to question the process. They wondered, 'Shouldn't we just promote people and be done with it?' You don't see the results from a process such as ours quickly."

When one black male was feeling isolated in his group several years ago, he took Ohab's advice and asked his white male supervisor to accompany him to a Martin Luther King Day celebration in Phoenix. The manager said "no." He didn't think he'd feel comfortable there. Ohab got on the phone and explained the impact of his "no" on the employee. The manager attended the event. The next year 300 Motorola people attended the Martin Luther King Day commemoration, and the year after that 600 people participated.

"This is how change happens, by crossing boundaries and taking risks," says Ohab. She eventually hired Vernetta Daniely, a systems analyst, to put an infrastructure in place that would champion the cause of diversity. Through the diversity champion process a calendar of multicultural events was established. Employees were encouraged to attend at least one a year. Hundreds of Motorolans now attend multicultural conferences, presentations, and meetings in the community. Ohab notes: "The champions of diversity are all the employees from all cultural, gender, and functional backgrounds who have developed their skills of leadership and influence the community by their behaviors." Explains Cynthia Wright-Brown, Senior Administrator: "This has given me an opportunity for expanded mentoring and contact with role models, such as Maya Angelou, or Dr. William Gray, head of the United Negro College Fund."

Issues to be addressed by Motorola in the future are diverse leadership styles, peer diversity interaction, mentoring and employee development, and effective teams of diverse styles. The team training that is going on at most corporations today has a lot to do with empowerment, an overused term but a good one: giving the employees greater freedom to work within given parameters. At Motorola empowerment is being implemented at its deepest root, letting employees determine from a diversity of styles which to chose in order to accomplish agreed-upon goals.

When British-born Gavin Woods, an operation's manager at SPS's MOS 21, looked into self-directed teams at other companies, he found disasters everywhere. "In the average application process everyone goes through a big training process and then they have a celebration and say, 'we're empowered.' We found that the relationship between a first-line supervisor and an operator on the factory floor was one of discipline. Until we eliminated that, we couldn't talk about empowerment. Instead of disciplining for mistakes, we learned how to build off them. The role that's most affected in the factory is the supervisor's because it changes so radically. Because they're so threatened, supervisors begin to sabotage the effort to make changes, whether consciously or unconsciously." Motorola found the same was true for middle managers.

"We started a process with the leaders of our work teams, talking about what it meant to change, thereby empowering the leadership," says Woods. "They had to begin to view themselves as coaches and mentors, as resources for the team—in a support role. I saw that people in other companies were dictating the empowerment process. We had our leaders plan their own pilot programs with their teams. The process is coming out of the people making the change."

To help guide the change process on the factory floor, Woods hired a team builder, Celina Saldana. "She's part consultant, part counselor, part teacher," he explains. "Her approach is focused on the people, while I focus on the business aspect."

Woods is a firm believer that you cannot separate the people issues from the business issues, although different people often have to focus on different issues. "I could shut down the entire plant by circulating one rumor," he laughs. "In the factory we measure activity, but our people produce our activity. I think roles have to be tailored around people, not the other way around. If we don't change the systems operating in the factory, then we don't empower the people. The systems have to support the change or the change process will derail."

This is radical thinking, especially at an engineering organization, where people are traditionally seen as functions plugged into the process or treated as cogs in the great, running machine. The systems Woods is speaking of are often invisible. These systems are the hidden boundaries, the underlying foundations that separate one team from another in the work process. These systems train workers to understand that different people of different backgrounds have different and many times more creative and innovative ways of achieving a goal. Being comfortable with differences and ambiguity, expressing mutual trust and understanding, benefiting from effective styles and efficient methods become the fuel with which the successful team operates.

With these understandings, work teams are better able to cross over to other teams, to learn multiple tasks so they can "cover" for others and help in other areas when their areas are slow. Workers become more at ease when stepping into new jobs, entering new situations, interacting with new environments, and learning from new cultures. The change process does not happen, not because people do not know intellectually what to do, but because they do not have the skills to work through the emotional uneasiness resulting from the new and the unknown. This emotional "loss" and "fear of the unknown," is what keeps most individuals and organizations from changing.

What we have seen in the Motorola experience is a company that zeroed-in on key elements that would achieve a high-performing, world class, and truly diverse organization.

Marygrace Ohab wondered out loud recently: "We had just received the Baldrige Award for quality production when we launched our diversity initiatives. How do you have quality products if you don't have quality of relationship with one another no matter how different we are?"

The success of Motorola's diversity initiatives is the result of strong corporate leadership, effective employee involvement, and efficient organizational structures and procedures. These efforts to make diversity inherent with bottom-line profit and business success are a tribute to the *people* of Motorola. Their courage, tenacity, and willingness to risk responsibly is benefiting them. Motorolans are an inspiration and an example to all businesses.

WORKSHOP

1. What present structures in your organization can you build upon to heighten the awareness of diversity as a business issue?

2. Who are those significant people who are essential in developing and implementing a process to promote diversity issues among the individual workers and in the organizational structures?

3. What efforts have you made to bring the white male into the movement of change within the workplace and the culture?

*There are no elements so diverse
that they cannot be joined
in the heart of a man.*
–Jean Giradoux
Siegfried

CONCLUSION

The work force is a human organism and also a structural entity. The workplace is a blend of group norms and individual needs; one aspect gives strength and power to the other. Rules and regulations govern the group as that unit works towards achieving a goal or a product. Individuals in that group need an ongoing, essential process of communication and persuasion to achieve the group's common goals. Reinvention of the work force, then, will be a unique intertwining of group and individual, of objects and people, of product and process.

Workplace is not an isolated entity. It includes the country's history, present experiences, and future plans. As part of this nation's culture, it influences and is influenced by that culture. To reinvent or change the workplace is to call into question other institutions of our society that have conditioned both employees who create the product or service and customers who buy that product or service.

With the beginning of a new millennium, the American workplace is at a critical junction. Over the past sixty years, because of available schooling, abundance of information and technology, television and communications, and easy travel at home and abroad, women and minority groups want greater access to the wealth and power of this democratic country. In the workplace, women and minorities want the training, opportunities, and jobs that will give them access to the economic wealth and power that has long been easier for white males to obtain.

In 1997, about 70 percent of Americans are white. That proportion is changing steadily. Although the population zones around the country vary markedly, some demographers predict that by the year 2050 Hispanics will be the largest ethnic group in a society with no majority population. The result of this shifting population is that Hispanics, Blacks, Asians, women—persons who had no role in the management of American corporations in 1940—are in the door and on the ground floor of American business today.

In a historical era quite different from today, white males inherited power positions. Now, white males find themselves interfacing with a world that is dramatically changing in population and being significantly impacted by technology. In the past, men obtained societal wealth and power because of their physical strength so necessary for the resource producing and the resource protecting of that time. Every family wanted male children to provide for them and to protect their wealth.

With the coming of the computer age, industrial societies around the world awoke to the fact that intelligence, not physical strength, was the essential ingredient needed to obtain wealth, power, and position in society. Without many of us being aware of it, the technological advances have propelled societies into a future where our present identities, roles, cultural norms, institutional positions, and individual behaviors are becoming obsolete. Basic human values remain unchanged over time. The behavioral expression of those values needs continual updating to fit the evolving knowledge and experience of today's world. Today's workers are analytic and intuitive, educated and skilled people. They are committed to making their companies work successfully so they may gain rewards and satisfaction. New information and communications technology give us the capacity to work differently and, therefore, to think differently about work. This brave new world cries out for leaders who can adapt to new cultural realities. It is a brave new business world that cries out for leaders who can work alongside their employees, sharing with them, learning from them, and serving their needs.

In one sense the diversity movement has come of age in this climate of imperative change. If any institution in our society, including the workplace, is to reap the benefits of this regeneration of the American democratic culture, the diversity of populations, styles, and talents must be conceptually embraced as a fundamental principle of action. We are in an era of fast-moving, pace-setting, constantly explosive innovated services and products. Worldwide customers of many different backgrounds are looking to satisfy a variety of needs. Continuing business success necessitates the creative dynamism that results from employees' diversity of talents, styles, views, and options.

To live in an environment that is constantly changing, to benefit from the blend of numerous differences will be neither comfortable nor easy. To profit from change, we must examine the old comfortable ways and take from them the parts that still are beneficial. Further, we need to reflect on new ways to see, implement, and evaluate procedures that may be better. What is fundamental and unique about this process is that the individual, group, company, and society must welcome, work with, reflect upon, process through, and embrace a world of paradoxes, a world of differences.

Charles Handy has called our time *The Age of Paradox*. I understand why. The roles of men and women, the interacting of different cultures, the role of institutions, and the structures of the workplace are all in a state of confusion. We are being asked to be tough enough for global competition. Yet we are asked to be gentle enough to work together in harmony with diverse peoples who gather in the workplace for a common goal. Our society has always applauded individualism. We now are being asked to pull together in cohesive groups or teams that are part of the American workplace.

We are encouraging corporations to be lean and mean. Corporations should be able to move and change as swiftly as a well-run military unit or a gifted sports team. War and sports imagery has pervaded the successful male workplace in the past. Today, we are hearing a different idiom that speaks more about collaboration rather than competition, inclusion rather than exclusion.

The very notion of power is being transformed and redefined to fit the new realities of a global, culturally different marketplace. Power must no longer be a personal prize. Power belongs to all. It must enhance a multicultural work force and self-directed work teams. This new definition of power will cause shifting of leadership roles for all workers especially executives, managers, and supervisors.

Historically, white males defined power in the workplace. Power was individualistic, competitive, object-oriented, and quantitative. No longer. The exigencies of our times shape the new American work force. Success is the result of collaboration in groups and on teams. To achieve successful goals that will profit all people, individuals are challenged to reconcile differences. We are called to heal the fragmentation.

Today's work force is challenged by a competitive international market that seeks no more than 3.44 defective parts per million units of production. This global market wants instantaneous response to market pressures. Customers demand satisfaction based on what they want and not on what the companies decide to give. This business world sees change and innovation as an everyday occurrence.

Many of the management fads and ideas of the previous decade have already run their course. While focusing on the structural aspect of the corporation, these organizational endeavors have ignored the human element of the workplace—its people. We once thought that the formulation of the right guidelines, formulas, structures, and programs were the essential elements of a successful business. The human complement, although always having been present, is quite new and different for many workplace leaders. They were brought up in a world where fairness meant to treat all people by the very same standard or rule. That rule guaranteed absolute order. That order became more important than the person. The person became simply one object in the plan for the "perfect order" that would ensure a successful organization.

Most of the American work force has been predominantly white and male. These men were raised in similar institutions with similar aspirations. They operated with a sense of the "same rules" for everyone. With all this harmony in the workplace, greater order allowed greater focus on company goals. The results were very successful companies and a prosperous American economy. In reality, this theory of homogeneity, which had made Japan so successful in the recent past, was basic to the American workplace fifty years ago.

Because of greater access to schooling, information, and the advantages of technology, the international world and the American world truly have changed. Many of the white males in 90 percent of upper management positions—holding the power, making the rules—seem to be living in utter denial about these realities. Many white men are finding that their sacred male behaviors are now being dismissed, attacked, or denied. They are accused of being valueless, un-American, self-centered, and greedy. Yet they have given their lives to making America one of the most prosperous nations in today's world. They even have given up their lives physically and emotionally so that others may enjoy that prosperity. For the first time, American white males face a paradox that is confusing and threatening.

In this new and evolving world, other paradoxes confuse the white male. Once clear and distinct boundaries are now vague and equivocal. Work roles around product and process, objects and people, now are overlapping. Distinctions between life at home and life at work are not so discrete. Gender roles of men and women are less defined.

Within the workplace, males historically have found the fulfillment of manhood. Paradoxically, white males who have called the workplace home now are called upon to open their homes to women and minorities. White men are asked to use their heritage and power as a central force to benefit the community—women and minorities.

Clearly the workplace has become the center in American society where all these paradoxes meet. All the issues of our society—economical, political, social, educational, ethical, philosophical, spiritual—come together in the workplace. Since the workplace is at the heart of the economy and, therefore, has a major responsibility for the survival of this country, it has become a chief agent for cultural change.

Formerly, religion was the chief change agent for a society and the stabilizer of the culture. Failing to recognize an educated, technological, and more democratic society, most organized religions have lost the power to lead. The corporation has filled in the vacuum of societal leadership vacated by religion. The mission of most religions is to inspire, support, and assist different people to live together in harmony for the common good as part of achieving a supernatural goal. The goal of workplace diversity initiatives is to educate and persuade all these different workers to collaborate in producing a profitable product or service so that employees and customers can benefit—a humanistic goal.

More and more one hears religious terms in the workplace. Books like *For Love and Profit* by Jim Autry teach about the "covenant" that companies can create with their workers. The whole basis of the work of Stephen Covey, of Mormon heritage, is based on values which one could call religious. Religious words and concepts like mission, dedication, commitment, and ritual abound.

Spirituality is the main component of religion. An example of a spiritual tenet in most religious traditions is: Love your neighbor as yourself. These spiritual tenets are values—love, faith, honor, hope, respect—that are central to humankind, to the institution of religion. Organized religion should be an interactive system that describes, clarifies, supports, and challenges individuals to live out in a community those spiritual values. Spiritual values are expressed through the use of rules and regulations, rituals and ceremonies, rewards and punishments. Thus people can be spiritual (living a life based upon certain values and practices) without being a part of a religious community (benefiting from others in a religious organization). People can be religious (following all the rules and regulations of a religious organization) without being spiritual (grounding one's life in spiritual values). Ideally, one strives to live out the paradoxes of individual spirituality within a community of religious forms in a congruent, cohesive, and mutually supportive manner.

Unintentionally, then, spirituality has come into society, into the workplace, and into the white male's system. Spirituality is that side of a culture which seeks to move beyond the immediate concrete fact and moment, beyond technology and innovation. Spirituality is that dimension which gives new and deeper meaning to what we do and what we have. Spirituality speaks to *who we are*. It completes the puzzle of what this world means. Spirituality is a world of people, of relationships, of process. This precisely is the world that most men and women unknowingly are seeking. Men, especially, need a sense of purpose for their lives as the new resource producers, resource protectors, resource directors. They need a purpose for living. They need a purpose for being. They need a soul!

One needs to enter the realm of the spiritual. The lives of people always have gained clarity and meaning when spiritual concepts were part of their heritage. A belief system acknowledges that there are powers beyond one's own intelligence, present understandings, and human control. Based on these belief systems many cultures have made sense of and gained strength from the sometimes monotonous routine of life and the unexplainable happenings that can occur.

Today's workplace is a very insecure environment—as is our entire society. Spirituality will give men—and women—the bedrock, the center, the stability and the focus for such a changing environment. Material things, power positions, celebrity status come and go. Spirituality matters. Relationships, connections with those important to us, remain. Could it be that this new millennium belongs not to technology but to spirituality?

Today's American society, especially its workplace, is positioned to achieve the balance between a relational world and an object world. The diversity of people cannot become effective unless we learn how to understand, respect, interact, and collaborate with each other for the common goals of productivity, prosperity, and true success. To do this is to be in relation to the other. This relational model speaks to the people who are making the product or providing the service. It speaks to the people who are buying that product or service.

Women and many minorities, who in their cultures and traditions have prized relationships, have that key element necessary for today's successful business. That they would be entering the work force now, that the American democratic culture is focused on the diverse nature of its people, is a strange coincidence. The relational gift that women and minorities offer men, white men in particular, is this world of relationships. It is a world that challenges and complements the male world of objects, organization, rules, and regulations. In the balancing of these two worlds each world will profit.

To enter this world of relationships, however, is to enter the complex world of paradoxes and differences. No two people are alike as two objects might be the same. You cannot treat two different people as you would two similar physics problems that might be solved with the same formula. To give up the order and control that comes from applying one rule, one formula, or one law requires a reevaluation of what it means to be "powerful."

To become truly powerful, one must start by renouncing the old methods that brought about domination and subordination. This renunciation will provide the space in which new formulas can be practiced.

The realm of relationships and spiritual tenets brings the individual to the core of being human—the soul. At this center one finds the answers to restlessness, boredom, disconnection, lack of meaning, and emptiness. At this pivotal point all men and women will find the peace they so desperately seek.

As we enter the twenty-first century, we are at a crossroads where men and women need to share the benefits of their roles. I am not asking men to become women, nor women to become men. What I am asking is that men learn relational skills from women; women learn skills for greater productivity from men. In this process men and women will better come to their own fullness as human beings. Human fulfillment is achieved through the integration of work and relationships, the integration of doing and being, and the integration of the human with the spiritual.

During the start of this nation, the federalists had the model of the Great Binding Law of the Iroquois Confederacy in front of them. As their heirs, we have the persisting complexities and rich possibilities of a diverse and democratic society confronting us. We are challenged to continue to live out the motto of their legacy: *E pluribus unum*. We approach the year 2000 having before us an evolving model of how to integrate so many differences and so many paradoxes into a meaningful pattern that will be fruitful for all Americans.

This bold new world that is unfolding will become the renaissance of the American economic system. It will offer all citizens a better environment in which to share and to receive. This bold new world calls for Americans to truly integrate the strengths and heal the weaknesses of white and black, female and male, homosexual and heterosexual, Asian and European, African and Latin American. Together we need to recommit ourselves to a renewed vision of this nation's democratic ideals. While profiting from our heritage, let us recognize that the time has now come for an end to the old world ways.

The year 2000 is upon us. A new world beckons. This new world clearly holds out for all of us new hopes, new beginnings, new challenges, new opportunities, and a new quality of life. Diversity is the central force! *E pluribus unum* is the rallying cry!

SELECTED BIBLIOGRAPHY

BOOKS

Aburdene, P., & Naisbitt, J. 1992. *Megatrends for women*. New York: Villard Books.

Adams, S. 1996. *The Dilbert Principle: A cubicle's—eye view of bosses, meetings, management, fads & other workplace afflictions*. New York: Harper Collins Publishers, Inc.

Adams, W. 1986. *The bigness complex*. New York: Pantheon Books.

Adler, N.J. 1986. *International dimensions of organizational behavior*. Boston: Kent Publishing.

Anfer, F.H., & Goldstein, A.P., eds. 1986. *Helping people change: A textbook of methods* (3rd ed.). New York: Pergamon Press.

Astrachan, A. 1988. *How men feel: Their response to women's demands for equality and power*. New York: Anchor NY.

Autry, J. A. 1991. *Love and profit: The art of caring leadership*. New York: Morrow Press.

Barnett, R., et al., eds. 1987. *Gender and stress*. New York: Free Press.

Barry, D. 1987. *Claw your way to the top*. Emmaus, PA: Rodale Press.

Baumli, F. 1985. *Men freeing men: Exploding the myth of the traditional male*. Jersey City, NJ: New Atlantis Press.

Block, P. 1993. *Stewardship*. San Francisco, CA: Berrett-Koehler.

Blotnick, S. 1984. *Corporate steeple chase*. New York: Viking Penguin.

Blotnick, S. 1988. *Ambitious men: Their drives, dreams, and delusions*. New York: Viking Penguin.

Bly, R. 1990. *Iron John*. Reading, MA: Addison-Wesley Publishing.

Boyett, J.H., & Conn, H.P. 1991. *Workplace 2000: The revolution reshaping American business*. New York: NAL-Dutton.

Brod, H. 1987. *The making of masculinities: The new men's studies*. New York: Routledge Chapman and Hall.

Carrigan, T., Connell, B., & Lee, J. 1987. Hard and heavy: Toward a new sociology of masculinity. *Beyond patriarchy: Essays by men on pleasure, power, and change*, edited by M. Kaufman. New York: Oxford University Press.

Carter, S., & Sokol, J. 1988. *Men who can't love*. New York: Berkley Publishing Group.

Champy, J. 1995. *Reengineering management: The mandate for new leadership.* New York: Harper Business.

Cohen, S.S. 1990. *Tender power*. Redding, MA: Addison-Wesley.

Connell, R.W. 1995. *Masculinities*. Berkeley, CA: University of California Press.

Cose, E. 1993. *Rage of the privileged*. New York: HarperCollins Publishers, Inc.

_____. 1996. *Color-blind*. New York: HarperCollins Publishers, Inc.

Covey, S.R. 1989. *The seven habits of highly effective people: Restoring the character ethic*. New York: Simon and Schuster.

Deep, S. 1990. *Smart moves*. Redding, MA: Addison-Wesley.

De Klerk, V. 1997. The role of expletives in the construction of masculinity. *Language and masculinity*, edited by S. Johnson and V.H. Meinhof. Cambridge, MA: Blackwell Publishers Ltd., 144–158.

Deutschendorf, H. 1996. *Of work and men*. Minneapolis: Fairview Press.

Doyle, J.A. 1989. *The male experience* (2nd ed.). Madison, WI: Brown and Benchmark.

Doyle, J.A., & Paludi, M.A. 1994. *Sex and gender* (3rd ed.). Madison, WI: Brown and Benchmark.

Drucker, P. 1959. *Landmarks of tomorrow*. New York: Harper & Row.

Dyson, M.E. 1996. *Race rules: Navigating the color line*. Reading Massachusetts: Addison-Wesley Publishing Company, Inc.

Ehrenreich, B. 1984. *Hearts of men: American dreams and the flight from commitment*. New York: Anchor NY.

Eichenbaum, L., & Orbach, S. 1987. *What do women want: Exploding the myth of dependency*. New York: Berkley Publishing Group.

Eisler, R. 1987. *The chalice and the blade: Our history, our future*. New York: Harper & Row.

Ellis, J.E. 1997. *America sphinx: The character of Thomas Jefferson*. New York: Alfred A. Knopf.

Farrell, W. 1988. *Why men are the way they are: The male-female dynamic*. New York: Berkley Publishing Group.

_____. 1993. *The myth of male power: Why men are the disposable sex*. New York: Simon & Schuster.

Fasteau, M.F. 1976. *The male machine*. New York: Dell.

Fausto-Sterling, A. 1992. *Myths of gender: Biological theories about women and men*. New York: Basic Books.

Fine, R. 1987. *The forgotten man: Understanding the male psyche.* Binghamton, New York: Haworth Press.

Fogel, G., Lane, F., & Liebert, R., eds. 1986. *The psychology of men.* New York: Basic Books.

Ford, H. 1922. *My life and work.* Garden City, NY: Doubleday, Page & Co.

Foster, H.L. 1986. *Ribbon', jivin', and playin' the dozen.* Cambridge, MA: Ballinger Publishing Company.

Franklin, C. 1988. *Men and society.* Chicago: Nelson Hall.

Franklin, C.W. 1984. *The changing definition of masculinity.* New York: Plenum Press.

Freire, P. 1982. *Pedagogy of the oppressed.* New York: Continuum Publishing.

Freud, S. 1931. *The interpretation of dreams.* New York: Carlton House.

Gaylin, W. 1992. *The male ego.* New York: Viking Penguin.

Gerson, K. 1994. *No man's land.* New York: Bantam Books.

Gerzon, M. 1992. *Choice of heroes: The changing face of American manhood.* Boston: Houghton Mifflin.

Gilbert, L., et al. 1985. *Men in dual career families: Present realities and future prospects.* Hillsdale, NJ: Lawrence Erlbaum Associates.

Gilligan, C. 1982. *In a different voice: Psychological theory and women's development.* Salt Lake City: HUP.

Gilmore, D.D. 1990. *Manhood in the making: Cultural concepts of masculinity.* New Haven: Yale University Press.

Goldberg, H. 1977. *The hazards of being male: Surviving the myth of masculine privilege.* New York: NAL-Dutton.

Graham, L. 1996. *Proversity.* New York: John Wiley & Son.

Gray, J. 1993. *Men are from Mars, women are from Venus: A practical guide for improving communication and getting what you want in your relationships.* New York: Harper Collins.

———. 1994. *What you feel, you can heal: A guide for enriching relationships.* Mill Valley, CA: Heart Publishing.

Grossman, H.Y., & Chester, N.L. 1990. *The experience and meaning of work in women's lives.* Hillsdale, NJ: L. Erlbaum Associates.

Gutek, B.A. 1985. *Sex and the workplace: The impact of sexual behavior and harassment on women, men, and organizations.* San Francisco: Jossey-Bass.

Hall, E.T. 1973. *The silent language.* New York: Anchor Books.

Halper, J. 1988. *Quiet desperation: The truth about successful men.* New York: Warner Books.

Handy, C.B. 1994. *Age of paradox*. Boston, MA: Harvard Business School Press.

Hammer, M., & Champy, J. 1993. *Reengineering the corporation*. New York: Harper Business.

Harragan, B.L. 1977. *Games mother never taught you: Corporate gamesmanship for women*. New York: Rawson Association.

Harrocks, R. 1994. *Masculinity in crisis: Myths, fantasies and realities*. New York: St Martin's Press.

Helgesen, S. 1990. *The female advantage: Women's ways of leadership*. New York: Doubleday.

Herdt, G. 1994. *Third sex, third gender: Beyond sexual dimorphism in culture and history*. New York: Zone Books.

Herrnstein, R.J., & Murray, C. 1994. *The bell curve: Intelligence and class structure in American life*. New York: Free Press.

Highman, E. 1985. *The organization woman: Building a career—an inside report survey by Arthur Highman*. New York: Hilman Sciences Press.

Hite, S. 1987. *The Hite report: A study of male sexuality*. New York: Alfred A. Knopf.

Hopcke, R. H. 1990. *Men's dreams, men's healing*. Boston: Shambala.

Hopkins, K.R., et al. 1988. *Opportunity 2000: Creative affirmative action strategies for a changing workforce*. Washington, DC: USGPO.

Horowitz, G., & Kaufman, M. 1987. Male sexuality: Toward a theory of liberation. *Beyond patriarchy: Essays by men on pleasure, power, and change*, edited by M. Kaufman. New York: Oxford University Press.

Iacocca, L.A., with Novak, W. 1984. *Iacocca: an autobiography*. New York: Bantam Books.

Jampolsky, G. & Jampolsky, L. 1996. *Listen to me: A book for women and men about father - son relationships*. Berkeley, CA: Celestine Arts.

Johnson, R.A. 1989. *He: Understanding masculine psychology*. New York: Harper Collins.

Johnson, S. 1997. Theorizing language and masculinity: A feminist perspective. *Language and masculinity*, edited by S. Johnson and V.H. Meinhof. Cambridge, MA: Blackwell Publishers Ltd., 8–26.

Jourard, S.M. 1971. *The transparent self: Self-disclosure and well-being* (2nd ed.). New York: Van Nostrand Reinhold.

Jung, C.S. 1964. *Man and his symbols*. New York: Dell Publishing Co.

Kanfer, F.H., & Goldstein, A.P. 1985. *Helping people change: A textbook of methods* (3rd ed.). New York: Elsevier.

Kanter, R.M. 1977. *Men and women of the corporation*. New York: Basic Books.

Kaufman, M., ed. 1987. *Beyond patriarchy: Essays by men on pleasure, power, and change*. New York: Oxford University Press.

Keen, S. 1991. *Fire in the belly: On being a man*. New York: Bantam Books.

Kelly, K., ed. 1987. *Females, males, and sexuality: Theories and research*. Albany: State University of New York.

Kidd, B. 1987. Sports and masculinity. *Beyond patriarchy: Essays by men on pleasure, power, and change*, edited by M. Kaufman. New York: Oxford University Press.

Kiesling, S.F. 1997. Power and the language of men. *Language and masculinity*, edited by U.H. Meinhof. Cambridge, MA: Blackwell Publishers Ltd, 65-85.

Kimbrell, A. 1995. *The masculine mystique: The politics of masculinity*. New York: Ballentine Books.

Kimmel, M.S. 1987. *Changing men: New directions in research on men and masculinity*. Newbury Park, CA: Sage Publications.

_____. 1987. The cult of masculinity: American social character and the legacy of the cowboy. *Beyond patriarchy: Essays by men on pleasure, power, and change*, edited by M. Kaufman. New York: Oxford University Press.

_____. 1996. *Manhood in America: A cultural history*. New York: The Free Press.

Kipnis, A. 1991. *Knights without armor: A practical guide for men in quest of masculine soul*. Los Angeles: Jeremy P. Tarcher.

Kleinberg, S. 1987. The new masculinity of gay men and beyond. *Beyond patriarchy: Essays by men on pleasure, power, and change*, edited by M. Kaufman. New York: Oxford University Press.

Kohn, A. 1992. *No contest: The case against competition*. Boston: Houghton Mifflin.

Kotkin, J. 1993. *Tribes: How race, religion, and identity determine success in the new global economy*. New York: Random House.

Kreitner, R., & Kinicki, A. 1991. *Organizational behavior* (2nd ed.). Burr Ridge, IL: Irwin.

Ladd, E. C. & Bowman, K. H. 1996. *Public opinion in America and Japan: How we see each other and ourselves*. Washington, D.C.: AEI Press.

Lee, R., & Daly, R. 1987. Man's domination and women's oppression: The question of origins. *Beyond patriarchy: Essays by men on pleasure, power, and change*, edited by M. Kaufman. New York: Oxford University Press.

Levant, R. 1991. *Between father and child: How to become the kind of father you want to be*. New York: Vicking Penguin.

Levant, R. & Pollack, W., eds. 1995. *The new psychology of men*. New York: Basic Books.

Lewan, L.S., & Billingsley, R.G. 1988. *Women in the workplace: A man's perspective*. Bridgewater, NJ: Remington Press.

Lewis, R.A., & Sussman, M.B. 1986. *Men's changing roles in the family.* Binghamton, NY: Haworth Press.

Lewis, R.D. 1996. *When cultures collide: managing successfully across cultures.* London: Nicholas Brealey Publishing.

Loden, M. 1985. *Feminine leadership, or, how to succeed in business without being one of the boys.* New York: Times Books.

Loden, M., & Rosener, J.B. 1991. *Workforce America! Managing employee diversity as a vital resource.* Homewood, IL: Business One Irwin.

Lowenthal, M.F., et al. 1975. *Four stages of life.* San Francisco: Jossey-Bass.

Lynch, F.R. 1989. *Invisible victims: White males and the crisis of affirmative action.* Westport, CT: Greenwood.

Madden, T.R. 1987. *Women vs. women: The uncivil business war.* New York: AMACOM.

McCarthy, B. 1988. *Male sexual awareness: Increasing sexual pleasure.* New York: Carroll & Graf.

McGill, M. 1985. *The McGill report on male intimacy.* Austin, TX: Holt, Rinehart, & Winston.

Melia, J. 1989. *Breaking into the boardroom.* New York: St. Martin's Press.

Meth, R.L., et al. 1991. *Men in therapy: The challenge of change.* New York: Guilford Press.

Michaels, L. 1993. *The men's club.* San Francisco: Mercury House.

Miller, L. 1985. *American spirit: Visions of a new corporate culture.* New York: Warner Books.

Miller, S. 1992. *Men and friendship.* Los Angeles: Jeremy Tarcher.

Milwid, B. 1992. *Working with men: Women in the workplace talk about sexuality, success, and their male coworkers.* New York: Berkley Publishing Group.

Money, J., & Tucker, P. 1975. *Sexual signatures: On being a man or a woman.* Boston: Little Brown.

Moore, R., & Gillette, D. 1993. *The warrior within: Accessing the knight in the male psyche.* New York: Avon.

Mornell, P. 1987. *Passive men, wild women.* New York: Ballantine Books.

Morrison, A.M., et al. 1992. *Breaking the glass ceiling: Can women reach the top of America's largest corporations?* Reading, MA: Addision-Wesley.

Murphy, R.T. 1996. *The weight of the yen.* New York: W. W. Norton & Company.

Murray, M. 1991. *Beyond the myths and magic of mentoring.* San Francisco: Jossey-Bass.

Myers, M.F. 1989. *Men and divorce.* New York: Guilford Press.

Myhlander, M. 1987. *The healthy male.* New York: Little, Brown & Co.

Naifeh, S., & Smith, G.W. 1984. *Why can't men open up?* New York: Clarkson Potter.

Naisbett, J. 1985. *Re-inventing the corporation: Transforming your job and your company for the new information society.* New York: Warner Books.

Norman, M. 1991. *These good men.* San Diego: Harcourt Brace Jovanovich.

Olsen, P. 1981. *Sons and mothers.* New York: Ballantine Books.

Osherson, S. 1987. *Finding our fathers: How a man's life is shaped by his relationship with his father.* New York: Fawcett.

Pearson, J.C. 1985. *Gender and communication.* Dubuque, IA: William C. Brown.

Peters, T.J. 1987. *Thriving on chaos: Handbook for a management revolution.* New York: Knopf.

Peters, T. 1994. *Tom Peter's seminar: Crazy times call for crazy organizations.* New York: Random.

Pearson, J., & Turner, L.H. 1991. *Gender and communication* (2nd ed.). Madison, WI: Brown and Benchmark.

Pleck, J.H. 1981. *The myth of masculinity.* Cambridge, MA: The MIT Press.

Pleck, J.H., & Sawyer, J., eds. 1974. *Men and masculinity.* Englewood Cliffs, NJ: Prentice-Hall.

Powell, C. 1995. *My American journey.* New York: Random House.

Purvis, E. 1992. *The male sexual machine: An owner's manual.* New York: St. Martin's Press.

Rieker, P.P., & Carmen, E., eds. 1984. *The gender gap in psychotherapy.* New York: Plenum Press.

Rix, S.E., ed. 1990. *The American woman, 1990–91: A status report.* Washington, DC: SLA.

Roscoe, W. 1992. *The Zuni man-woman.* Albuquerque: The University of New Mexico Press.

Ross, J.M. 1992. *The male paradox.* New York: Simon and Schuster.

Rotundo, E.A. 1987. Patriarchs and participants: A historical perspective of fatherhood in the United States. *Beyond patriarchy: Essays by men on pleasure, power, and change,* edited by M. Kaufman. New York: Oxford University Press.

Sadker, M., & Sadker, D.M. 1994. *Failing at fairness: How America's schools cheat girls.* New York: Macmillan.

Sargent, A.G. 1981. *The androgynous manager.* New York: AMACOM.

Schaef, A.W., & Fassel, D. 1990. *The addictive organization: Why we overwork, cover up, pick up the pieces, please the boss, and perpetuate sick organizations.* San Francisco: Harper SF.

Schlesinger, A.M. 1992. *The disuniting of America.* New York: W.W. Norton & Co.

Schor, J.B. 1993. *The overworked American: The unexpected decline of leisure.* New York: Basic Books.

Shapiro, E.C. 1995. *Fad surfing in the boardroom.* Reading, MA: Addison-Wesley Publishing Company.

Shapiro, S. 1984. *Manhood: A new definition.* New York: Putnam Publishing Group.

Silverberg, R.A. 1986. *Quiet desperation.* New York: Warner Books.

Skovhold, T.M., et al., eds. 1980. *Counseling men.* Monterey, CA: Brooks/Cole Publishing.

Solomon, K., & Levy, N.B., eds. 1982. *Men in transition: Theory and therapy.* New York: Plenum Press.

Staples, R. 1982. *Black masculinity: The black male's role in American society.* Oakland, CA: Black Scholar Press.

Stearns, P.N. 1990. *Be a man! Males in modern society* (2nd ed.). New York: Holmes and Meier.

Stewart, R.J. 1991. *Celebrating the male mysteries.* Twin Lakes, WI: Arcana Press.

Stoltenberg, J. 1990. *Refusing to be a man: Essays on sex and justice.* New York: NAL-Dalton.

Tannen, D. 1986. *That's not what I meant.* New York: Ballantine Books.

———. 1990. *You just don't understand: Men and women in conversation.* New York: Ballantine Books.

———. 1994. *Talking from 9 to 5.* New York: William Morrow and Co.

Tanenbaum, J. 1990. *Male and female realities: Understanding the opposite sex.* Costa Mesa, CA: Tanenbaum Associates.

Thiederman, S. 1990. *Bridging cultural barriers for corporate success: How to manage the multicultural work force.* New York: Free Press.

Thompson, K., ed. 1991. *To be a man.* San Francisco: Jeremy P. Tarcher.

Tichy, N. 1993. *Control your destiny or someone else will.* New York: HarperCollins Publishing, Inc.

Tiger, L. 1989. *Men in groups.* New York: M. Boyars.

Trompenaars, F. 1994. *Riding the waves of culture: Understanding cultural diversity in business.* Burr Ridge, IL: Irwin Professional Publications.

U.S. Department of Labor. 1991. *A report on the glass ceiling initiative.* Washington, DC: USGPO.

_____ . 1992. *Pipelines of progress: A status report on the glass ceiling.* Washington, DC: USGPO.

Weatherford, J.M. 1988. *Indian givers: How the Indians of the Americas transformed the world.* New York: Crown Publishers.

Weiss, D.E. 1991. *The great divide: How females and males really differ.* New York: Simon and Schuster.

Weiss, R.S. 1990. *Staying the course: The emotional and social lives of men who do well at work.* New York: The Free Press.

Whitehead, B.D. 1997. *The divorce culture.* Westminster, MD: Random House, Inc.

Williams, C. L. 1989. *Gender differences at work: Women and men in nontraditional occupations.* Berkeley: University of California Press.

Wolfe T. 1987. *The bonfire of the vanities.* New York: Farrar, Straus, Giroux.

Yankelovich, D. 1981. *New rules: Searching for self-fulfillment in a world turned upside down.* New York: Random House.

JOURNALS AND PERIODICALS

Aburdene, P. 1990. How to think like a CEO for the 90s. *Working Woman*, September, 134–137.

Adler, J., et al.. 1981. Drums, sweat, and tears. *Newsweek*, 24 June, 46–51.

_____ . 1981. Heeding the call of the drums. *Newsweek*, 24 June, 52–53.

Allen, B.P. 1995. Gender stereotypes are not accurate: a replication of Martin (1987) using diagnostic vs. self-report and behavioral criteria. *Sex Roles*, May, 583–600.

American Management Association 1990. Rx for affirmative action. *Human Resources Forum*, October, 1–3.

Associated press 1989. No lack of racism in sports? *Denver Post*, 15 September, 8D.

Atwater, L., & Brewster, T. 1991. Lee Atwater's last campaign. *Life*, February, 58–62.

Belfry, M., & Schmidt, L. 1988. Managing the diverse workforce. *Employment Relations Today* 15(4):337–339.

Bem, S.L. 1981. Gender schema theory: A cognitive account of sex typing. *Psychological Review* 88:354–364.

Bennett, A. 1989. Corporate chiefs calling it quits earlier. *Wall Street Journal*, 22 December, B1, B4.

_____ . 1993. GE redesigns rungs of career ladder. *Wall Street Journal*, 15 March, B1–B2.

_____ . 1993. Path to top job now twists and turns. *Wall Street Journal*, 15 March, B16.

Bennett, R. 1994. They did what had to be done. *Readers Digest 145*, November, Issue 871, 13.

Bhargava, S.W., & Jesperson, F. F. 1993. Portrait of a CEO. *Business Week*, 11 October, 64–65.

Bleakley, F.R. 1993. The best laid plans. *Wall Street Journal*, 6 July, A1.

Blonston, G. 1993. Companies to workers: More with less. *Boulder Daily Camera* 8 August, 1E.

Boards add more minorities, women. 1990. *Denver Post*, 28 April, 2C.

Bongiorno, L. 1992. Where are all the female B-school profs? *Business Week*, 7 December, 40.

Bound, J., & Holzwer, H.J. 1993. Industrial shifts, skill levels, and the labor market for white and black males. *Review of Economics and Statistics* 75(3):387–396.

Braham, J. 1989. No, you don't manage everyone the same. *Industry Week*, 6 February, 28–35.

Briton, N.J. & Hall, J.A. 1995. Beliefs about female and male nonverbal. *Sex Roles*, January, 79–90.

Burnette, E. 1995. Black males retrieve a noble heritage. *APA Monitor*, June, 1.

Byrne, J. 1993. The horizontal corporation: It's about managing across, not up and down. *Business Week*, 20 December, 76–79.

_____ . 1996. Strategic planning. *Business Week*, 26 August, 46–53.

Byrne, J., & Hawkins, C. 1993. Executive pay: The party ain't over yet. *Business Week*, 26 April, 56–64.

Cameron, D. 1992. Not gender difference but the difference gender makes - explanation in research on sex and language. *International Journal of the Sociology of Language* 94:13–26.

Cameron, K.S., & Freeman, S.J. 1991. Cultural congruence, strength, and type: Relationships to effectiveness. *Research in Organizational Change and Development* 5:23–58.

Chavez, L. 1994. Dividing the united: Multiculturalists carve up the country's common culture. *Rocky Mountain News*, 7 February, 77A.

Cohen, L.R. 1983. Nonverbal (mis)communication between managerial men and women. *Business Horizons*, January-February, 14–16.

Copeland, L. 1988. Valuing diversity, part I: Making the most of cultural differences at the workplace. *Personnel* 65(6):52–60, June.

_____ . 1988. Valuing diversity, part II: Pioneers and champions of change. *Personnel* 65(7):44–49, July.

Corvin, S., & Wiggins, F. 1989. An antiracism training model for white professionals. *Journal of Multicultural Counseling and Development* 17:105–114.

Crispell, D. 1992. The brave new world of men. *American Demographics*, January, 38–43.

Davies, J. 1985. Why are women not where the power is? An examination of the maintenance of power elites. *Management Education and Development* 16(3): 278–288.

Davis, A. 1997. English-only rules spur workers to speak legalese. *Wall Street Journal*, January, B1.

Denison, D.R., & Spreitzer, G.M. 1991. Organizational culture and organizational development: a competing values approach. *Research in Organizational Change and Development* 5:1–21.

Dingle, D.T. 1989. Peak performance. *Black Enterprise*, May, 64–70.

Dorgan, W.J. 1994. Power and power bases. *Modern Machine Shop*, July, 114.

Drucker, P.F. 1994. The age of social transformation. *Atlantic Monthly*, November, 53–80.

Dumaine, B. 1990. Creating a new company culture. *Fortune*, 15 January, 127–128, 130–131.

Eagly, A.H., Makhijani, M.G., & Klonsky, B.G. 1992. Gender and the evaluation of leaders: A meta-analysis. *Psychological Bulletin* 111(1):3–22.

Eastland, T. 1996. Endgame for affirmative action. *Wall Street Journal*, 28 March, A11.

Edmondson, B. 1990. Hail to the chief. *American Demographics*, February, 11–12.

_____ . 1996. Work slowdown. *American Demographics*, March, 4–7.

Edwards, A. 1991. Cultural diversity in today's corporation: The enlightened manager. *Working Woman*, January, 45–47, 51.

Efron, S. 1990. Politics are changing for Asian-Americans. *Los Angeles Times*, 16 August, A3, A39.

Ehrlich, E. 1990. Welcome to the woman-friendly company. *Business Week*, 6 August, 48-55.

Ellis, C., & Sonnenfeld, J.A. 1994. Diverse approaches to managing diversity. *Human Resources Management* 33(1):79–109.

Erkel, R.T. 1990. The birth of a movement. *Networker Magazine*, May/June, 27–35.

Eskey, K. 1992. Women still hit glass ceiling in corporate arena, labor chief says. *Rocky Mountain News*, 12 August, 52.

Eassland, T. 1996. Endgame for affirmative action. *Wall Street Journal*, 28 March, A11.

Eskelson, A. 1996. The best teacher: mediating effects of experience with employed women on men managers' responses to subordinates' mistakes. *Sex Roles*, February, 237–252.

Exeter, T. 1993. The declining majority. *American Demographics*, January, 59.

Experts divided on jobs in the '90s. 1989. *New York Times*, 16 April, 29, 31–32.

Farnham, A. 1994. How to nurture creative sparks. *Fortune*, 10 January, 94–96, 98, 100.

Fierman, J. 1990. Do women manage efficiently? *Fortune*, 17 December, 115–118.

Fine, M.G. 1991. New voices in the workplace: Research directions in multicultural communication. *Journal of Business Communication* 28(3):259–270.

Fine, M.G., Johnson, F.L., & Ryan, M.S. 1990. Cultural diversity in the workplace. *Public Personnel Management* 19(3):305–319.

Fineman, H. 1995. Race and rage. *Newsweek*, 3 April, 23–34.

Fiol, C.M. 1991. See the empty spaces: Towards a more complex understanding of the meaning of power in organizations. *Organization Studies* 12(4):547–566, Fall.

Francese, P. 1992. Income winners. *American Demographics*, August, 2.

French, H.W. 1997. Africa's culture war: Old customs, new values. *New York Times*, 2 February, 4:1.

Fuchsberg, G. 1990. Many businesses responding too slowly to rapid work force shifts. *Wall Street Journal*, 20 July, B1.

_____ . 1992. Total quality is termed only partial success. *Wall Street Journal*, 1 October, B1, B5.

_____ . 1994. It's the quality, not the quantity, of your work hours. *Wall Street Journal*, 27 July, B1.

Fukunishi, I. & Rake, R. 1995. Alexithymia and coping with stress in healthy persons: allexithymia as a personality trait is associated with low social support and poor responses to stress. *Psychological Reports*, June, 1299–1305.

Gains, Jr., S.O. 1995. Prejudice: From Allport to DuBois. *American Psychologist* 50(2):96–103, February.

Galen, M., & Palmer, T. 1994. White, male & worried. *Business Week*, 31 January, 50–55.

Gardner, M. 1987. Male-only clubs keeping women below a "glass ceiling." *Christian Science Monitor*, 20 February, 29.

Gates, D. 1993. White male paranoia. *Newsweek*, 29 March, 48–53.

Geber, B. 1990. Managing diversity. *Training: The Magazine of Human Resources Development* 27(7):23–30, July.

Gelman, D. 1994. The mystery of suicide. *Newsweek*, 18 April, 45–49.

Gerdes, E.P. 1995. Women preparing for traditionally male professions: physical and psychological symptoms associated with work and home stress. *Sex Roles*, June, 787–807.

Gilman, R. 1987. The trouble with men. *Context*, Spring, 5–9.

Glazer, N. 1995. Race, not class. *Wall Street Journal*, 5 April, B1.

Goldman, K. 1990. Female voice-overs: Still hard to find. *Wall Street Journal*, 10 April, B6.

Good, G.E., Dell, D.M., & Mintz, L.B. 1989. Male role and gender role conflict: Relations to help seeking in men. *Journal of Counseling Psychology* 36(3): 295–300.

Good, G.E., Robertson, J.M., O'Neil, J.M., Fitzgerald, L.F., Stevens, M., DeBord, K.A., Bathels, K.M., & Braverman, D.G. 1995. Male gender role conflict: Psychometric issues and relations to psychological distress. *Journal of Counseling Psychology* 42(1):3–10.

Granfield, M. 1992. '90s mentoring: Circles and quads. *Working Woman*, November, 15.

Harris, A. 1994. Break the glass ceiling for senior executives. *HR Focus*, March, 1–5.

Harwood, J., & Brooks, G. 1993. Ms. President: Other nations elect women to lead them, so why doesn't U.S.? *Wall Street Journal*, 14 December, A1, A9.

Heery, W. 1994. Corporate mentoring can break the glass ceiling. *HR Focus*, May, 17–18.

Henkoff, R. 1994. Getting beyond downsizing. *Fortune*, 10 January, 58–60, 63, 64.

Herz, D.F., & Rones, P. 1989. Institutional barriers to employment of older workers. *Monthly Labor Review*, April, 14.

Himelstein, L. 1996. Shatterproof glass ceiling. *Business Week*, 28 October, 55.

Himelstein, L. and Forest, S. 1997. Breaking through. *Business Week*, 17 February, 64–70.

How the men in your office really see you. 1991. *Working Woman*, November, 101–103.

Huey, J. 1993. Managing in the midst of chaos. *Fortune*, 5 April, 38–41, 44, 46, 48.

Hymowitz, C. 1990. When firms cut out middle managers; those at the top and bottom often suffer. *Wall Street Journal*, 5 April, B1.

Ipsaro, A. 1986. Male client-male therapist: Issues in a therapeutic alliance. *Journal of Psychotherapy* 23(2):257–66.

Jacob, R. 1994. Why some customers are more equal than others. *Fortune*, 19 September, 215–224.

Jacobs, M.A. 1995. EEOC ruling reopens question of when discrimination is legal. *Wall Street Journal*, 19 April, B10.

Jaschik-Herman, M.L. & Fisk, A. 1995. Women's perceptions and labeling of sexual harassment in Academia before and after the Hill-Thomas hearings. *Sex Roles*, September, 439–446.

Jeanquart-Barone, S. 1993. Trust differences between supervisors and subordinates: examining the role of race and gender. *Sex Roles*, July, 1–11.

Kadar, A.G. 1994. The sex-bias myth in medicine. *Atlantic Monthly*, August, 66–70.

Keen, S., & Zur, O. 1989. Who is the new ideal man? *Psychology Today*, November, 54–60.

King, P. 1989. What makes teamwork work? *Psychology Today*, December, 16–17.

Kirkpatrick, D.D. 1996. Women occupy few top jobs, a study shows. *Wall Street Journal*, 18 October, B16A.

Kleiman, C. 1989. Women a rarity in blue-collar jobs. *Denver Post*, 15 May, 4C.

Kort, M. 1989. The best professions for women. *Savvy Woman*, August, 32–34.

Kroeger, B. 1994. The road less rewarded. *Working Woman*, July, 50–55.

Laporte, S.B. 1991. Cultural diversity: Twelve companies that do the right thing. *Working Woman*, January, 57–58.

Lee, M. 1993. Diversity training brings unity to small companies. *Wall Street Journal*, 2 September, B2.

Lehner, U.C. 1993. Belief in an imminent Asian century is gaining sway. *Wall Street Journal*, 17 May, A12.

Leighty, J.M. 1986. Close friendships between men don't come easy, studies indicate. *Denver Post*, 15 May, 2C.

Leinberger, P., & Tucker, B. 1991. The sun sets on the silent generation. *New York Times*, 4 August, 11.

Loeb, M. 1994. Where leaders come from. *Fortune*, 19 September, 241–242.

Long, V.O. 1989. Relation of masculinity to self-esteem and self-acceptance in male professionals, college students, and clients. *Journal of Counseling Psychology* 36(1): 84–87.

Lublin, J.S. 1993. Diversity training extends beyond U.S. *Wall Street Journal*, 12 March, B1.

Luthar, H.K. 1996. Gender differences in evaluation of performance and leadership ability: autocratic vs. democratic managers. *Sex Roles*, September, 337–361.

Lynch, F.R. 1991. Tales from an oppressed class. *Wall Street Journal*, 11 November, A12.

———. 1992. Race unconsciousness and the white male. *Society* 29(2):30–35.

Macoby, M. 1993. Managers must unlearn the psychology of control. *Research-Technology Management* 36(1):49–51.

Magnet, M. 1992. The truth about the American worker. *Fortune*, 4 May, 48–51, 54, 58, 64–65.

Mall, E. 1994. Why getting ahead is (still) tougher for women. *Working Woman*, July, 11.

Mander, J. 1991. Our founding mothers and fathers, the Iroquois. *Earth Island Journal*, Fall, 30–32.

Mansnerus, L. 1993. Why women are leaving the law. *Working Woman*, April, 64–67.

Martell, R.E. 1996. What mediates gender bias in work behavior ratings? *Sex Roles*, August, 153–169.

May, A.M., & Stephenson, K. 1994. Women and the great retrenchment: The political economy of gender in the 1980s. *Journal of Economic Issues* 27(2):533–543.

McGowen, K.R., & Hart, L.E. 1990. Still different after all these years: gender differences in professional identity formation. *Professional Psychology Research and Practice* 21(2):118–123.

McGuire, P.A. 1987. Men's rights: Male bashing and the need for mutual respect. *Baltimore Sun Magazine*, 15 February, 8F.

McNerney, D. 1994. The bottom-line value of diversity. *HR Focus*, May, 22–23.

Miller, A., & Kruger, P. 1990. The new old boy. *Working Woman*, April, 94–96.

Morris, B. 1995. Executive women confront midlife crisis. *Fortune*, 18 September, 60–86.

Nelton, S. 1988. Meet your new workforce. *Nation's Business*, July, 14–17, 20–21.

Noble, B.P. 1994. Putting women on the agenda. *New York Times*, 1 May, 21.

Nousaine, M. 1985. Will the real superman please stand up? [Review of Mario Puzo's film trilogy]. *Tarrytown Letter*, October, 15–18

Oliver, J.A. 1992. To reach minorities, try busting myths. *American Demographics*, April, 14–15.

O'Brien, P. 1993. Why men don't listen. *Working Woman*, February, 56, 58–59, 82.

O'Neil, J. 1980. Male sex role conflicts, sexism, and masculinity: Psychological implications for men, women, and the counseling psychologist. *Counseling Psychologist* 9:61–80.

O'Reilly, B. 1992. Your new global workforce. *Fortune*, 14 December, 52–54, 58, 62, 64, 66.

_____ . 1994. The new deal: What companies and employees owe one another. *Fortune*, 13 June, 44–47, 50, 52.

Otten, A.L. 1991. Women lead growth in college enrollment. *Wall Street Journal*, 13 March, B1.

_____ . 1992. Men claim desire to become less macho. *Wall Street Journal*, 31 March, B1.

Parker, B., & Chusmir, L. 1991. Motivation needs and their relationship to life success. *Human Relations* 44(12):1301–1312.

Pasztor, A. 1991. On the battlefield, pep talks take on a sensitive tone. *Wall Street Journal*, 4 February, A1, A12.

Perry, N. J. 1991. The workers of the future. *Fortune*, Spring/Summer, 68–72.

Phillips, C. 1990. Anti-gay message goes unchallenged. *Los Angeles Times,* 5 August, 8, 77–80.

Pittman, F. 1990. The masculine mystique. *Networker Magazine*, May/June, 40–52.

Pleck, J.H., & Brannon, R., eds. 1978. Male roles and male experience. *Journal of Social Issues* 34(1).

Ragins, B.R., & Sundstrom, E. 1989. Gender and power in organizations: A longitudinal perspective. *Psychological Bulletin* 105(1):51–88.

Rice, J.W. 1991. When "fatherly" concern is not welcome. *Wall Street Journal,* 25 February, A8.

Richman, L. S. 1992. America's tough new job market. *Fortune*, 24 February, 52–54, 58, 61.

Rifkin, G. 1994. Workplace diversity: The forgotten white male. *Harvard Business Review*, July/August, 8.

Rosenberg, W. 1994. Making manhood visible: a review essay. *Masculinities*, Fall, 71–79.

Rosenthal, H.F. 1995. Emotion triggers vary by gender. *Denver Post*, 27 January, 10D.

San Francisco Examiner. 1990. Coed classes can impede women. *Rocky Mountain News*, 13 March, 33.

Saris, R.N., Johnston, I. & Lott, B 1995. Women as cues for men's approach or distancing behavior: a study of interpersonal sexist discrimination. *Sex Roles*, August, 289–298.

Schele, A. 1990. Male bonding: Can you beat it? *Working Woman*, December, 30–32.

Schlender, B.R. 1992. The values we will need. *Fortune*, 27 January, 75–77.

Schrof, J.M. 1993. Feminism's daughters: Their agenda is a cultural sea change. *U.S. News & World Report*, 27 September, 68–71.

Schwartz, J. 1990. New priorities. *American Demographics*, October, 13.

Segal, R. 1990. It's a world's man. *Men's Health Magazine*, December, 46–47.

Segell, M. 1989. The American man in transition. *American Health,* January/February, 59–63.

Sharpe, M.J. & Heppner, P.D. 1991. Gender role, gender role conflict, and psychological well-being in men. *Journal of Counseling Psychology* 38(3):323–330.

Shellenbarger, S. 1991. Fathers (not managers) know best. *Wall Street Journal,* 12 September, B1, B6.

_____ . 1992. Men find more ways to spend time at home. *Wall Street Journal*, 12 February, p. B1.

Shellenbarger, S., et al. 1993. Work and family. *Wall Street Journal Reports*, 21 June, R1–R14.

Sherman, S. 1993. A brave new Darwinian workplace. *Fortune*, 25 January, 50–56.

Sifneos, P.E. 1996. Alexithymia: past and present. *American Journal of Psychiatry*. July, 137–142.

Smith, L. 1994. Stamina: Who has it, why you need it, how you get it. *Fortune*, 28 November, 127–139.

Solomon, C.M. 1991. Are white males being left out? *Personnel Journal*, November, 88–91, 94.

Solomons, H.H., & Cramer, A. 1985. When the differences don't make a difference: Women and men as colleagues. *Management Education and Development* 16(2):155–168.

Stewart, T.A. 1994. Managing in a wired company. *Fortune*, 11 July, 44–56.

_____ . 1997. Get with the new power game. *Fortune*, 13 January, 58–62.

_____ . 1997. When change is total, exciting - and scary. *Fortune*, 3 March, 169–170.

Stout, H. 1990. U.S. universities failing to educate minority students. *Wall Street Journal*, 7 December, B7.

Straus, H. 1989. Freaks of nurture. *American Health*, January/February, 70.

Sue, D.W. 1990. Culture-specific strategies in counseling: A conceptual framework. *Professional Psychology: Research and Practice* 21(6):424–33.

Swisher, K. 1995. Diversity training: Learning from past mistakes. *Washington Post National Weekly Edition*, 13 February, 20.

Thomas, D.A., & Ely, R.J. 1996. Making differences matter: A new paradigm for managing diversity. *Harvard Business Review* 74(5):79–90.

Thomas, R. R. 1990. From affirmative action to affirming diversity. *Harvard Business Review* 90(2):107–117.

Tifft, S.W. 1994. Board gains. *Working Woman*, February, 37–39.

Trost, C. 1989. Firms heed women employees' needs. *Wall Street Journal*, 22 November, B1. B4.

Wade, J.C. 1996. African American men's gender role conflict: the significance of racial identity. *Sex Roles*, January, 17-33.

Waldrop, J. 1994. What do working woman want? *American Demographics*, September, 36–37.

Warner, M. 1997. Working at home - the right way to be a star in your bunny slippers. *Fortune*, 3 March, 165–166.

Watson, W.E., Kumar, K, & Michaelson, L.K. 1993. Cultural diversity's impact on interaction process and performance: Comparing homogeneous and diverse task groups. *Academy of Management Journal* 36(3):590–602.

Watts, P. 1987. Bias busting: Diversity training in the workplace. *Management Review*, December, 51–54.

Wheeler, M.L. 1996. Diversity: Making the business case. *Business Week*, 9 December, Special Advertising Section.

White, J.B. & Hymowitz, C. 1997. Watershed generation of women executives is rising to the top. *Wall Street Journal*, 10 February, A1.

Whitehead, R., Jr. 1988. New collars. *Psychology Today*, October, 44–49.

Women gain clout as top advisers. 1989. *Denver Post*, 25 February, 2A.

Working for foreigners. 1991. *Wall Street Journal*, 7 January, A10.

Wynter, L.E. 1994. Recognizing whites as an ethnic group. *Wall Street Journal*, 15 June, B1.

Yoder, J.D., Aniokudo, P. & Berendseu, L. 1996. Looking beyond gender: the effects of racial differences on tokenism perceptions of women. *Sex Roles*, October, 389–400.

York, T. 1994. White men still wield most power. *Baltimore Business Journal*, 8 April, 54.

Youman, R. 1985. Making contact. *New York Times*, 10 November, 74.

INDEX

Aburdene, Patricia, 94–95
Achievements, 84
Adams, Walter, 77
Adaptation, 135
Affirmative action, 18–19, 141
    in new national policy, 151
    turbo-charged, 141
African American Million Man March, 17
African Americans, 170–71
    income gains, 171
    "not walking the talk," 173
    religion and, 173
    sell-outs, 200
    women, 170, 173
    See also Minorities
Aggressiveness, 64–65
Agrarian work model, 71
Alexithymia, 30
Anger
    going beyond, 49
    unexpressed, 49
    See also Feelings
Asian Americans, 90, 200
Asian culture, 36–37
Assimilation, 130
    in diversity cycle, 234
    strategy limitations, 234
Assimilation model, 142–43
    letting go of, 144
    "Life with Father," 146
Atwater, Lee, 11–13, 23, 210
Authentic diversity, 133–34, 149
Authority, white male, 16–17
Autry, Jim, 255

"Backlash" stories, 18
Balance, 71
    home and work, 219
    Kikuyus culture, 37
    work/home, 153
Bardeen, John, 45
Barneby, Mary Rudie, 203
Bedford, Brian, 231, 240
Belonging, 63
Berdaches, 40
Bergman, Stephen, 84
Biases, 57
Biblical values, 17–18
"Bigger is better" assumption, 77
Biological differences, 60–61
    in children, 60–61
    puberty, 61
Biological sex
    as basic element, 5
    defined, 4
Block, Peter, 82
Boundaryless, 80, 210
Brattain, Walter, 45

Braun, Kathryn, 203
Brock, James, 77
Bryne, John, 78, 80
Business culture
    military culture vs., 31
    movement in, 32

Captain Kickass, 148
Catalyst Institute for Research, 52
Categorizations, 62
"Celebrating differences," 125
Champy, Jim, 76, 78, 79
Change, 57–58, 221
    agents for, 163–83
    attitudinal, 76
    commitment to, 179–81
    corporations and, 253
    emotions and, 75
    failure to, 183
    fear of, 154
    influence in, 244
    obstacles to, 79
    organizational, 231–49
    perspective, 244
    as process, 75–76, 244
    profiting from, 253
    reasons for, 75
    recognizing, 75
    risks and, 247
    women and, 221
    workplace and, 127, 163
Check-point phenomenon, 195
Children, 97
    biological differences in, 60–61
    women desire for, 219
Closed cultures, 128–30
    advantages of, 129
    disadvantages of, 129–30
Cohen, Lynn Renee, 178
Collusion, 155–57
    defined, 155
    through denial, 156
    excluding behaviors and, 156
    silence and, 157
    support methods for, 155
"Common ground," 144
Communication
    backing off and, 178–79
    body size and, 178
    eye contact and, 179
    frustrations, 177
    male/female, 6, 113, 177
    miscommunication cues, 178–79
    non-verbal, 167, 178–79
    personal space and, 178
    rappin', 167
    silence and, 167
    smiling and, 179

279

styles catalogue, 175–77
styles of, 65, 166–69
touching and, 179
woofin', 167
See also Relationships
Computers, 46, 76
    gender roles and, 46
    home work and, 153
    respect and, 115
Connell, R.W., 5, 225
Conversation, 174
Copeland, Leonard, 90–91, 156
Corporations
    assimilation and, 130
    change and, 253
    culture of, 144
    entrepreneurial world vs., 227
    flattened hierarchy of, 78, 84
    hierarchical male structure and, 75
    human element in, 165
    humanity and, 73
    lack of heart in, 72
    "lean and mean" attitude, 108
    leaving, 77
    mentoring in, 199–200
    personal life and, 220
    process engineering, 78
    reengineering, 72, 77, 190
    self-destructive values in, 147
    success definition, 72
    trusting, 191
    white male bashing and, 123
Cose, Ellis, 147, 169
Counseling, 54
Covey, Stephan, 133, 135, 154, 255
Cramer, Audrey, 202
CYA (cover your ass), 198

Day care centers, 95
Deming, Professor N. Edward, 129
Democracy, 75
Demographics, 89–101
Denial
    collusion through, 156
    of white men, 4
De Toqueville, Alexis, 127
Differences
    acknowledging, 145
    biological, 60–61
    celebrating, 125
    commonness and, 126
    in diversity cycle, 234
    focusing solely on, 126
    ignoring, 145, 146
    interfacing with, 165
    working style, 145
Discrimination, 18–19
    covert, 130
    effects of, 19
    overt, 130
    redressing imbalance and, 149

reverse, 18
Diversity, 22, 258
    advantage, 137
    authentic, 133–34, 149
    benefits, 157–58
    best practices factor and, 233
    challenge of, 66
    control and, 154
    creative thinking factor and, 232–33
    customer-orientation factor and, 233
    defined, 220
    demographics of, 89–101
    equation, 19–20
    global market factor and, 233
    implementation pressures, 172
    initiatives, fostering, 181
    initiatives, weak point, 142
    management commitment to,
        181–83
    for men, 220
    Motorola model and, 236
    movement, 252
    principles, 157, 220, 232
    reasons for practicing, 232–33
    societal factor and, 233
    success and, 232–33
    talent pool factor and, 232
    teams, 81, 243
    training, 164, 246
    for women, 220
    work force, 136
Divorce, 218
Double standards, 41, 148
Drucker, Peter, 81, 170
Duty, 199

Education, 168–69
Edwards, Anthony, 164–65
Eisler, Riane, 33–34
Ellis, Joseph J., 38
Emotions. *See* Feelings
Empowerment, 27
Endurance, 49
Entrepreneurs
    women, 94
    world of, 227, 229
E pluribus unum, 124, 164, 221, 226, 257,
    258
Estrogen, 60
Exclusion
    frustration of, 80
    practice of, 18
    white male feelings of, 17
Eye contact, 179

Family
    crisis of, 212
    women rule of, 211
Fear, 164
    of change, 154
    of confrontation, 155

of losing something, 155
of reflection, 30–31
See also Feelings
Feelings, 22, 23
    anger, 49
    basic, 51
    bottling up of, 48
    change and, 75
    constriction, cost of, 49
    contacting, 50
    different cultures and, 51
    failure, 195
    fear, 30–31, 154–55, 164
    inadequacy, 195, 223
    inferiority, 57
    lack of experience with, 51
    men and, 85, 225
    vulnerability/weakness, 111
    women and, 85
    world of, 30
Femininity, 5, 59
Fierman, Jaclyn, 203, 204
Flattened hierarchy, 78, 84
Ford, Henry, 189, 190, 231
Formal Organization, 192, 195
Fuchsberg, Gilbert, 99
Fundamentalism, 212

Gardner, Howard, 167
Gartin, Larry, 238
Gender
    biological differences, 60
    defined, 5
    human goals and, 6
    mentoring and, 200
    politics, 178–79
    relations, 5
Gender roles, 253
    computers and, 46
    defined, 5
    definition of, 33
    European culture, 40
    "hardwired," 59, 83
    impact awareness, 95
    less definition in, 254–55
    sex and, 114
    shifting, 96–97
    work roles and, 29
Generalizations, 7, 8
Gillette, Douglas, 58, 59
Gilmore, David, 47, 65
Glass ceilings, 80, 193, 195
    defined, 80
    hitting, 193, 195
    shattering, 203–4
Goals
    organization, 134
    personal, 218
    successful, 253
    team, 134
Goldin, Claudia, 204

"Good ole boys" clubs, 193, 197, 198
Goodwin, Marjorie, 174
Greer, W.T., 203, 240–41
Groups
    diverse, 180, 241
    homogeneous, 180, 241
    PLU, 180
    profiles of, 7
Gutek, Barbara, 113–14, 178, 220
Gutman, Bobbi, 235, 236

Halper, Jan, 108, 110, 114
Hammer, Michael, 76, 78, 79
Handy, Charles, 253
"Hardwired" roles, 59, 83
Harragan, Betty Lehan, 31
Hightower, Tracie, 239
Hill-Thomas matter, 114
Hispanics, 89–90
    "coconuts," 200
    population, 251
    See also Minorities
Homophobia, 49, 224–25
Homosexuals, 172
Hudson Institute, 90
Human interaction. *See* Communication;
    Relationships
Hymowitz, Carol, 78, 79

Iacocca, Lee, 191, 197
Immigration, 90–92
    illegal, 92
    legal, 91–92, 93
    revamping laws, 91
    socialization processes and, 92–93
Inclusion, 17, 21
Indifference, male, 17
Industrial Revolution, 42, 194, 215–16
Initiation rites, 62, 63, 64
Integration
    defined, 130
    in diversity cycle, 234
Interviews
    Bert, 118–20
    Bob, 227–29
    Carol, 159–61
    Jack, 24–27
    Joan, 184–86
    John, 138–39
    Keith, 206–7
    Nancy, 102–4
    Randy, 86–87
    Richard, 68–69
    Ron, 53–56
Intimacy, 217, 219
Iroquois Confederacy, 39, 257

Japanese culture, 128–29
Jefferson, Thomas, 38–39
Johnson, Sally, 166
Jourard, Sidney, 198

Keiretsu, 36
Kikuyus culture, 35
    males/females in, 35
    power balance of, 37

Law and order, 16
Levant, Ronald, 85
Loden, Marilyn, 17, 143
Loneliness, 54, 71, 210
Lower management, 192
Loyalty, 199, 216
    pushing, 222
    rediscovering, 224

Magna Carta, 37–38
Male community, 63–64
Management
    "art of," 193
    authoritarian, 31
    commitment to diversity, 181–83
    as facilitators, 82
    fads, 254
    finding, 83
    lower, 192, 193
    middle, 82, 192
    "science of," 193
    as social function, 82
    upper, 181–83
    white male, 84
Mander, J., 39
Manhood
    democratic, 214
    fulfillment of, 255
    heroic, 214
    model of, 216
    redefining, 223
    successful, 218
Marriage, 97–98
Martin, Edith, 203
Masculinity, 59
    code of, 216
    defined, 5
    definition of, 42–43, 62
    proving, 111
    as resource producer, protector and
        director, 42–43
    validation of, 111
McGill, Andrew, 83
McGraw, Diane, 240
"Medieval economy," 215
Men
    accumulation and, 13–14
    aggression of, 64
    in agrarian work model, 71
    American, as seen by foreigners,
        109
    approach to life and work, 12
    behavior as labeled by women, 113
    biological differences, 60–61
    communication style, 175–77
    communication with women, 6,

113, 177
    conversation for, 174
    death and, 109
    diversity for, 220
    divorce and, 218
    emotional relationships with men, 111
    emotions and, 85
    guardedness, 171
    "help" connotation for, 177
    human goals of, 6
    identities of, 116
    indifference and, 17
    isolation of, 216, 217
    Kikuyu, 35
    learning from, 210
    learning from women, 85
    loyalty to, 26
    military hierarchy outlook of, 26
    older, lexicon of, 47
    power definition, 15
    power system, 201, 202
    reliance on words, 73–74
    as resource directors, 29, 43, 209, 222
    as resource producer, 33, 42, 209, 222
    as resource protectors, 29, 33, 42, 222
    respect for women, 112
    roles, shifting of, 96–97
    self-judgment by, 114
    sexual harassment confusion, 74
    stress of, 107
    suicide and, 109
    vision of themselves, 213
    "who he is" question, 84–85
    woman's view of, 31
    working styles of, 145
    See also White men
Men's groups, 224
Mentoring, 199–200
    gender/race and, 200
    subordinates, 200
    women/minorities and, 201
Middle management, 82, 192
Military, business culture and, 31
Minorities
    African Americans, 170–71, 200
    Asian Americans, 90, 200
    computers and, 46
    differences of, 125
    exclusion frustration, 80
    Hispanics, 89–90, 200
    immigration and, 90–92
    Native Americans, 66–67, 200
    old world behavior support, 42
    recruiting, 99
    in upper management, 201
    white male model and, 146
    white male power and, 14
    white males view of, 1–2
    in work force, 99
    in workplace, 89
Money, John, 59

Moore, Robert, 58, 59
Motorola model, 235–49
    change influence, 244
    change process, 244
    diverse leadership characteristics, 237
    diversity process, 236, 245
    diversity teams, 243
    diversity training, 240, 246
    empowerment in, 247
    "green zone," 238
    homogeneous groups in, 241
    motivation for, 235
    multicultural activities and, 247
    power shifts, 242
    "red zone," 238
    work teams, 248
Multicultural workplace, 93–94
    encouragement of, 182
    national/international, 209
    See also Workplace

Naisbitt, John, 95, 116
National work policy, 151–53
    affirmative action in, 151
    safeguards, 151
    work/home balance in, 153
    work week in, 152
Native Americans, 66–67
    "apples," 200
    See also Minorities
Niche markets, 136
Non-verbal communication, 167, 178–79
Norling, Jim, 242
Norms
    defined, 7
    group, 7–8
    using, 8
    workplace, 142

Ohab, Marygrace, 239–40, 242–47, 249
O'Reilly, Charles, 147
Osterman, Paul, 81

Parnell, Myrtle, 165
Partnership, 189
Patriarchy, 34–35, 83
People Like Us (PLU), 180, 181
Performance, 22, 222
    judgments, 61
    reward for, 30
Personal space, 178
Peters, Tom, 77, 98, 133, 136, 163, 183
Physiology, power and, 43
Pleck, Joseph, 111, 216
PNP (positive, negative, positive) principle, 46
Potential, realizing, 133
Powell, Colin, 19, 44
Power
    exclusive, 202
    female system, 201
    global marketplace and, 253

male system, 201, 202
    material, 205
    nonawareness of, 14
    nurturance, 33
    over, 51
    personal, giving away, 15
    physiology and, 43
    positional, 199
    religion and, 255
    in resource distribution, 35
    rules and, 15–16
    shifting of, 16, 242, 253
    societal, 16
    spiritual, 205
    systems, 203
    transforming idea of, 51
    trust and, 149
    of white men, 14, 146–47, 202
Prager, Emily, 61
Prejudices, 62, 242
Process
    change as, 75–76, 244
    engineering, 78
    orientation, 79
    stages, 75–76
    teams, 78–79
Product/process schism, 73
"Promise Keepers" program, 17, 212
"Pseudo warriors," 58
Puberty
    biological differences at, 61
    male bodies at, 65
Public schools, 168–69
Purvis, Kenneth, 64, 65

Quotas, 141

Racism, 170
Reflection, 22, 23
    defined, 30
    fear of, 30–31
    importance of, 22
    lack of, 29–30
    promotion of, 23
    rewards and, 30
Relationships
    importance of, 22
    lack of experience in, 216
    life without, 22–23
    men with men, 111–12
    minimization of, 42
    rules of, 217
    as set of steps to follow, 73
    women and, 79, 85, 177–78, 201
    workplace, 153–54
    world of, 30, 257
Religion
    African American, 173
    "good ole boys" clubs, 197
    influence of, 2
    male dominance, promotion of, 223

male initiation of, 211
power and, 255
spirituality and, 255–56
women equality and, 18
Resource directors, 29, 43, 209, 222
Resource producers
men as, 33, 42, 209, 222
women as, 115
Resource protectors, 29, 33, 42, 222
Respect, 63
building, 179–80
computers and, 115
men for women, 112
women for men, 112
"Reverse discrimination," 18
"Revolution of rising expectations," 142
"Right gender right clan" principle, 16, 37
Roles. *See* Gender roles
Roscoe, Will, 40
Rosener, Judy, 143
Rules
of business, 217
cultural, 128
in hierarchical structure, 192
law and order and, 16
lower management, 192
middle/upper management, 192
new, for women and minorities, 84
power and, 15–16
of relationship, 217

Safire, William, 93
Schizophrenia, 39
Schlesinger, Arthur Jr., 90, 126–27, 142–43
Schor, Juliet, 214, 215
Seattle, Chief, 66–67
Self-organization, 132–33
Self-reflection. *See* Reflection
"Sex role spillover," 178, 220
Sexual harassment, 74
Shapiro, Stephen, 214
Shimer, Julie, 236
Shockley, William, 46
Sifneos, Dr. Peter, 30
Silence
collusion and, 157
communication of, 167
conspiracy of, 198
Smiling, 179
Solomons, Helen, 202
Spanish culture, 36
Spirituality, 255–56
Standards
double, 41, 148
ethical, 148
workplace, 21
Statistics, 6–7
Stereotyping, 7, 169
Stress, male, 107
Success
corporate definition of, 72–73

diversity and, 232–33
male, 95, 195
personal, 190
workplace, 107–8
Suicide, 109
Synergy, 133

Tannen, Deborah, 174
Teams, 51, 81
defined, 81
diversity, 243
goals of, 134
self-managing, 83
Testosterone, 64–65
Thomas, R.R. Jr., 136, 149
Thompson, Chuck, 239
Total Quality Management (TQM) movement, 129
Touching, 179
Training programs, 150
diversity, 164, 179, 246
ongoing, 179
Trust, 189–205
corporations and, 191
destruction of, as bond between men, 216
exhibiting, 196
gender differences and, 172
importance of, 126
loyalty and, 199
power scheme and, 149
scrutiny for, 201
upper management and, 196
Tucker, Patricia, 59

Upper management, 181–83
anxiety of, 196
breaking into, 204–5
rules, 192
trust and, 196
women/minorities in, 201
See also Management

Vietnam veterans, 58–59
Views
of men, 31, 113
of women, 1–2, 34, 113

Warriors, 190
aggressive potentials, 58
characteristics of, 48, 58
culture, 32
"hardwired," 59
homosexuality and, 48
ideals of, 58
Japanese, 58
model modification, 34
"pseudo," 58
spirit, reframing, 210
spiritual component, 58
value conditioning, 47–48

virtues, 47, 57
Welch, Jack, 80
White men
    achievement of, 213
    alienation of, 1
    appreciation for, 20
    authority and, 16–17
    "backlash" stories, 18
    balanced understanding of, 3
    bashing, 123
    biases, 57
    change of, 11
    crisis of, 4
    cultural isolation of, 3
    in denial, 4
    double standard, 41
    exclusion, 17, 18
    failures and exploitations, 19
    feelings of, 3–4
    fishbowl analogy of, 15
    inclusion of, 17, 21
    management, 84
    new frontiers for, 209–26
    power of, 14, 146–47, 202
    reconciliation, 20
    "reverse discrimination" of, 18
    trust with, 172–73
    understanding themselves, 2
    as unknown majority, 14
    as winners, 222
    See also Men
"Woman's place is in the home" phrase, 42
Women
    acting like men, 145
    African American, 170, 173
    in agrarian work model, 71
    behavior as labeled by men, 113
    biological differences, 60–61
    change and, 221
    communication style, 175–77
    communication with men, 6, 113, 177
    computers and, 46
    conversation for, 174
    differences of, 125
    diversity for, 220
    divorce and, 218
    emotions and, 85
    entrepreneurs, 94
    equality, 18
    exclusion frustration, 80
    family rule by, 211
    human goals of, 6
    Iroquois Great Law and, 39
    Kikuyu, 35
    learning from, 210
    learning from men, 85
    life as ongoing process and, 74
    management training for, 99
    movement, 45
    old world behavior support, 42
    patience for male change, 75
    perspective of, 63, 74
    power system, 201
    in relationships, 79, 85, 177–78, 201
    respect for men, 112
    roles, shifting, 96–97
    "sluts," 200
    trusting of same race, 172
    in upper management, 201
    view of men, 31
    views of, 113
    as weak, 34, 222
    white male model and, 146
    white male power and, 14
    white males view of, 1–2
    "who she is" question, 84
    workforce entry of, 94
    working styles of, 145
    in World War II, 44
Woods, Gavin, 247–48
Words, reliance on, 73–74
Work force
    aging of, 98
    diversity, 136
    lost potential, 134
    minorities in, 99
    "monkeys in a zoo" image, 132
    new additions to, 98
Workplace
    boundaryless global, 210
    as center of American society, 127
    change and, 127, 163
    critical junction of, 251
    equality promise, 142
    as insecure environment, 256
    minorities in, 89
    multicultural, 93–94
    national policy governing, 151–53
    norms, 142
    performance evaluations, 131
    relationships, 153–54
    standards, 21
    success, 107–8
    training programs, 150
    twenty-first century, 209
    women coming into, 89–96
"Work role spillover," 220
Workshops, 27, 55–56, 69–70, 87–88,
    104–5, 120–21, 139–40, 161, 186–87,
    208, 230, 249
Work time, 215
World War II, 43–44
Wright-Brown, Cynthia, 247

X chromosomes, 60

Yankelovich, Daniel, 110
Y chromosomes, 59